Boccaccio's Two Venuses

Stultum credere poetas nil sensisse sub cortice fabularum
—Genealogie, XIV, X

Vanus a Venere etymologiam trahit
—Isidore of Seville, *Etymologiarum*, X, 280

Boccaccio's Two Venuses

ROBERT HOLLANDER

New York ∽ Columbia University Press ∽ 1977

Library of Congress Cataloging in Publication Data

Hollander, Robert.
Boccaccio's two Venuses.

Includes bibliographical references and index.
1. Boccaccio, Giovanni, 1313–1375—Criticism and interpretation. 2. Love in literature. I. Title.
PQ4293.L72H6 858'.1'09 77-5144
ISBN 0-231-04224-8

Columbia University Press
New York Guilford, Surrey

Printed in the United States of America

For D. W. Robertson, Jr.

Contents

Acknowledgments

Despite the basic nature of my disagreement with Boccaccio's previous interpreters, it is clear that my study is often and greatly dependent on their labors. Few major figures are as well served by their best critics as is Boccaccio, and it is meet that I here record my sense of personal indebtedness, even if, with a single exception, my contact with these *studiosi* does not include personal acquaintance. I can only hope that my naming of four great scholars will not seem invidious to others who are worthy. My labors have been both softened and invigorated particularly by the efforts of Giuseppe Billanovich, Vittore Branca, Giorgio Padoan, and Antonio Enzo Quaglio. It may seem foolish to thank them for their impersonal and unintended mercies to me, but my certain knowledge of what their work has meant to me demands that I do so.

To those who have given me the money and the time to pursue these studies I offer this book in repayment, along with heartfelt thanks. The National Endowment for the Humanities awarded me the fellowship that took me and my family to Rome for some nine months, a gestation period that has produced this squalling but I hope healthy infant. I would like here to record my gratitude to the selection panels of my peers and to the staff of the Endowment, who combined to entrust me with the opportunity to complete a study of Dante's poetics in relation to the more traditional poetic theory of the *Trecento* (a task which I have completed), but who had no idea that this illegitimate child was also growing inside me. I did not either. It is as much a surprise to me as it will be to them. I must also thank Princeton University, first for allowing me the services of an undergraduate research assistant in the spring term of 1974: Ersilia Zott '75 prepared the bibliographies which were a starting point for my research. And it was the full year of leave which Princeton allowed me to take which meant that the germ of an idea could be elaborated in this book, rather than lying fallow in unwritten pages. My debt to Princeton extends further, to the Princeton University Committee on Research in the Humanities and Social Sciences, which has now for a second time contributed generously toward the cost of publication of my work.

Libraries which I have used in the preparation of this study include my own University's easeful Firestone, which is clearly one of the world's great libraries attached to a smaller university. In Italy I was fortunate to be able to avail myself of the resources of the Riccardiana and the Nazionale in Florence, the Accademia dei Lincei and the Nazionale in Rome. To the directors and the staffs of all these institutions I extend my gratitude. But my principal source of material was the magnificent Biblioteca Apostolica Vaticana, in whose reading rooms I have now spent nearly two years' worth of contented mornings, and where I long to be again. To all there, from Alfonso Stickler, the Prefect of Studies, and Monsignor José Ruysschaert, the Vice-Prefect, to Alberto Cerilli, the cordial keeper of the gate who greeted me each morning, I send *auguri cordialissimi.*

Back in America, I sought the counsel of friends and colleagues, all of whom responded with useful comments after reading my manuscript or parts thereof: Paolo Cucchi, Joan Ferrante, John Fleming, Alban Forcione, Charles Klopp, Giuseppe Mazzotta, David Quint, D. W. Robertson, Jr., Charles Singleton, Janet Smarr, Chauncey Wood, Theodore Ziolkowski. It is a fortunate scholar who is able to count on helpful readers of such high caliber. Yet I would be remiss if I did not make special mention of Charles Klopp, my colleague in Italian here for seven years and now at Ohio State. Although he probably disagrees with my conclusions more than anyone whom I have named, he spent days with my manuscript and produced a heavy sheaf of suggestions for revision that were of inestimable aid to me. I am greatly in his debt.

There remains the traditional task of the married academic writer of acknowledgments. Since wives have so often been crowned with obligatory sprigs of laurel in pages which these must perforce resemble, I am delighted to make it plain that mine responded to my disappearance into the labyrinth of Boccaccio with bemused skepticism, a reaction that also characterized her reading of the finished MS. However, since I have never seen Jean happier than during this past year in Rome, I can only conclude that my nightly and lengthy news bulletins concerning my life among the *opere minori* were not as dreadfully monotonous as they now seem to me to have been. I thank her for her patience. But my real indebtedness to her far outstrips her mere comforting, and makes this last dependence on her love and judgment only another in a long and happy train. May we long continue to burn in the flames of two loves.

Hopewell, N.J.
21 December 1975

Boccaccio's Two Venuses

Introduction

Boccaccio's *opere minori in volgare,* while receiving more attention than his Latin works, still suffer from neglect by comparison with the *Decameron,* even though the range and size of this *corpus* should have guaranteed it wider attention. This is not to say that it has been unattended—the bibliographical notices included in footnotes will make that clear enough—but that it has been underattended and perhaps therefore often misconceived. A brief description of what the *corpus* includes follows: [1]

1) ***Caccia di Diana*** (1334? 1338?). Pastoral allegory that reflects the medieval tradition of the dream vision. 18 *canti* in *terzine* (1047 lines).

2) ***Filostrato*** (1335?). "Epic" treatment of the love of Troiolo and Criseida. In 9 parts, 713 stanzas of *ottava rima* (5704 lines).

3) ***Filocolo*** (1336–38?). Prose romance. In 5 books (615 pages).

4) ***Teseida*** (1339–41?). "Epic" treatment of the love of

Palemone and Arcita for Emilia. In 12 books, 1138 stanzas of *ottava rima* (9104 lines).

5) ***Comedia delle ninfe fiorentine*** (1341–42). Pastoral allegory that reflects the tradition of the dream vision. 50 *canti,* mixed prose and *terzine* (155 pages).

6) ***Amorosa Visione*** (1342). Allegorical dream vision. 50 *canti* in *terzine* (4406 lines).

7) ***Elegia di madonna Fiammetta*** (1343–44?). Prose elegy. In 9 chapters (ca. 200 pages).

8) ***Ninfale fiesolano*** (1344–46??). Pastoral. In 473 *ottave* (3784 lines).

9) ***Corbaccio*** (1354?). Satirical dream vision in prose. No formal divisions in the text (ca. 100 pages).

In addition to these nine works, all of which will be discussed in the first three chapters of this study, there are the *Rime,* some 150 of which are probably attributable to Boccaccio, composed over something like a thirty-five year period (from ca. 1340 until shortly before Boccaccio's death in 1375). When we reflect that most readers of Boccaccio, even in Italy, are acquainted with few of these works aside from those that appear in excerpt in school anthologies (in other countries even such acquaintance with the *opere minori* is probably unusual—although of course English and American Chaucerians may have read through either the *Filostrato* or the *Teseida,* or perhaps both), we may fairly speak of them as being underattended. Perhaps no other major writer has had his "minor" works so little read and ill regarded. And the quotation marks in the preceding sentence may be taken to reflect the puzzlement of the author of the present study. A more accurate designation would be the "less read" works of Boccaccio; a writer of his compass does not write "minor" works. As W. H. Auden is said to have remarked, we do not read a good book, a good book reads us. If that is true, we are not very well read by the great bulk of Boccaccio's output, which has paid the price of having been the companion of an undisputed masterwork, and of which we have been minor readers.

The history of modern critical response to the *opere minori* (having made objection to the term I shall accede to past and current usage and employ it) may be roughly divided into two parts—that which preceded the pioneering work of Vittore Branca and that which followed. Almost all who went before, beginning perhaps with G. B. Baldelli in 1806, found the minor works of primary interest as the means of putting together a patchwork of an amorous "biography" of Giovanni Boccaccio and "Maria d'Aquino," that is, "Fiammetta." [2] Beginning in the mid-1930's Branca began to veer from this dominant position. Giuseppe Billanovich's *Restauri boccacceschi* (Roma, 1945) opened the post-war era of Boccaccio studies with the central recognition that Boccaccio was a writer, not an "autobiographer," and tried to lead readers back to the texts as literary objects, rather than "autobiographical" ones.[3] The last thirty years of Boccaccio criticism have been highly active ones, involving major breakthroughs in identifications of autographs, ascriptions, source studies, and clarifications of the nature of literary relationships both within the *corpus* and between it and its precursors. But while the "biographical" scaffolding that was built up over a century and a half around the *opere minori* has been almost entirely taken down,[4] another one has been reared on its shards. For the "new" Boccaccio of the *opere minori*—with only a few exceptions—is taken to be in the most important respect not at all different from the old one, for he continues to be considered an enthusiastic champion of sexual love. That Fiammetta is Maria d'Aquino, an actual Neapolitan lady, is no longer the palatable notion it once was, and few defend it. But that she, or some lady, is the literary carnal aim of Boccaccio's desire is hardly disputed. The aim of Boccaccio's "youthful" fiction is generally, indeed very nearly universally, understood to be the praise of carnal love.[5] My study will argue that such was not Boccaccio's aim. I believe that the intent of his *opere minori in volgare* was to make an ironic attack upon the religion of love, an attack which is at times interspersed with praise of marital love. That sentence summarizes my basic interpretation accurately and would fit into a telegram. The problem is that few of Boccaccio's readers would accept the message as having any relationship to their own sense of Boccaccio's *opere minori*. And for that reason I have written at greater length.

The phrase "the religion of love" will occur with some frequency in the text that follows. At the outset I would like to clarify what I intend by the phrase. First of all, I do not wish to join the debate concerning the actuality of such a "religion," of the so-called "courts of love," in short of the historical footing of adultery in the middle ages. What I do intend to indicate is a literary tradition, one in which ladies and gentlemen swear their loyalty to the Lord of Love, placing him above all other gods in their esteem. It is not my contention that all writers who in their works describe cultish veneration of Amor, or of the carnal Venus, present a negative view of such behavior such as I find in Boccaccio's fiction. Rather, it is precisely my point that it was Boccaccio's intention to develop a systematic parody of this kind of literary behavior. (A necessary corollary implies that Boccaccio would, in fact, have found actual behavior modelled upon the literary "religion of love" at least fatuous; but, once again, I must insist that it is beyond my purpose here to conflate life and literature.) Thus the phrase "the religion of love" serves to draw attention to a literary phenomenon. And if I may allow one instance to serve for many, I would make exemplary the words of Amore to l'Amante in *Il fiore:* "Worship me, for I am your god. Set aside any other faith; believe not Luke, nor Matthew, nor Mark, nor John." [6] The religion of love, here explicitly, elsewhere implicitly (as in Francesca's speech in *Inferno* V), entails a worship of the Lord of Love that displaces any other form of piety.

What strikes a reader immediately about all of the *opere minori* is that without exception they are concerned with carnal love. Lascivious sexuality is described or said to have occurred or to be longed for in all of them—and not merely as a partial or fleeting aspect of the subject of the works, but as the central concern of its major characters. However, within all the works there are clear indications that such behavior as going pale, wasting away, and longing for death if one cannot possess the sexual favors of one's beloved is not merely a bit daft, but clearly immoral, in the sense that it is destructive as well as self-destructive. In the body of criticism, however, there is only now and again even the slightest awareness of the negative valence of such indications, for most of Boccaccio's critics, having been taught by earlier critics, have never even asked the necessary initial question about the works, namely, is such amorous behavior in itself praiseworthy in Boccaccio's view?

Another clue which these critics have tended to disregard is found in the mythographic indications offered in the texts. In all the works—in each and every one of them—Venus and/or Cupid, her son, are present either as "characters" or else as deities who appear, in dream or in epiphany, to characters in the works, or they are venerated in temples to which the characters go in order to make sacrifice to them.[7] Even without recourse to any mythographic tradition, one can see in the very text that such deities are vain, cruel, and dangerous, and that those who worship them have a terrible time indeed—suffering the pangs of spiritual torture and sometimes physical death. To think, for instance, of the *Filostrato* and of Troiolo, his allegiance to Venus earns him a brief interlude of sexual pleasure, which is followed by betrayal by Criseida and a brutal death at the hands of Achilles. One supposes that Boccaccio's readers are either masochists or simply bad readers when they find such behavior and such suffering noble and good. There seems no other way to account for the paeans to the glories of love that the work has occasioned. That the presence of this sort of goddess (or that sort of a son of a goddess) has not brought better criticial response is itself surprising. But what makes the usual critical procedure extraordinarily difficult to fathom is that Boccaccio, in several of the works, presents *another* Venus as well, a heavenly Venus who presides over matrimony and the getting of children. She has received sparse attention, and even those who see that she is there fail to see that she is at odds with her other and carnal self, or that she is of any real importance to the meaning of the work.

But I anticipate my arguments within. And that is enough as an indication of my basic interpretive position. This book offers itself as a general interpretation, based on nine specific instances, of the meaning of the *opere minori in volgare.* That is to say what the purpose of this study is. I should also say what it is not.

First, and most importantly, this is not a study of the *Decameron.* What I am here attempting to say already involves too large a territory to get under any sure control and is likely to be controversial enough without entering into the vast terrain of *Decameron* studies. Yet I may be allowed the hope that at least some readers will look upon this study as a kind of prolegomenon toward some rethinking of the *Decameron.* On occasion I have pointed to parallels between various of the *opere minori* and the *Decameron* with an eye to that concern. But my own view of the *Decameron,* while it reflects a good deal of the attitudes expressed here, finds it more resistant to my thesis than the rest of the fiction, and the work remains, in the eyes of this reader at any rate, possibly the most enigmatic text in continental medieval fiction, richly difficult to fathom.

Second, my aim is not to deal with the problem of Boccaccio's sources *per se.* Still, this subject will appear fairly frequently in conjunction with analyses of particular texts, usually as a means of clarifying—or at least attempting to clarify—a particular signification. This is a way of saying that I have tended to leave to one side the most important study of all, for source study, well handled, is probably our best single hope of penetrating the aesthetic ordering principles of literary texts: how A, B, and C all enter into X, and in what way X is like and unlike A, B, and C. Since in Boccaccio's case A and B are certainly Dante and Ovid, the matter is of some promise and considerable interest. Dante alone is the "source" of what must be hundreds, what may be thousands, of Boccaccio's words, phrases, thoughts. Rarely has one author been so frequently present within another's works.[8] And Ovid, if not as often present, is at least as strong and probably stronger a shaping influence, for in his matter, which is love, Boccaccio is the Italian Ovid. (The way in which he understood Ovid will be a subject of inquiry in the fourth chapter.) While this aspect of the *opere minori* is not within my chosen boundaries, it will obtrude on more than one occasion.

Third, this is not a study of the Latin works. There are three main reasons for this exclusion. We have quite enough to do with what is before us; the Latin works have long been understood in precisely the light which I here propose for the *opere minori in volgare;* and I do not wish to argue from the Christian and moralizing focus of the late works back to the earlier ones. Not that it is my understanding that their focus is different in any but stylistic ways from the earlier works; but if one were to argue from them he would open himself to the charge of having presented in evidence precisely the matter which is in dispute, since the traditional view of Boccaccio's *œuvre* finds the early work pagan, the late work Christian, and claims a pivotal "conversion" to account for the change. Therefore I have taken pains to avoid the charge that I have treated Saul as Paul, even though I do not believe, in the case of Boccaccio's literary career, that there ever was a Saul. Yet, on occasion, it has proven useful to show how little difference exists between the supposed Saul and Paul, to which purpose passages in the *Genealogie* and the *Esposizioni* of Dante's *Commedia* have seemed particularly well fitted.

Fourth, I have deliberately—with only one or two failures of compliance—ruled out the use of Chaucer's reading of Boccaccio, as this is represented by his reworkings of our poet, as support for my own reading. While it seems clear that in most particulars Chaucer read Boccaccio very much as I do, if one has recourse to such a tactic he enters still another hotbed of debate among medievalists—the question of Chaucer's Christian intent. While it is surely clear which way my own inclinations lie, it seemed more prudent and certainly less confusing to fight one battle at a time. It is quite large enough for me.

There are many other things that might be here, but are not; these four seem those which are most naturally linked to my subject. And the last of them leads to a brief explanation of the dedication of this book. Professor Robertson was not my teacher (a callow undergraduate, I preferred to read Chaucer on my own rather than subject myself to the Robertsonian disciplines available in McCosh Hall), is not my friend (this merely happens to be the social fact—I surely feel friendly enough toward him), and is in fact the object of several less than cordial remarks in a book I wrote on Dante some years ago (and on the subject about which we disagreed then I believe we still disagree just as strongly today). But this is his book, not because he caused it, which he did not, but because he could have written it. Had he done so, it would have undoubtedly been a much better book. Some time ago an ill-advised reviewer of my Dante book referred to it as "Robertsonian." He happened, in that circumstance, to have been quite wrong. But it is a charge that I more than willingly accept for this one. *Quis tale opprobrium dabit, honorem mihi cedet.*

Indications concerning Procedures and Texts

As the reader will note, I have not moved chronologically through Boccaccio's *opere minori in volgare.* I have chosen not to for three reasons. First, no one is really certain of their exact chronological order. Second, my thesis, which sees no real difference in their several meanings, does not require that I do so, or that I attempt to establish such an order. Third, certain conjunctions, *Caccia di Diana-Corbaccio, Filostrato-Teseida. Comedia ninfe-Amorosa Visione,* seemed desirable for various reasons, and these desired conjunctions, along with other concerns (to treat the *Filocolo* first after the introductory and at least hypothetically exploratory first chapter, to get to the *Elegia di madonna Fiammetta* early, to have the *Teseida* leading into the discussion of the allegorical works) moved me to order my discussion as I have.

A major procedural issue—one that has been very difficult to solve—has been caused by my desire to address this book to at least two audiences. One is American and English, is not particularly well acquainted with the *opere minori,* and would ostensibly like to have enough sense of what happens in the works in order to follow my argument. The second is Italian, and requires no such assistance, but will want to see the relationship of Italian scholarship to that argument. The evidence that these two audiences have been kept in mind is present in two possibly disconcerting features of this book: its use of plot synopsis and the large amount of material relegated to the footnotes.

One who comes from Dante studies finds the bibliographical plenty in Boccaccio studies almost skimpy and certainly well ordered. The three basic bibliographies are as follows (others exist, but these cover almost all publications concerning Boccaccio, and are more than adequate):

Guido Traversari, *Bibliografia boccaccesca* (Città di Castello: Lapi, 1907).

Covers items through part of 1906.

Vittore Branca, *Linee di una storia della critica al "Decameron" con bibliografia boccaccesca completamente aggiornata* (Milano-Genova-Roma-Napoli: Società Anonima Editrice Dante Alighieri, 1939).

Adds items missed by Traversari and covers items through 1938.

Studi sul Boccaccio, Vol. I (1963) to present—the last published issue is Vol. VII (1973)—contain ample and descriptive bibliographies prepared by Bittore Branca and Giorgio Padoan.

Adds items missed in the first two bibliographies, above, and is the major source of current bibliographical information.

Citations from Boccaccio's texts are made, whenever possible, from *Tutte le opere di Giovanni Boccaccio* (Verona: Mondadori), of which Vols. I, II, III, VI, and X have now been published, under the general editorship of Vittore Branca. These texts are the result of outstanding scholarship and should be the standard texts of Boccaccio for some time. Appended is a list of the contents of each volume, with the name of the editor of each text following its title in parentheses.

Vol. I "Profilo biografico" (V. Branca): *Caccia di Diana* (V. Branca); *Filocolo* (A. E. Quaglio).

Vol. II *Filostrato* (V. Branca); *Teseida* (A. Limentani); *Comedia delle ninfe fiorentine* (A. E. Quaglio).

Vol. III *Amorosa Visione* (V. Branca); *Ninfale fiesolano* (A. Balduino); *Trattatello in laude di Dante* (P. G. Ricci).

Vol. VI *Esposizioni sopra la Comedia di Dante* (G. Padoan).

Vol. X *De mulieribus claris* (V. Zaccaria).

Citations from texts not yet published by Mondadori are from the following texts:

Elegia di madonna Fiammetta, ed. F. Ageno (Paris: Tallone, 1954), as reprinted (with two changes in the text) in the *Opere,* ed. C. Segre (Milano: Mursia, 1966).

Corbaccio, ed. T. Nurmela (Helsinki: *Annales Academiae Scientiarum Fennicae,* Vol. CXLVI, 1968).

Rime, ed. V. Branca (Padova: Liviana, 1958), also as reprinted in Segre's edition of the *Opere.*

References to critical notices in the Mondadori edition are given as, e.g., "*Opere,* VI, 829," and references to Boccaccio's text follow the numeration used in the editions listed here.

Citations of the *Divina Commedia* are from Petrocchi's edition (*La Commedia secondo l'antica volgata* [Roma: A. Mondadori for the Società Dantesca Italiana, 1966–68]), as printed in C. S. Singleton's revised edition of C. H. Grandgent's bilingual text (Cambridge, Mass.: Harvard University Press, 1972).

Readers of English who are without Italian will find some of the *opere minori* translated—if not always reliably so. The following is a list of English translations.

Filostrato: N. E. Griffin and A. B. Myrick (Philadelphia, 1929).

Teseida: Bernadette McCoy (Sea Cliff, N.Y., 1974).

Elegia di madonna Fiammetta: Edward Hutton's revision of Bartholomew Yong's sixteenth-century translation (London, 1926).

Ninfale fiesolano: D. J. Donno (New York, 1960); Joseph Tusiani (Rutherford, N.J., 1971).

Corbaccio: Anthony Cassell (Urbana, Ill., 1975).

Currently in preparation or awaiting publication (according to Louis L. Gioia, cited in the *Boccaccio Newsletter,* 2, 2 [Fall, 1975]):

Filostrato (R. P. apRoberts and Anna B. Seldis).

Filocolo (Rocco C. Blasi).

Comedia ninfe, Caccia (Bernadette McCoy).

I may note here that translations found within are my own unless there is indication to the contrary.

The Flames of Two Loves

IF IT CAN be demonstrated, or at least argued, that all of Boccaccio's vernacular fictions conform to the same matrix of meaning, we would do well to study two of his works that have generally been taken to have very different significances. The one vernacular fiction often seen as incongruent with Boccaccio's usual fictional concerns is the last, the *Corbaccio.* Further, because it was written after the *Decameron* and because most treatments of the *opere minori* are pleased to move from good, to better, to best (or from mediocre, to surprisingly good, to best), and thus to neglect the work which follows the "best," or the *Decameron,* it is rarely given more than scant attention. In brief, the *fortuna Corbacci* has been a stunted one for these two major reasons: It fails to support the usual view most critics have of Boccaccio's status as *scriba Amoris,* and it has the misfortune to be the only vernacular fiction to follow the great *Decameron.* At the other end of Boccaccio's productive life in fiction lies, if not absolutely certainly, the *Caccia di Diana.* Here too we have a work which has received scant attention, first, because until recently it was not generally considered to be among Boccaccio's genuine works; second, because it seems to most of its readers (even to its rescuer and perhaps best reader, Vittore Branca) to be inferior stuff. This first chapter will offer analyses of what are at least likely to have been the first and the last of Boccaccio's vernacular fictions and will try to suggest that the gulf of time (roughly a quarter century) that separates them does not result in their being—at least insofar as it is their significance that interests us—as different from each other as has generally been supposed.

It is only recently that the *Caccia di Diana* has been widely accepted as Boccaccio's own work. It is, as is so often the case, Vittore Branca who must be given the credit for a major contribution to Boccaccio studies. In 1938, in a study which is in need of only slight *aggiornamenti,* Branca demonstrated, against the majority of "authoritative" opinion, that the *opuscolo* is surely Boccaccio's.[1] Once we are as sure as Branca has allowed us to be that the *Caccia* is by Boccaccio, we realize that the little work, which continues to receive the slightest of notice, whether we consider it particularly good, or even particularly good Boccaccio, at least ought to be studied seriously in order to see in what ways it does or does not conform to its better known and more highly regarded sisters. Probably written, as Branca has argued, around 1334,[2] and thus by a would-be poet of barely more than twenty years of age, the *Caccia* is comparable to the lesser works of many an acclaimed author. Its technical insufficiencies seem shameful only to those who expect Shakespeare to have composed *King Lear* in his apprenticeship rather than *Venus and Adonis* or *The Rape of Lucrece* and help explain why those who denied authenticity felt moved to do so. Yet what we have to deal with here is more than likely Boccaccio's first work in the vernacular, a literary object, in other words, of more than passing interest.

In eighteen *canti* of *terza rima,* all but one of nineteen *terzine* and thus fifty-eight lines,[3] Boccaccio describes a hunt led by Diana, and its happy (or perhaps, as I shall suggest, disastrous) conclusion in the disappearance of Diana and the triumphant advent of Venus. Let us begin at the beginning. As is always the case in Boccaccio's vernacular fiction, the first presence we confront is that of the narrator. In the fresh fields of spring we see a sad and solitary figure seeking relief from the pains of love.[4] This is our "frame," and it is one familiar to

Boccaccio's readers, who are probably accustomed to finding in that first framing element a sad lover who will shortly tell the tale of love that is Boccaccio's customary subject. The narrator is not here, nor is he elsewhere, with the single exception of the *Amorosa Visione,* named in the text.[5] All that we can surely say of him is that he is in love, that he has written (at least that may be Boccaccio's and our own mutual pretense) the poetic narrative which follows. He is a poet of love for the simple reason that he is in love.[6]

The action of the *Caccia di Diana* begins quickly—much more quickly than is usually the case in Boccaccio's fictions—with the verbal formula one usually associates with medieval dream visions: "when I *seemed to hear* [we usually find a visual rather than an auditory verb following the copulative] a gentle spirit come calling loudly in its flight." [7] This spirit convokes by name those ladies of the court of Naples who have been chosen as consorts by none other than the lofty goddess Diana. Her name should probably strike us as something of a surprise, for the vernal setting, the love-struck narrator, the list of ladies—all of these would make Venus a more likely goddess to convoke this gathering. In her time, she will do so. For now she is totally absent from the scene and from the poem (she will not even be mentioned until she is summoned by our narrator's beloved in the seventeenth canto). Diana's *nuncio* calls to assembly thirty-three Neapolitan ladies,[8] the first thirty-two of whom are named, and were actual presences in the Angevin court of Boccaccio's time.[9] The thirty-third lady is not named. But for the narrator she is clearly the most important of them all, since she is his own, that is, the one in whose thrall he suffers the pain of love. She is not named here or later.[10]

Line six of the first canto has given us the cause of the narrator's *duolo amaro: amor.* Line 46 introduces us to his lady, the last one summoned by *il messo di Diana.* The six lines which describe her quality would seem to be conventional enough: Amore honors her more than any other because of her *somma virtute* that has such a powerful effect upon the other ladies; for their *salute* (Boccaccio seems to be playing with Dante's high sense of the word, which includes "well-being" and "salvation" in its range of meanings, in the *Vita Nuova*) she acts as their leader and guardian.[11] And the conventional anonymity of the beloved is maintained by the combined forces of Diana's messenger and the narrator: "and he did not call her by name, because higher praise would befit her name than I am here able to recount." [12] The lady is thus associated with the Lord of Love, son of Venus. We may well wonder why she has been summoned by Diana, traditional rival of Venus,[13] to be one of her consorts. The first canto of the *Caccia* has established the precondition for a struggle between the forces of chastity, marshalled in the hunt, and those of Venery, devoted to another kind of hunting, one that ends in the toils of carnal affection. The struggle is so long delayed in coming to a head (the rebellion of the ladies against Diana occupies the concluding lines of the sixteenth canto, and the triumphant advent of Venus will occur halfway through the penultimate canto) that readers tend to neglect its presence altogether, or, if they do perceive it, to underestimate its importance.[14] Before examining the conclusion, we should look briefly at the intervening matter.

The second canto moves us from the fields of spring to a lovely valley, enclosed by four mountains (one for each major point on the compass), in which the requisite greenery and floral decoration is of course present. Nor do we do without an abundantly flowing fountain. The surrounding mountainsides are so thickly treed (and the trees are so thickly leafed) that the sun's rays can barely penetrate this pleasant place. Here birds sing their carols, breezes gently blow, and every kind of animal is to be found.[15] The surrounding is, one might argue, morally charged but morally neutral; what you choose to do here will tell us what you are. It is here that Diana, "che 'l tiepido foco/ne' casti petti tien" (II.22–23), receives her thirty-three recruits. She is the keeper of less than ardent flames. And while a Romantic reader may see fit to despise flames in ladies' breasts which burn less than hot, it is at least likely that Boccaccio expects us to admire the moderation that Diana urges in her followers.[16] She commands the ladies to bathe in the waters of the fountain, to cleanse themselves with "freschi liquori." They do so, then put on purple vestments [17] and garlands of olives and flowers. At this point the goddess divides the group into four platoons. The first, led by the "bella donna," the narrator's lady, is sent to climb the mountain to the south, the second, under Isabella degli Scrignar, is directed to the western peak; the third, led by Fior Curial, is sent north; Diana's own party moves to the smallest of the four mountains, the one lying to the east.[18]

In the action that follows (III–VIII) we observe the four hunting parties at their effortful play, first Diana's, then that of the "bella donna," that of Isabella Scrignara, and finally Fior Curial's. In the ninth canto we return to the narrator, hidden among the green fronds of the base camp, who sees another group approach. He is at first afraid that it may be composed of evil fok, but is reassured to discover that it too is made up of pretty ladies. Their names occupy two cantos, and one must agree, following Vittore Branca, that Boccaccio, if not attempting to storm Olympus, is making an assault of some kind upon the Neapolitan court [19] in his painstaking salute to fifty-eight of its ladies.[20] The following cantos (XI–XV) recount the adventures in the hunt of this new group. It is with a certain relief that we find the sixteenth canto bringing us to noon, when, because of the increasing heat of the sun, Diana calls for a rest from their sport. She sends one of her party to call in all the others. Once they have all descended. Zizzola d'Anna, who alone had gone to hunt that day without being called by Diana's messenger, also joins the group, bringing her own numerous prey.[21] As the fifty-nine ladies, returned to their starting point, sit around their mountain of prey ("un gran monte"—XVI.32), Diana rises, her face joyful, to address them. It is the first and last time in the poem that she will say anything of moment.[22] She makes appeal to the "donne gentili e donzelle" (in XVI.12, the ladies, called back from the hunt, are referred to as "le donne e le pulcelle"), reminding us that the huntresses are either married ladies or virgins of the court: "It is my desire that you make sacrifice of your prey to Jove, king of the high kingdom, and to honor me, who should be worshipped by you in a fitting manner. This I beg of you, this I seek as earnestly as I am able; make haste so that you may assume your seats in my choir." [23] This modest proposal causes the turning point in the work. For in response the narrator's lady, identified only as "la donna piacente," rises in her place, her face troubled, to say: "Nothing like this shall come to pass! Until this moment, as you have commanded, so have we, gathered here, in fact done. Now we have no further desire to follow your deity, since our breasts and souls are inflamed by a different fire." [24] At this Diana, *turbata* in her turn (she and the "bella donna" share the same adjective at lines 47 and 57, thus underlining their roles as the primary antagonists of the first sixteen cantos), concludes the canto by leaving the *brigata* and returning to the heaven whence she had come.

Had the poem ended even here we would have beheld enough in the way of action (as fanciful as it may have been) to see at least a possible moral point to it all. Under the auspices of Diana, of the chaste life, the ladies of the court have spent a successful morning killing every kind of animal. The moral sense of such endeavor is, at least in one branch of medieval convention, evident: their ordered hunting of the beasts of nature corresponds to their ordering of their own carnal lives.[25] They should all seek, in short, to be governed by Diana, "che 'l tiepido foco/ne' casti petti tien" (II.22–23), whether they be *donne,* and thus chastely contented with their husbands, or *donzelle,* and thus virgins until they be wed. The dead bodies of their prey, in one sense approximate to the bodies of the men at court whom their beauties "kill," are to be sacrificed for the sake of chastity, not enjoyed. This solution is patently unwelcome to the "bella donna." She has been hunting, we can only surmise, for the pleasure of the prey. Her abrupt, even colloquial response ("E' non sarà così niente!") reveals that she is no friend of Diana or chastity. Rather than Diana's proposed sacrificial fire, she seeks the flames of lust. Against such opposition, Diana's sudden withdrawal should probably be seen not as the defeat of the goddess, but as her scornful response to the disloyal ladies. She deserts them, for they are not worthy. Their behavior, as Branca's note makes evident, is similar to that of the ashamed Dante in the Earthly Paradise.[26] The action of Canto XVII continues with the urgings of "la donna gentile" (is the verbal formulation dependent on "la gentile donna" of the *Vita Nuova,* Dante's "wrong" lady?). She advises the assemblage to seek the aid of "Venus santa Dea, madre d'Amore" (XVII.8) by sacrificing the prey in *her* honor. This direct contravention of Diana's wish—that the prey be sacrificed to Jove, or God,[27] and for the sake of chastity—is surely not casually put. The new plan, nonetheless, pleases all the ladies. They set fire to their catch, and pray to Venus: "O holy Goddess, heeding the worth of our sacrifice, do not disdain our words, which express our desires; compassionate in your joyful office, receive us, in your beneficence, by merit of our humble prayers. Drive low thoughts out of our breasts and by your power make our minds sublime and our hearts liberal and gentle. Oh, allow us to feel the pleasure of your effects, and make our minds content in loving." [28]

That is quite enough for Venus. She shortly descends, standing nude on a little cloud, [29] and, suspended just above them, speaks: "I am she of whom each of you seeks grace in her prayers; and I promise you, by the high gods, that each who is worthy of following me shall be granted what she seeks." [30] Venus turns to the fire, says things which the narrator either cannot hear or cannot understand ("non so che disse"—XVII.38), thus pointing to her skill and power in the casting of spells,[31] and, presto, the burning beasts turn into handsome young men who run about upon the grasses and flowers. *They* now bathe in the *fiumicello* in which the ladies had bathed while they were under Diana's tutelage. But instead of a *purpurea veste* (II.29) each of these now puts on a *vermiglio drappo* (XVII.44–45).[32] And then Venus addresses them: "Be subjects of these ladies, love them until you merit victory and pity by your effort." [33] Venus has put them under the rule of the familiar "religion of love." Having delivered herself of this code of behavior, she too goes back to her heaven. Her visit, so different in purpose from that of Diana, has a strikingly dissimilar result. For where Diana disappeared without leaving any sign of her ministry in the hearts and minds of the fifty-nine ladies, Venus withdraws "lasciando a' petti/di tutti segno d'etterna memoria." [34] In the *Caccia di Diana* it is Venus who triumphs, despite the title of the work, at least in the minds of the ladies.

The last canto begins by revealing the effect of her victory on the narrator. Summarizing the actions which he has observed since he last spoke to us (in Canto IX), he culminates his brief description of the events of the last eight cantos with "il sovrano/miracol . . . , maraviglioso ad intelletto umano" (XVIII.4–6) that Venus's metamorphosis of the dead animals into living men represents to him. He wonders to find himself in the same *mantel* as that worn by the other men (see XVII.44–45: "d'un vermiglio/e nobil drappo si facean mantello"). He sees himself offered to the "bella donna," and, most surprisingly, "di cervio mutato in creatura/umana e razional esser per certo" (XVIII.11–12), changed from a stag into a human and rational being. Boccaccio would certainly seem to be playing with his Ovid here, for what we have is a reversal of the myth of Actaeon (*Metamorphoses* III,138f.), the hunter who saw Diana plain and was turned into a stag for the pleasure and subsequently torn to death by his own dogs.[35] The business is accomplished in so sophisticated a manner that the fairly obvious parallels have apparently hitherto gone unnoticed. If Diana turned a man into a stag, Venus turns this hiding stag into a man. The effect, comparable to that achieved by running a film backwards, is rather stunning—especially since it preserves the Diana/Venus antithesis so neatly. At this moment the reader, whether he is aware of the Ovidian parallel or not, should feel at least mildly uncomfortable: up to this point his narrator has been, he must reflect, a stag. If it does nothing else, this bizarre revelation forces the reader to attempt to penetrate Boccaccio's intention in the *Caccia.* And one of the first facts he can now grasp more clearly is that the animals who populate this allegorical vision from the first to the penultimate canto are what we have previously intuited. They are representations of men. And our forest glade is, *in senso allegorico,* no such place at all, but the court of Naples. The masque-like events we have witnessed recede in this perspective and make the triumph of Venus all the more important (and, some might conclude, dangerous), for she rules not merely in the fictive glade but in the very center of civilization, where men are governed, in one of the most compelling tropes of the middle ages, by their bestial, not by their rational, natures.

The narrator's response to his new human condition, that of hopeful lover, may or may not represent the thoughts and feelings of his creator, Giovanni Boccaccio. The rest of the final canto is devoted to what is a conventional (and certainly Boccaccian) check list of a *laus dominae: angelica bellezza, . . . discreta e saggia nel suo ragionare e signorevol donna nello aspetto, lieta e baldanzosa nello andare* (XVIII.16–21).[36] Even God (*l'etterno Signor*), the narrator believes, takes particular joy in having made her (XVIII.26–27). Four of the seven capital sins (*superbia, accidia, avarizia, ira*—1.34) are banished from the narrator's mind when he sees her. (Does that leave *gola, invidia,* and, more importantly, *lussuria* still at work in him?) The praise, while unstinting, may not be above reproach. The narrator appeals to those of us who are, like him, lovers. His words are worth attending: "For these reasons I devoutly pray that everyone who is, as am I, a subject of that lord who makes every ignoble mind gentle will pray on my behalf that I long remain in her affection, and that I be capable of honoring her. For I shall always make this same prayer for him who possesses his beloved in joy, or who desires to possess her, and also for those who are rebels to their ladies: that they have peace, with anguish no longer their scourge." [37]

Does Boccaccio consent in these sentiments? Their ironic possibilities are several. Replacing "l'etterno Signor" (Himself more like a gallant than the Creator in his joy in the "bella donna") we find the lord of Love. Replacing prayers of penitence we have prayers for lovers. And perhaps in the last group of these, those who would escape the toils of love, we have another clue.[38] Diana, who was rebelled against by the ladies, would certainly side with these. For the love of which the narrator speaks is the mere gross fulfillment of the carnal, dressed up in the finery of fraud. The last lines of Canto XVII show us the beasts-turned-into-men, "some taking various delights in the fields, some sighing and picking little flowers, all awaiting the promised gifts" (XVII.55–58). Now we all know what these are: the sexual favors promised by Venus. (Since she has already promised the same to the ladies, we know that none or few will have too long to wait.) And our narrator, who congratulates himself on having turned from beast to man ("uom ritornai/di brutta belva"—XVIII.23–24), is he really such a rational creature? In a nice touch, the tenses of the verbs in the last canto have turned from past to present, lending the entire process of lofty praise and carnal hope a sense of urgency. The poem concludes with the narrator gazing on the *pietate* he sees enacted on the green fields (are the others already receiving their "promised gifts"?), while he hopes for his own *salute* from the "bella donna," a *salute* that has little or nothing to do with anything but sexual gratification.

Whatever we make of the *Caccia di Diana* (and few have made very much of it at all), we ought to think either that it means something or that it means nothing. While the second hypothesis is of course logically possible, all that we know of literary efforts—at least until our own time, which may have produced some intentionally meaningless works—tends to make us doubt its validity. If we can agree that the *Caccia* means something we have only two likely possibilities. One is that the work is an ironic presentation of the lustful enthusiasm of those who are devoted to Amore, the other is that it is a positive celebration of the triumph of natural human urges.[39] (Our views of Venus and Diana are essential in making a judgment between the two interpretations.[40]) The reader need hardly be reminded that this second view is the most widely accepted view of *all* Boccaccio's vernacular fiction, with the exception of the *Corbaccio.* Without at this point developing a framework which might attempt to justify the choice of the other alternative, may I simply suggest that there might be some merit in the interpretive position that is sketched out in the foregoing presentation of the *Caccia?*

What is put forth here may not seem to constitute the rudiments of a convincing reading. It may at least seem a possible reading. Let us turn from what is likely the first to what is almost certainly the last of Boccaccio's vernacular fictions, one that has long been understood as revealing a frame of mind that has little good to say about carnal love. Although minor uncertainties concerning the *Corbaccio* continue to exist,[41] the work is clearly, at least within the interpretive context of the present study, the vernacular work of Boccaccio that presents fewest problems. There are no or few ambiguities in the meaning of the piece, from the narrator's opening remarks to the long misogynist harangue that occupies roughly one-half of the text.[42] We begin, as we always do in Boccaccio's fictions, with a "narrator's frame." Once again the narrator is not named.[43] He begins obliquely, with a general proposition: The man who fails to acknowledge openly benefits he has received, unless he has some appropriate reason for not doing so, shows himself to be an ingrate. Therefore, so that he will not be accused of that failing, he will describe, in the following *trattato,*[44] the special grace conceded him by the Virgin, who had interceded on his behalf with God.[45] This narrator acknowledges openly the favor of Heaven. By telling of it, he continues, he will not only repay part of his debt, but will doubtless be of help to many readers. So that this may in fact be the result, he seeks, in devout prayer, divine aid in writing the work, solely that it may bring honor and glory to His most holy name, utility and consolation to the souls of those who may read it.

This paraphrase of the first paragraph of the *Corbaccio* shows, both in tone and expressed intent, antithetic desires to those we usually find in the statements of purpose made by Boccaccio's narrators. To suggest that the difference is polar in nature would not be to exaggerate. And if that is the correct characterization, it in turn suggests a reason for the difference: Boccaccio's earlier narrators were guilty of inverting the order of values which Boccaccio himself holds to in his works. This is the view of the matter which I shall argue for in the fourth chapter of this study; here let us merely reflect upon the enormous difference between what we have encountered here and what we find in the opening six lines of the *Caccia,* since we have just come from that work. Where the narrator of the *Caccia* is in love, the narrator of the *Corbaccio* has been favored by an intervention of the Virgin, the result of which is that (as we are shortly to be told) he has been freed from the chains of carnal love—the *duolo amaro* of *amor* no longer pains him. To be brief, we can say that the attitudes of the two narrators (if not of their single author) are utterly opposed, the first being "pro Amore," the second "contra Amorem." [46] Whether we choose to believe that the latter narrator expresses Boccaccio's sentiments or not, he, even more clearly than the narrator of the *Decameron,* expresses overt and clear Christian purpose. If I have argued for an ironic reading of the narrator's view of the events of the *Caccia* (as I will for the narrator's view in most of the vernacular fictions), I must certainly agree that such a reading is possible here also. That is, it is conceivable that in the *Corbaccio* Boccaccio is making fun of those who attack Love (since he is one of the praisers of Venus). Such a hypothesis does not seem immediately reasonable.[47] And almost all of the limited number of critical responses [48] to the work do in fact take the narrator's view as being the anti-venereal product of Boccaccio's old age.[49]

Let us examine the second framing element of the dream vision that constitutes the major element of the *Corbaccio,* the "situational frame," as it were.[50] Turning from his purpose in writing the *trattato,* the narrator briefly describes the crisis in his personal life which led him to his "conversion." Alone in his room, weeping, sighing, regretful, he directs his thoughts to the "accidenti del carnale amore." [51] A widow who has brutishly turned aside his epistolary protestations of love (the hilarious business will be recounted at length during the dream sequence) is the cause of his affliction. His own *bestialità* and her *crudeltà,* considered in pain, lead him to the conclusion that death must be preferable to a life such as his own has become.[52] Having chosen a method of doing away with himself,[53] he fears he may thereby go from bad to worse ("di malvagia vita a peggiore"). The choice he must make, between a life cursed by love and death in damnation, leave him in a "battaglia" of conflicting thoughts [54] which only begins to be resolved when "uno pensiero" adds a striking new element to the internal drama.

"Deh, stolto," it begins, in a delightful parodistic joining of the language of address of love poems to the jarring saltiness of *stolto.* The "thought," which delivers itself of sane advice for two pages, is described in the following glowing terms by the comforted narrator: "A wondrous thing in the minds of mortals is divine consolation: this thought, sent forth, in my opinion, by the most merciful Father of light, having lifted from my mind's eyes almost all darkness, made my sight sharp and clear. . . ."(47). The phrase *divina consolazione* and the function of the "thought" point clearly in the direction of Boethius. And a Boethian bourgeois, the sixty-year-old "guide" whom we shall shortly meet in the ensuing dream action, will continue the motif (he and the "thought" speak with similar unembellished, bone-crunching simplicity). This second frame is thus Boethian in character as well as message. The internalized "thought" presents a clear analysis of the narrator's present condition, making it plain that his unhappiness is not the lady's fault but his own, that his death would only give her pleasure, and that he should consequently give over "questo tuo folle appetito" (43)—his lust for the *donna*—and these thoughts of suicide. It is in these directions that his own best selfish interests are seen to lie.

The narrator, strengthened, leaves his lonely room, his face as serene as it can be after so much pain, and seeks the company of his fellows. One can almost smell the sweet air of Florence and sense the pleasant feeling of escape, of unilateral movement toward the pleasant and the good.[55] He and his friends, like those tale-tellers in the *Decameron,* move away from the place of pain and death to gather in "dilettevole parte." There, also like those other speakers, they speak with order and discretion. The subjects which they discuss take the following arrangement: the changefulness of *fortuna* (one of the persistent topics of the *Decameron,* and certainly one that continues the Boethian strain initiated by the "thought"), the foolishness of those who embrace her eagerly and rest their hopes in her. From moral philosophy they move to natural philosophy, discussing the "perpetue cose della natura" (50), and thence to theology ("da queste passammo alle divine"—50), the outermost reaches of which are simply too exalted for human comprehension by less than the most sublime intelligences. Like the ravaged Boethius, the narrator turns from the world's deceits to the steadfastness of philosophy.[56] Only the advent of evening brings their discussion to a halt; the narrator describes his condition: "as though I had fed on divine food, all my former unhappiness fled, now almost [57] forgotten, I returned to my customary lodging, consoled" (52). The participle *consolato* reminds the reader once more of the role of a Boethian conception of philosophy in the entire "situational frame."

What follows is one of Boccaccio's triumphs. Those who love Dante will rarely or never observe their *poeta* being "sent up" in better or more loving ways. Boccaccio has inherited the dream vision from a long tradition in medieval literature,[58] and he has inherited—it is by far his most precious inheritance from the recent past—Dante's *Commedia.* As various tales in the *Decameron* show his uneasiness with the otherworldly setting of the *Commedia,*[59] here too Boccaccio returns to his Dante in a mildly corrective way, as though to say, "Dante, I know that you present your poem as a vision, but I also know that you made it up." In something like this frame of mind Boccaccio "redoes" the first two cantos of *Inferno.* Since it is not the purpose of this study to consider Boccaccio's omnivorous use of the greater poet, I shall leave the reader to his own instruction and pleasure. The reconstructions of Dante are numerous, evident, and delightful to behold. And Boccaccio's own contribution to the craft of handling the literary dream is vastly underrated. The only present-day sensibility one thinks of easily as being competent to handle the Dantesque machinery of otherworldly procedures, the quick leaps in comprehension that reveal the gradual awakening of the dreaming character to his horrible situation, the completely Boccaccian awareness of the humor of that situation, based in a sure grasp of the relation of dream to life, is Fellini's. Let a moment suffice. The narrator is certain that he knows his "Virgilio" [60] from somewhere. And then, with a blinding shock of recognition, he realizes that he "knew" him indeed—he is the shade of a dead Florentine acquaintance. He wants to run but, "siccome sovente avviene a chi sogna, che gli pare ne' maggiori bisogni per niuna condizione del mondo potersi muovere," he cannot move a muscle (84). It is difficult to think of a more "modern" dream vision in all of medieval literature, or of a funnier one.

The narrator's dream leads him along a lovely path into a *locus amoenus* which quickly turns into an infernal landscape.[61] The place is densely Dantesque ("una solitudine diserta, aspra e fiera, piena di salvatiche piante, di pruni e di bronchi, senza sentiere o via alcuna, e intorniata di montagne asprissime"—61). Horrid sounds assault his ears ("mi pareva . . . sentire mugghi, urli e strida di diversi e ferocissimi animali"—63).[62] He is terror-stricken, and must be content either with grieving at his own condition or calling on God's aid. At this moment a man who looks sixty or more, wearing a vermilion garment that seems even brighter than garments painted by "i nostri maestri," appears to him (67).[63] Calling the narrator by name,[64] he speaks: "What evil fortune or destiny has brought you to this desert? Where has your good sense flown?. . . . Can't you understand that here one finds physical death, that here one loses one's soul, which is much worse?" (74). The narrator, weeping and shamefaced, replies that he has been brought to this low estate by "il falso piacere delle caduche cose." It is an admission worthy of the errant narrator of the *Amorosa Visione,* but he is much too happy with the corruptible things of this world to make such an admission or (it is probably the better word) confession. Where we are is becoming clear enough. We are in hell on earth. All the borrowings from the *Inferno* are underlined by a colloquial version of Virgil's "facilis descensus Averno" to make this point clear.[65] And the particular hell in which the narrator finds himself has particular affinity with the fifth canto of the *Inferno* (for obvious reasons it seems to have been Boccaccio's favorite *locus* in Dante). Its various names, which are supplied by the guide, make that clear enough. It is known variously, he explains, as "il laberinto d'Amore" (appropriated by Boccaccio as the subtitle of the work), "il porcile di Venere," "la valle de' sospiri e della miseria." The labyrinth of Love is not a pleasant place.[66] You cannot leave it, the guide tells him, unless a heavenly light lead you out (95). Something like this has been his own fortunate fate, it appears, since he now purges himself in Purgatory (101). The narrator begins to understand his own good fortune in being offered such a light. In a passage that helps to clarify Boccaccio's earlier uses of the language of the religion of love, he expresses his nascent gratitude to God for sending the *guida* to him to help bring about his *salute* (not the carnal gratification so often implied by the word in its uses by lovers).[67] His words remind us of that other religion by negating it. He speaks of (109) "la benignità del mandatore" (God, not Amore), his "umiltà" (before God, not a *donna*), "l'altezza e la potenzia del mio Signore" (God, not the Lord of Love), "la mia viltà" (not a lover's hopeful protest but a believer's penitence), "Colui che . . . mi si mostrava pietoso e liberale" (not a prayer to a lady to be so, but thanksgiving to God for His grace). The words constitute not only a litany of sorts, but also a "counter-litany" to the "litany" of the religion of love. Yet the narrator is only beginning to come round. Within a page he makes a serious and indicative error when he believes that the inhabitants of the *valle* must be those who have been exiled by Amore from his court.[68] As for the noises that he hears, he supposes them to be made by the beasts who inhabit this place. That is enough for our *guida,* who offers the foolish narrator [69] some unvarnished home truths in what can be treated as a commentary on this hellish place, or, to speak more to the point, on the religion of love. Although its message is obvious, it is worth having in full.

> Truly I understand that the ray of the true light has not yet reached your intellect, that you, as do many fools, consider this thing, which is the worst of miseries, to be the greatest happiness. You believe that in your concupiscent and carnal love there is some good; therefore, open your ears to what I now will tell you. This miserable valley *is* the court that you call "Love's"; those beasts, which you say you have heard and still hear bellowing, *are* those miserable creatures—of whom you are one—who are ensnared by false love; their voices, insofar as they speak of such love as that, have no other sound in the ears of sane and educated men than that which they now have in yours. And thus a little while ago I called this valley "the labyrinth"

> because in it men, as they used to of yore, become trapped, without knowing how they may ever escape.[70]

His meaning is clear enough: Carnal love is hell. The rest of the activities described in the *trattato* may be judged against this clear statement. Thus, when the narrator describes the awakening in himself of the flame in the heart he felt for the sexually attractive widow, he is different from Boccaccio's other love-sick protagonists only in that he is learning and will eventually have learned the way in which he should consider such emotions. All of his description of the birth of lust in himself sounds exactly as it sounds in the mouth of the narrator of the *Caccia,* of Troiolo, of Fiammetta (in the *Elegia*). There is a single and pivotal difference: His account begins with the phrase "da falsa opinione vinto" (150). And we thus have a way of disapproving, and of experiencing his own growing disapproval, of lust.

The *guida* knows full well the attractions of love. But the narrator is rebuked because at least his age (something past forty) and his studies should have been proof against "questa matta passione" (180). He is, after all, a poet, and poetry, "no less than the other sciences, should have shown you the nature of love and the nature of women. . . . Consider ancient as well as modern tales and behold how many evils, fires, deaths, undoings, ruinations, murders this damnable passion has caused. And yet crowds of you miserable mortals—among whom yourself—having thrown aside your intelligence, call him 'god,' and as though to the highest granter of aid, sacrifice your minds to him in your need and pray to him with utter devotion" (195–96). That poetry, both ancient and modern, should have shown the narrator the falseness of love and of the religion of love may not seem, to many, a Boccaccian sentiment. But what if it had always been Boccaccio's sentiment? Let us at least admit the possibility. The *guida* concludes this part of the *somnium* with a mocking picture of the Lord whom lovers worship. His effigy, as it was made by the ancients—if philosophy or experience had not been warning enough—should have been sufficient admonition in itself. Look at him. He is young, nude, has wings, veiled eyes, and a bow (198).[71] He is dangerous, in short, if we put ourselves in range.

We shall not here consider the attack on women that fills, for some four dozen uninterrupted pages, or something more than half the text, the remainder of the *Corbaccio.*[72] In his verbal assault upon his own former wife the *guida* means to warn us against all *femmine* who style themselves *donne*—of whom there are precious few.[73] The venom of his diatribe, which takes its first image of disgust in the menstrual instruments of the fourteenth century and ends with the praise of true gentility (which is where we began and which is seen to consist in the positive use of the free will—hardly the position of the "court of love"), has long been noticed, if not universally admired. Its purpose, within the pretext of the fiction, was to turn the narrator's lust into hate. And certainly our narrator seems to have required something like this version of a sermon on Hell to amend his lustful ways. One positive image of womankind inserts itself into the tirade, as an *exemplum* of all the feminine virtues that the *guida* finds almost entirely lacking on this earth (indeed he says that virtuous women are more rare than phoenixes—268): the blessed Virgin.[74]

The *somnium* ends with a Dantesque ascent. The *guida* moves easily to the summit of one of the surrounding mountains, drawing with him his charge (who makes the ascent only with the most painful difficulty). From Boccaccio's version of the Earthly Paradise the narrator, now in the veritable *locus amoenus,* looks down at the valley of Love and sees it for what it is—an inferno. Now his *guida* (as, in the same place, Virgilio had done for Dante) sets him free. As he wishes to throw himself down at the feet of the spirit in gratitude, his Macrobian dream concludes (551–54). We move back into the "situational frame." Having decided that his dream was a true one, he returns to the company of his friends. They expound the dream with him (clearly along the lines the *guida* has already laid down). In a few days the narrator is completely cured of his carnal affection for the widow and has regained the liberty[75] he had lost by loving her. If he is given the time, he will punish her properly (a promise fulfilled in the book which we hold in our hands). The work ends with the usual *congedo* (except that in this one the amatory values which usually inform the narrator's final words are turned upside down). He hopes that the "piccola mia operetta" will be of use to the young and will bear witness to his "beneficio . . . ricevuto" of the Virgin (as Boccaccio closes his circle by returning to the first line of the work). But then he warns his book to avoid finding its way into the hands of bad women—especially the widow's—where it will be poorly received. This is a distinct reversal of the pattern of Boccaccio's usual *congedo,* in which the narrator prays that his work *will* find its way into the hands of his lady.[76] And the work ends with the promise, repeating itself, of still harsher treatment of the widow.

If the meaning of the *Corbaccio* is clear enough to all of its readers, Boccaccio's intention in writing it is not. In attempting to confront the problem, one might reasonably conceptualize possible views of Boccaccio's career in vernacular fiction as follows: Either he was always a follower of Venus (and thus had undergone either a "conversion" of some sort before writing the *Corbaccio* or is ironizing the simple-minded Christianity of his narrator, whose dream is far from being a true one—the second possibility, though logically possible, has only recently been proposed by Cassell), or he was never a follower of Venus (and thus in the *Corbaccio* is only saying overtly what he had previously said ironically). A third possibility is that there is no consistent interest in saying anything at all to be found in Boccaccio's fiction—he was "just a writer," and thus may have played with some of the *topoi* literary critics like to deal in, but we make a mistake to take such behavior seriously. For certain readers (they are likely to be on good terms with the partisans of "Jolly Geoff Chaucer") the last formulation has its appeal. In actual fact the major view of the *Corbaccio* has been the first one. And the most enlightened views of its relationship to the earlier works stress its opposition to their values. Perhaps the most trenchant passage written in this vein was composed some thirty years ago by Giuseppe Billanovich.[77] If he has led us to consider the *Corbaccio* in the light of the tradition of Ovid's *Remedia amoris* and its medieval sisters, his argument holds to the point of believing that Boccaccio (like Ovid and Andreas in this) is apologizing for the praise of sensuality which we find in his earlier works. While Billanovich is not ultimately clear (and thus ultimately most suggestive) on this point, a later *studioso,* Giorgio Padoan, one of Boccaccio's most schooled readers, has returned to Billanovich's interpretation and reinforced it, seeing the *Corbaccio* as the rejection of the amorous tradition of the earlier works.[78] The "conversion theory," in whatever form it is advanced,[79] has much to recommend it, insofar as we perceive that Boccaccio's intent, at least through the *Decameron,* is, if not lascivious, at least venereal, that is, that he holds carnal love to be a positive good—whether in relationship to higher goods or simply in itself. But it is at least possible that such an appreciation of Boccaccio's intent is itself at fault. Without doing more than repeat that suggestion, which has been made several times in this chapter, and which will shortly be argued at some length, I might offer another way of seeing the difference between the *Caccia* (to which I shall limit myself for the moment) and the *Corbaccio.* Simply assume, for the purposes of experiment, that the *Caccia* is as ironically anti-venereal as the *Corbaccio* is openly so. The fact remains that the early work (in this like most or all of the preceding vernacular fictions) *feels* like a very different sort of thing indeed. It seems light-hearted in tone, whatever its meaning. And certainly I could say at least as much (if not a great deal more) about the *Corbaccio*'s "neighbor," the *Decameron.* There is so much happy (along with a good deal of destructive and sad) sensuality found there. Hasn't the author of the *Corbaccio* moved away from that, if not to "a new moralizing attitude" (to use Padoan's words), then to a *more* moralizing one? And here the answer must be affirmative.

If so, what can I say, within the boundaries of my own hypothesis, to explain the change? Must I agree to the theory of a "crisis" or a "conversion"? Not necessarily. All that I must grant is a change in tone and method, brought about by the growing conviction that to treat moral matters convincingly, one must sound more like a cleric.[80] This hypothesis, or explanation, takes its sense of the reason for the change in Boccaccio's tone from within and without the writer's own persuasions. That is to say that the tone of Boccaccio's late works—of the classicizing Latin works as well as of the *Corbaccio*—is more outwardly Christian both because the author himself felt the need to take such a position (either because he genuinely felt that need or because he felt pressed by his detractors, whose traces are already evident in the prologue to the Fourth Day and in the Conclusion of the *Decameron*—or, as is most likely to be the case, for both these reasons) and because the more sober audience which he now sought to address expected such literary behavior. To attempt to assay the varying weights of these considerations would be difficult, if not impossible. But to see them as all being present is probably just. However, to argue that the explicit Christianity of the *Corbaccio* is altogether a change from the position taken in the early works may simply be the result of our having misread these works.[81] And it is to an examination of the characteristics of their patterns of signification that we now proceed.

Christian Romance and Pagan Delusion

WHETHER OR NOT it has been convincing, the preceding chapter had the advantage of a certain clarity of line. That is, we were able to follow the general outline and some of the more salient particulars of two not terribly complicated and rather short works. This is not to suggest that what resulted is a thorough analysis of either work, but enough of one, I would hope, at least to make an interpretive position clear. In this second chapter we shall be dealing with four of Boccaccio's fictions, *Filocolo, Fiammetta, Filostrato,* and *Teseida.* While my guiding concern shall be to uncover the truth about Venus (which is twofold) as it is revealed in these four texts, I shall also attempt to show that in three of them (and in a major portion of the *Filocolo*) the carnal Venus is attacked indirectly, precisely by the use of irony.[1]

If in both the *Caccia* and the *Corbaccio* Venus appears or is mentioned but once, she is so frequently present in the *Filocolo*[2] as to be one of the major "characters" in the work. Her name (in that form, not including the appellation "Citerea") occurs at least fifty-three times.[3] And her function in this early romance of Boccaccio's is complex and diverse, offering the reader an opportunity to grasp the author's intention in his teasing treatment of carnal love.[4] Yet hardly any of the infrequent studies of the *Filocolo* have paid more than the slightest attention to her role in the work.[5] She makes her first appearance in the narrative portion of the romance only in the last paragraph of Book One.[6] When they are six years old, the king puts his son Florio and the Christian orphan, Biancifiore, whom he has been raising as his own child, under the tutelage of one Racheio, a grammarian. Since the children were born on the same day, their mutual arrival at the age of six is described as a return to the astral influence of Venus.[7] While their birth occurred in pagan surroundings, it had the auspicious overtones of Christian mystery mingled with pagan divinity.[8] If they were born under Venus, we expect that they will have loving dispositions. And our grammarian helps to make sure of that. Book One ends with a climax of sorts: Florio and Biancifiore, having been taught how to read, take up a most important text indeed, "il santo libro d'Ovidio," in which the art of kindling "santi fuochi" in cold hearts is told (I, 45, 6).

If the *Ars amatoria* is to be their moral guide, we may expect them to fall passionately in love.[9] Turning the page, one finds the groundwork being laid by none other than Venus herself (II, 1, 1). On her mountain she calls her winged son to her and sends him down to earth, seeing that these two Ovid-reading youths seem more apt to her service than to that of "i freddi fuochi di Diana." The familiar struggle between these two goddesses is thus implanted in the lengthy plot of the romance. Venus tells Cupid to disguise himself, as he did when he took on the form of Ascanius. The reference to the inflammation of Dido, with its anti-Roman (and, for a medieval reader, anti-Christian) overtones will have a larger context once we come to Book Five. For Florio, in this like Aeneas, will crown his labors of love by becoming an emperor. But now we have no such context. Venereal love, though balanced by Diana's name, has no apparent opposition in the text. Disguised as Florio's father, King Felice, Cupid does his work, and the two children fall under the spell of his "segreto veleno" (II, 1, 2—the word *poison* surely has negative implications). While the son is thus occupied, the mother too descends from heaven (these are the first of the many *discese* of the gods which dot the pages of the *Filocolo*) to keep the king busy while Cupid does his work. She does so by bringing him a dream in which the main plot of the *Filocolo* is clearly foreshadowed, including even the lovers' final conversion to Christianity.[10] The two children, in Boccaccio's delightful replay of *Inferno* v, close their Ovids and kiss—no more than that, for they are as yet too young to be allowed to know the hidden pleasures of sex.[11] They are now under control of the venereal flame, and Diana's coldness would come too late to cool them off (II, 4, 8). However, the notion of carnal affection between their son Florio and the lovely little stranger is anathema to the king and queen. Florio's labors of love begin (he compares himself to Hercules at II, 15, 3) with their forceful opposition and will not end for hundreds of pages. Through the following one hundred and more pages of Book Two, in adversities one trembles to recall and gladly will not recount, the separated lovers are *dévots* of Venus. At the conclusion of this book we get an inkling of the direction in which their solution lies. Biancifiore, saved from death at the hands of the seneschal by Florio, makes the rounds of the temples with the queen, offering "debite grazie" (a motif of which Boccaccio is fond) and making sacrifices. They do not do quite thorough enough a job in their religious observances, however, for they unknowingly omit the temple of Diana.[12] Their failure here will have nearly dire effects and leads to the delaying of a happy ending to the love shared by Florio and Biancifiore for two more lengthy books of adventure.

When Diana finally appears as an actor in this drama of love, some fifty pages later, she does so accompanied by a phrase that points clearly to the seriousness of Biancifiore's omitted sacrifice: "Diana, alla quale niuno sacrificio era stato porto come agli altri iddii fu. . . ." (III, 24, 1). The anger she has hidden in her breast is now given vent when she descends to the Apennine cave of "fredda Gelosia," [13] who then comes forth to put jealousy into Florio's loving heart and further complicate the plot. And from this point on Diana begins to play an important role in the proceedings. When the king, Florio's father, arranges to marry Biancifiore to the Carthaginian merchant Sardano (the intrigue which will allow Boccaccio to go "east" for his setting of the fourth book of the romance), she vainly objects that she has vowed eternal virginity to Diana in the hope of forestalling his aim (III, 46, 3). This is of course a lie. Her own ensuing prayer to Diana (III, 51, 7) makes plain that while she is still a virgin, she looks forward to yielding her maidenhead to Florio.[14] And it once again reminds us that Biancifiore is in her present difficulty because she failed to honor Diana. On the next page, moved by "i pietosi prieghi" which we have just heard, Diana decides to temper her wrath. To do so, she pays a friendly visit to Venus (III, 52). It is striking to find these two old enemies together and acting in consort, especially in light of their antagonistic rivalry in the *Caccia di Diana.* Now they appear together to the dreaming Biancifiore in order to reassure her (III, 53). As in the *Aeneid,* such heavenly reassurance is a long time in making its promises fact. Yet what is important, and even imperative, to note is that the restoration of each lover to each is now apparently impossible under the aegis of Venus alone.[15] The nature of the cooperative relationship of these two goddesses becomes clearer later in the narrative. For now we can observe that as the second book ended with notice of Biancifiore's failure to make sacrifice to Diana, Florio (having recently taken on the alias of "Filocolo") [16] and his companions prepare for their laborious journey in search of Biancifiore by making sacrifice to "Jove supreme, Venus, Juno, Neptune, Eolus, and to every other god" (III, 76, 1). Cynically we might say that they are only covering their bets. But in the world of Christianized pagan romance, their behavior is only correct. For if each of the gods sees the need for his own honor only (or at most the sharing of honor with another god whose help happens to be required in a given task [17]), the wiser of the mortals understand that all the gods must have their due. That would seem to be Boccaccio's version of "pagan orthodoxy."

The course of Filocolo and his companions does not run straight. Misadventure forces them to winter in Naples. Nearly eighty pages, or more than one-eighth of the *Filocolo,* is given over to this sojourn, during which the principal "event" is a "court of love," presided over by the beautiful and wise Fiammetta.[18] The most recent and most intelligent treatment of the famous "questioni d'amore" is that of Victoria Kirkham.[19] While there are some quibbles (which will be dutifully recorded [20]), even from the cordial point of view of this study, that may be lodged against Kirkham's findings, the importance of her article is considerable. One does not wish to recapitulate her thesis, for it deserves close attention. Her major contribution is to make us see that in the *Filocolo* the worship of Cupid is to be conceived as worship of a false god.[21] We do well to listen to her: "The *questioni d'amore* thus appear to be structured around a double perspective involving on the one hand the relative, or peripheral, supremacy of Cupid, and on the other the absolute and central supremacy of God." [22] And let us look briefly at the exchange between Caleon and Fiammetta. Caleon, obviously inflamed by sexual longing for her, wants to know whether it is to a man's own good ("a bene essere di se medesimo") to fall in love (IV, 43, 16). Fiammetta's answer centers in what Quaglio characterizes as "la tradizionale dottrina dell'amore." [23] The second of these three kinds of love ("onesto, per diletto, per utilità") is the one under discussion. "Questo è il nostro iddio," says Fiammetta, here speaking in her quality as carnal lover (IV, 44, 6), and promises to say shortly whether their worship is good or not. (Her definition of "honest love" clearly points us toward her eventual answer—it is the love that joins God and his creatures, the love, we might add, which St. Paul calls charity.) After describing the variability of "amore per utilià," which, linked to mutable Fortune, lays waste many a good thing and should be referred to as hate rather than love,[24] she opposes this religion of love in ways that have relevance to all of Boccaccio's work. No one who wishes to live the virtuous life should subject himself to this kind of love, for it is without honor, leads to sorrows, awakens vice, gives plentiful vain care, and unworthily takes away freedom—freedom, which should be held more precious than anything else; let him who can live free, following that which in all things increases freedom, and let vicious vassals follow vicious lords (IV, 44, 8–9).[25] Nothing could be clearer than Fiammetta's denunciation of the religion of love, despite her own involvement in the game of the *questioni*.[26] Caleon is of a far different opinion. For him *amore per diletto* should be followed, not shunned, by those who seek a glorious end and as an "aumentatrice di virtù" (IV, 45, 2). His examples follow: Mars, turned from a harsh warrior to a gentle lover by his love for Venus; Medea, who helped Jason; Paris and Menelaus, lovers of Helen; Achilles' wrath soothed by Polixena's prayers. He concludes with Orpheus, "who merited the regaining of his lost wife" (IV, 45, 3–7).[27] The point about Caleon's pedantry is that it tends to prove Fiammetta's point rather than his own. To take only one of his examples, Paris's love for Helen had disastrous results. Indeed, if one goes through Caleon's list of great love affairs—all of which he considers to have been ennobling—one sees that they produced exactly those effects which Fiammetta had described a few moments before. Boccaccio's irony is (or should be) clearly visible here, and its object is the religion of love,[28] which Boccaccio attacks on two counts: It is a false religion (as opposed to Christianity) and it is a fraudulent religion (it claims the noblest of intentions but seeks only sexual release). It may surely be argued that Caleon's defense of Cupid is rendered ineffectual by its own feeble and incorrect argument, that is to say that in his speech we are dealing with an obviously ironic Boccaccio. That this is not some sort of latter-day imposition of an interpretation which violates the sense of the text is guaranteed by the fact that Fiammetta herself takes up Caleon's exemplary figures, one at a time (and adding a few of her own) in order to demonstrate the danger and fatuousness of *amore per diletto.* Because what she says does not square with what most critics have assumed Boccaccio is saying, her (and Boccaccio's) message is generally ignored.

One of the main arguments of this study is that we, Boccaccio's readers, are the ones who must supply such arguments as Fiammetta delivers here when they are not present in the text (it was my pleasant experience, as I worked through this passage, to find my own ironic reading of Caleon's speech reinforced by Fiammetta's reaction), the necessary ironic commentary to the praise of carnal love. The "questioni d'amore" have an important role in the *Filoclo,* both thematically and morally (as Victoria Kirkham has pointed out). In them—at their very center—Filocolo/Florio for the first time hears a clear negative commentary on the lessons of Ovid's *Ars amatoria.* More positive instruction awaits him further on. The last lines of Fiammetta's response to Caleon lead us and him in this direction when she speaks of the light that appeared to Aeneas (*Aeneid* II, 590f.) to lead him out of darkness and destruction. That light was Venus.[29] And in Fiammetta's remark we have one of Boccaccio's first articulated suggestions that there are two Venuses. For her son, with whom she is usually identified, the winged and blind Cupid, has just been seen as her own enemy.[30]

In her lonely tower *la belle captive,* Biancifiore, awaits the admiral's pleasure. At the door to her chamber we find a statue of Cupid. He is conventionally portrayed—nude, golden-winged, his bow and arrows in his hands—"ma egli non ha gli occhi fasciati come molti il figurano" (IV, 85, 8). The small iconographical departure from the usual,[31] which Boccaccio puts before us so teasingly, will make its significance felt shortly. The eyes of this Cupid are eyes that give forth an amazingly bright light. This change in his aspect accounts for the brightness of the room when Filocolo at last, some four hundred pages from the beginning of the romance, is alone and naked with his sleeping beloved. Kisses—one hundred or more for every word he speaks (and since he speaks well over one hundred a medieval kiss-counter might well have trembled for the condition of his lips) cover the face and upper body of the sleeping girl, and the highly wrought Filocolo even ventures to touch "quel luogo ove ogni dolcezza si richiude" so that "gli pare trapassare di letizia le ragioni degl'iddii" (IV, 118, 6). If we heed Boccaccio's many "biographers" this scene is merely another version of Boccaccio's actual seduction of the actual Maria d'Aquino. What they fail to notice is the text, for Filocolo's lust stops at the portals of joy so that he and Biancifiore may be married.[32] To be sure, this marriage is of a private and thus extraordinary nature.[33] Nonetheless, at the very moment of probable and certainly expected carnal union Filocolo draws back from mere carnality in the name of a better kind of love: "I haven't exhausted myself for so long a time to gain a paramour, but to take a wife, from whom I shall never part" (IV, 120, 3). He marries her with her talismanic ring in the symbolic presence of "Imeneo e la santa Giunone e Venere, nostra dea." Diana is here replaced by the combined forces of Hymen and Juno, the presiding deities of the nuptial deflowering and of marriage respectively, and who are accompanied by a Venus who has similar associations. But we are told that Diana too rejoices because the two lovers had remained chaste until they were pledged in marital love (IV, 122, 2). In the absence of a proper temple, Filocolo chooses the bright-eyed statue of Cupid to be the representative of

Hymen, Juno, and Venus (IV, 120, 4). As a result there seem to be two Cupids in the *Filocolo,* at least in the sense that Filocolo "uses" the statue of the god, who is usually the enemy of marriage, to represent higher forms of love (and thus offering a small paradigm of Boccaccio's "use" of pagan myth). It is further worth noting that Venus, who had so long held sole place in the prayers of the two lovers, is now in the company of gods who lend her a new (and better) nature, and is named last among them. (At IV, 121, 3, she is even omitted from the list, when only Hymen and Juno are named.) It is only once these nuptials have been celebrated that Boccaccio will finally allow nature to follow its course. The lovers take pleasure of one another for a "fitting space of time" (IV, 122, 3), and fall asleep in one another's arms. The scene seems purposefully anti-climactic, as though to downplay the importance of merely sexual love. And even Venus now seems to have changed her nature. When she appears to aid them in their further difficulties (for of course there are some) she is not nude, nor partly clad in purple, but is wrapped in the whitest of clouds (IV, 134, 2).[34] If there is a program here, the change in her appearance would seem to be the result of the change in their perception of her deity—she now governs marital love, not the love that is kindled by readings of the *Ars amatoria.*

Book Four concludes with the softening of the jealous admiral's ire and the subsequent wedding feast for the two lovers in Alexandria. The wedding is accompanied by prayers of the populace of that city "to Hymen, holy Juno, and some other gods" (IV, 160, 1), and the happy couple, their *fatiche* at an end, desire only to return to Verona and Filocolo's father. Indeed, there seems little more that Boccaccio can do with his tale. He has used up all the source material available in the French and Italian versions of the romance. Yet the narrative still has over one hundred pages to run.

If the *Filocolo* is little read, its fifth book seems hardly to be read at all. It has little in the way of "action," as there is no romantic problem to resolve (since the lovers are united). The portion of the text which has had the largest amount of attention bestowed upon it is the section involving the return to Naples (V, 13–31), which, beginning with Crescini,[35] has been mined for "autobiographical" references. The four ladies with the backwards names (Alleiram, Airam, Asenga, Annavoi) should probably have drawn more attention to what they do (defy the gods, for which they are justly punished) than to who they might be. The major "events" of the fifth book occur, importantly enough, in Rome (V, 50–77). There Filocolo comes as a pilgrim. The sense of his pilgrimage will shortly be made clear. Where he had earlier once described himself as "un povero pellegrino d'amore" (IV, 16, 9), under the tutelage of the priestly Ilario (who, after informing Filocolo politely that he is an idolater for worshipping pagan gods, gives a lengthy précis of the events of Christian history, beginning in Creation and concluding with a version of the Creed—V, 53–56) he will become a pilgrim in a stricter sense. "Accesi del celestiale amore" (V, 58, 2—the contrast of celestial and carnal love could not be more clear), he and Menedon spread the Word among their fellows. They soon have themselves baptized.[36] The only pagan of note left in sight is poor old King Felice, and it is only in his mouth that we still hear the names of the old gods, when he worries that his son has been subverted by the Christians (V, 78, 8–9).[37] God Himself appears in a vision to the last of the pagans (V, 80), and Felice's conversion is only pages away (V, 84, 2), bringing with it the conversion of all the citizens of Marmorina (Verona). That is all I shall say of the fifth book. Perhaps it is enough in order to indicate the character of its Christian tone and meaning.[38] It may not be the most exciting part of the *Filocolo,* but it seems absurd to pay it no mind, as so many readers have done.[39]

If the reader has found the presentation of even this much of the *Filocolo* laborious, he should be aware that it constitutes a more than brief treatment of the complicated action of the romance. Left to one side are considerations not only of what is far from my purpose, but of many scenes and formulations which would help to reinforce my reading.[40] From as much as we have examined, it is probably just to conclude, whatever the aesthetic merit of the *Filocolo,*[41] that in it Boccaccio has constructed what we might call, to borrow from the title of Alban Forcione's recent study of Cervantes' *Persiles,* a "Christian romance,"[42] in which the deity with whom we begin, the Venus of the *Ars amatoria,* is superseded by a better Venus, who in turn yields to the true God. Since that is what happens in the text, it is a little surprising that the first reading of the *Filocolo* which moves clearly in this direction is Kirkham's.[43]

The relevance of the foregoing remarks to our concern with Boccaccio's uses of the figure of Venus should be evident. What we are able to perceive in the *Filocolo* is at least the emergence of a notion that Boccaccio will clearly state in his commentary to the *Teseida*—there are two Venuses.[44] But before we examine the presence of this *topos* in the *Elegia* and the *Teseida* we might think for a moment of the ways in which Boccaccio makes his meaning felt in the *Filocolo.* The perhaps surprising fact is that so much of his intention is, if not baldly stated by the narrator, readily apparent from the words and actions of the characters. For instance, the changing behavior and perceptions of Venus, while not unsubtle, are fairly easy to follow. And so, while there are any number of allegorical moments in the work, its basic gestures toward our understanding are made through straightforward statement, which is joined to a certain amount of ironic statement. The latter predominates in the early part of the work, in which pagan principles are devotedly adhered to by the young lovers, while in the fifth book this mode has yielded almost entirely to narration in which moral principles are handed directly to the reader by the new Christians. It is difficult (and dangerous) to schematize broadly here. And in order to see the differences in Boccaccio's uses of various modes, we do well to study what is perhaps his greatest accomplishment in the ironic mode, the *Elegia di madonna Fiammetta.*

With the exceptions of the *Teseida* and the *Filostrato,* which take place in the pre-Christian era, the *Elegia* is the work of Boccaccio which makes least overt reference to Christianity.[45] This is not to say that Christian values should be absent from our understanding of the work, which is probably at least as satirical as the *Corbaccio.* After Boccaccio himself, who left his meaning clearer than we have managed to take it, no one has come closer to revealing the negative view of carnal love in the *Fiammetta* than Walter Pabst.[46] The very title of his study points toward the double sense of Venus that long ago should have been perceived as central to Boccaccio's fiction. And while one may find some aspects of his study troubling, one has also the sense that it is among the most suggestive pieces ever written about the *Fiammetta.*[47] The contributions of the leading Italian student of the work, Dario Rastelli, are of another order. In his first article on the *Elegia* he patiently traces the history of much of the wrongheaded response it has received (with origins in Hegel and Burckhardt), and which may be typified as being Romantic in spirit rather than responsive to the medieval qualities of the work.[48] This valuable survey of prior critical attitudes clears the way for a more systematic study of the text. A later article does a similar service for the situation of the *Elegia* among its "biographical" critics.[49] However, it is probably fair to say that Rastelli, if he has restored the *Fiammetta* to some of its medieval preoccupations and to many of its medieval rhetorical conventions, has not offered any major new interpretation.[50]

In the rather busy lists of *Fiammetta* criticism there is an earlier instance of something that is at least vaguely similar to the Pabst-Quaglio dispute. During Boccaccio's last anniversary celebration an article by Giuseppe Gigli appeared in one of the major publications in honor of the occasion.[51] In this brief and altogether unimposing piece the author, basing his arguments entirely within the biographical mode of reading the *opere minori,* dared to suggest that the *Elegia* was Boccaccio's revenge on Fiammetta for having spurned him.[52] If one is to accept a biographical reading of the works, this is, of course, the only argument that makes any literal sense. The commemorative volume was, naturally, fairly widely reviewed. Poor Gigli, with his four pages (out of nearly three hundred), felt the wrath of the outraged—many of those who reviewed the volume pierced him with a bitter shaft or two.[53] The point is not that Gigli was a particularly perceptive critic (for he was probably not as perceptive as most of his detractors), is not that he was right (he most likely was not, since there was probably no "actual" Fiammetta or Maria d'Aquino to account for the narrative line of the *Elegia*), but that early twentieth-century students of Boccaccio did not like to be forced to think again once they had made up their minds. Hauvette's high dudgeon is hilarious—unless one is as solemn and wrong-headed a reader as he. Not to see the many caustic elements that perforate Fiammetta's pretensions to amorous nobility is to miss one of the better pleasures of modern fiction—for the *Elegia* is "the first modern psychological novel" [54] written in the middle ages (or at least the first medieval psychological novel), and it is (and here I part company with Pabst, who tends to see Fiammetta as a tragic character, victimized by Venus) a very funny one. In this sense Gigli is not far off the track when he thought of the similar satiric intent of the *Corbaccio,* for the *Elegia* is a stinging treatment of the religion of love.

Fiammetta, as Raffaello Ramat has suggested, is a sick woman.[55] In earlier times a doctor (whether of medicine or theology) would have had little difficulty in diagnosing her disease. She has a terrible case of *melanconia* or *tristitia,* the desperate sadness that results from carnal love.[56] She is in that sense a victim. But unlike the heroine of Seneca's *Phaedra,* on whom she is partly modelled,[57] or of Racine's *Phèdre* ("Vénus tout entière à sa proie attachée"),[58] she is not so much caught in a trap as hoist on her own petard. The difference between Phaedra (or Phèdre) and Fiammetta is the difference between classical (or neo-classical) dramatic fatality and the Christian medieval "drama of choice," in the sense that all medieval moralizing literature, from Augustine's *Confessions* and Prudentius' *Psychomachia* to Dante's *Commedia,* Petrarch's *Canzoniere,* and Chaucer's *Canterbury Tales,* has as its central subject matter the direction of the (free) will away from the sinful to the good. The "moral drama" of the character Fiammetta concerns her unwillingness to make the correct choice.[59]

Fiammetta, who narrates her own sad tale of love and woe, tells us that she had been living happily and chastely with her husband (I, 1). That this decent sort of fellow is never named in the course of the narrative—while we hear Panfilo's name often enough—gives some clue to Boccaccio's intentions. For here we have a parodistic and perverse reflection of the religion of love, in which lovers must seek to hide the name and identity of their adulterous partners: Fiammetta "hides" the name of her lawful spouse, and not from desire to save his reputation from the blot of cuckoldry but from sheer lack of interest in him—at least this is the impression that one receives. Her woe, she recounts (and would have us believe), is the fault of Fortune, who insidiously roused the previously favorable gods against her (I, 2). The night before she fell into the clutches of passion, she had a dream. Like Proserpina (and Dante's Matelda?), picking flowers in a lovely field, she decided to lie down on the grass. As Eurydice was bitten in the foot by a hidden serpent,[60] so is she bitten by a serpent, under the left breast. Her ensuing act is what is most arresting. Having been bitten, she takes the *fredda serpe* and puts it in her bosom, thinking thus to make herself better.[61] The snake then resumes its biting, drinks much of her blood, and goes off. The dream is a clear foreshadowing of the sexual behavior of Panfilo, who "loves 'em and leaves 'em." But is the serpent the only guilty party? Or does Fiammetta, even within the simple concealments of her own dream, act in such a way that she too must be considered responsible? Whether or not the dream should be understood in that way, her ensuing actions tell us more about her nature. In the light of morning she dresses to go to church,[62] having discarded the warnings of the dream as "sciocchezze de' sogni," taking pleasure in her own beauty (she thinks she resembles the goddesses seen by Paris in the valley of Mount Ida—I, 4).[63] Disregarding what she will later perceive was another sign sent her by the gods (a flower which falls from the garland on her head), she proceeds to the service, where she is admired by men and women alike as though she were Venus or Minerva (I, 5).[64] If Fiammetta has told us that her life with her husband had been chaste, we are probably a little surprised at the vanity of her behavior in church (shortly before, as she adorned herself, she was, in her own words, like a preening peacock—I, 4), where she is utterly inattentive to the service (I, 8).[65] But on this occasion she will pay for her self-love. In Panfilo's eyes she reads the words "O donna, tu sola se' la beatitudine nostra," [66] and she is caught. But not yet vanquished. She has one more chance to avoid the trap of passion. It is offered in the form of a warning which she is given by her loyal Senecan nurse, whose long speech counsels against sexual passion, and includes the just and appropriate observation in the form of an admonition, "Pensa che parte della sanità fu il volere essere guarita." [67] That is exactly the problem: Fiammetta does not wish to be cured. The nurse gives the best possible advice in her hectoring sermon against young men and women who have chosen the way of Love (I, 15).[68] Her words remind us of Pabst's observations: "vi avete trovato Amore esser iddio al quale piuttosto giusto titolo sarebbe furore. . . . Costui, da infernale furia sospinto, con súbito volo visita tutte le terre, non deità, ma piuttosto pazzia di chi il riceve. . . ." We may choose to dismiss the nurse as an old fool—but then we are foolish ourselves. "You have made Cupid a god; he is a madness sent from hell." That is her message and, in light of the fact that later Fiammetta will often ruefully exhibit similar sentiments (which is not to mention the force her argument has on its own merits), it seems impossible not to take it seriously. The nurse's speech goes on to make explicit the two kinds of love. "Ora non veggiamo noi Venere santissima abitare nelle piccole case sovenente, solamente e utile al necessario nostro procreamento? Certo sì; ma questi, il quale, per furore, Amore è chiamato, sempre le dissolute cose appetendo, non altrove s'accosta che alla seconda fortuna." Here, as in the *Filocolo,* Venus—the matrimonial Venus—and Cupid are seen as enemies.[69]

Having been told the truth in no uncertain terms, Fiammetta responds predictably: "O vecchia, taci, e contro agl'iddii non parlare." Cupid is her lord and master and is not to be blasphemed. The nurse, reminiscent of Diana in the sixteenth canto of the *Caccia di Diana,* leaves Venus's minion to herself.[70] Is Fiammetta a victim? In her speech the nurse has said, "And you call him the son of Venus, saying that he draws his force from the third heaven, as though you wished to make necessity an excuse for your madness." [71] Her point is clearly (she will make it again at VI, 15) not only that lovers are deceived, but that they deceive themselves.[72] Fiammetta, hesitating for a moment in response to her wise words, wishes to call her back, but suddenly the goddess of love is before her in her room—she has not the inclination for more temperate thoughts (I, 16).

The importance of Venus's appearance to Fiammetta can hardly be overstated.[73] Here, as in the *Filocolo* when she represents carnal affections, she appears nude, partially wrapped in purple.[74] The speech that she gives in praise of her son's power (it is no mystery which of the two Venuses we have to deal with here), fittingly enough filled with classical allusions, is similar, in its insistence on the total hegemony of Amore, to Caleon's (*Filocolo,* IV, 45), although it is a more splendid and extended piece of classicizing rhetoric, covering three large pages of text (I, 17). The only deity, she says, who has not been wounded by her son is Diana. And she, Venus adds, is said by some not so much to have fled from him but to have hidden herself—so great is his power. What can poor Fiammetta use against her persuasion? "Né ti faccia a ciò tiepida [a word we frequently find in Boccaccio describing the effects of Diana] il dire: 'Io ho marito, e le sante leggi e la promessa fede mi vietano queste cose.' " Venus robs her of the Christian chastity she might fall back on in her own defense,[75] but it does not seem to be an argument that she really wants to employ. When she finally speaks on her own behalf, all she can say is "Sia come ti piace" (I, 18). After which she falls to her knees and prays to her new "deità celeste," in a perverse version of a prayer to the Virgin, having forgotten that this Venus is more likely to have arisen from hell than descended from heaven. (In hindsight, and with an understanding similar to her nurse's, she will later have no doubt but that the apparition in her room was not Venus, but Tisiphone.)[76] Between the words of the nurse, which may be taken as they are delivered, and the words of Venus, which should be taken with more than a little cynicism, the entire moral climate of the *Elegia* is present in the form of a choice: Fiammetta may worship either Venus she chooses. She chooses the wrong one. Boccaccio does not suggest that the choice is an easy one—Venus and her son are enticing and powerful presences in all of us. Nonetheless, we surrender to them not because they are strong but because we are weak. Boccaccio, who seems to anticipate renaissance painting in his love of nude bodies, but who actually continues a late medieval treatment of female flesh that is if anything even more frank and "realistic" than that found later, shows us the culminating moment of Venus's visit in such ways that we perceive the meretriciousness of the goods she sells. Fiammetta compares her to the false Ascanius lighting poor Dido's hidden flames, and then describes the semi-striptease which she performs, showing forth, held in her arms between her breasts, a picture of . . . Panfilo (I, 19). It is such tawdry business that one cannot take the "religion" which includes it seriously.

What is clear is that Boccaccio's carnal Venus is the opposite of the celestial goddess Fiammetta supposes her to be; she is a demon.[77] From Fiammetta's choice flows all her later distress—and there are eight chapters of distress to follow. By the end of the first chapter, Fiammetta is a devotée of Venus, burning incense at her altars (I, 25) when she is not making love with Panfilo.[78] And while she now looks back in horror at the way in which she banished the wise counsel of her nurse, the extraordinary thing about her behavior is that she never gives up her love for Panfilo—on the last page of the book she is still hoping for his penitence and return. The *Elegia* is the documentary history of a disease with no cure, rather, of a patient who refuses to be cured.[79] If Fiammetta's goddess has affinities with the Furies, she herself is not exactly a model of celestial thought and behavior. Not that Panfilo is either. After less than a year of Fiammetta's favors he has obviously had all that he wants. He must, he artfully explains to her, return to Florence and support the lonely suffering of his aged father (II, 4). If his story seems cooked, Fiammetta's response is hardly kind: I will die if you leave me; since your father is so old, perhaps it would be kinder to leave him alone to die (II, 6). The two of them are hard to accept as the serious figures of romance they have so often been made out to be.[80] Panfilo's response is droll—I would gladly let him die, but I would be severely blamed for such behavior. The bauble of reputation seems cause enough for Fiammetta, and she accepts his empty promise to return in four months.[81] He swears his fealty in the counterfeit oaths of the religion Fiammetta embraces: Even if he himself could possibly ever want another woman, hardly even Jove himself could bring such love to pass, "con sí fatta catena ha il mio cuore Amore legato sotto la tua signoria" (II, 9). It should be clear to readers of the *Elegia* that Panfilo is a rogue, Fiammetta, a fool.

Alone, Fiammetta is a sight to behold. Is it pathos or bathos we witness when we see her, in the misery and confusion of Panfilo's departure, embrace her servant, thinking her him, and bid her *adieu* (II, 14)? The confusion would seem to be mainly comic in intent.[82] And the windy sighs of the third chapter, the lonely nights ("who would believe that Love taught me astrology, science of serious minds, not of those which are caught up in his madness?" she wonders at one point—III, 10), all the trappings of woe might be touching if Fiammetta were not such a self-deceiver. Of course Panfilo does not return when he said he would, and of course she hears rumors that he has married (V, 2). The most telling touch in this scene occurs when the report of his marriage is made: One of the nuns who happens to hear the news fights back tears. Fiammetta takes the obvious implication—Panfilo has been more amorously active in Naples than she had thought, as even his name might have suggested to her when she first gave it to him (I, 23). Her illness grows worse. Even the joys of Baia do not help; her husband calls in the doctors, to no avail. The fact is that since Panfilo has gone, everything is a cause of sadness in her ("di tristizia cagione"—v, 23). It is this sadness, or melancholy, as I have suggested above, which is the prime symptom of her disease.[83] In church one day she weeps. Ladies near her think she despairs of God's mercy. Her attempt at a dignified gesture in response is typically self-deceiving and fraudulent. Choking back her tears, she raises her head; she is careful to tell us that she did not look around the church as she was wont. Why not? Because she knows, she continues, that Panfilo is not there. Nor does she look to see the effect her beauty makes on others in the church. On the contrary, she is attentive to Christ (a surprising change of heart and mind if it were to be a true one) and prays to Him . . . for Panfilo's return (V, 34). The whole scene, with Fiammetta's self-consciousness and her attempt to turn Christ into her pander (as she herself admits in her prayer, she knows that her request is "ingiusta . . . nel cospetto di te giustissimo giudice"—v, 35) [84] draws, or should draw, not our sympathy but our laughter.[85] Her prayer to Jesus is the last desperate act of the lengthy and increasingly desperate fifth chapter, and leads naturally to her attempted suicide (VI 16–21). Admittedly none of her misfortunes is funny in itself, but because of the ironic treatment of his heroine's behavior Boccaccio makes us understand that her own romantic version of the truth is not to be trusted. It is continually undermined by a plain contrary fact (for example, Panfilo never had any intention of returning) or by her performance of extravagances worthy of burlesque, accompanied by wracked outcries against the tyranny of Amore. After a while her insistence on her own pain becomes comic, not least of all because that pain is not a necessary one.[86] Her attempted suicide is a case in point. Having prayed for the courage of death, she finds Tisiphone standing before her,[87] and is encouraged to the deed. She has time for a final prayer—addressed to her bed ("O bed, go with God, Whom I beg to make you more gracious to the next lady than He has made you to me").[88] Following Tisiphone, she rushes outdoors to do away with herself and is only saved by her nurse and her maidservants, whose immediate rewards are to have their scalps ripped open and their faces torn bloody by their mistress's nails (VI, 20), a likely reminiscence of Ovid's concern for the unfortunate *ornatrix* of *Ars amatoria* III.239. The *Elegia* is relentless in its pursuit of the fact of Fiammetta's delusion. When the nurse tells her that Panfilo has returned, she gives a prayer of thanksgiving to Jove, Apollo, Venus, and Cupid: "Whoever perseveres, hoping in you, cannot fail in the end" (VII, 3). Since the work does not take place in the pre-Christian era, the prayer is, like the rest of Fiammetta's prayers, most likely to be considered blasphemous. (The only time she has turned to Christ, as we have noted above, was to seek His aid in her carnal hopes.) In a few pages, after having put on joyful garments once again, she will learn that the friend of the fellow on the beach wasn't Panfilo at all—the nurse had not quite caught his name the first time (VII, 8). With that bit of vaudeville the "action" of the *Elegia* concludes. The eighth chapter is filled with Fiammetta's version of Venus's vainglorious "triumphus Cupidinis" (I, 17). But now all of Love's triumphs are seen to be sad events indeed for those who are conquered by him. She identifies most with Dido (VIII, 5),[89] perhaps the prime medieval exemplum of the love that leads to death.[90] And she herself seems to be more directed to such a death than to be interested in life.

The *Corbaccio* opened with what may be considered a later "portrait of Fiammetta": a lover, shut up in his room, given over entirely not even to the pleasures of carnal love, but to the self-indulgence of lonely posturing, the unloved lover protesting his love and its pain. Consolation comes within a page to this lover. The role of his *pensiero* is roughly equivalent to the role of Fiammetta's nurse; it too brings wise counsel, and, reinforced by the *guida* in the narrator's dream, moves him from devotion to the love that leads to death to a kind of conversion. Like the Israelites of Psalm 113 he is led out of bondage into freedom. Fiammetta, offered this choice, denies it. She is resolute in maintaining the values of a love and of a religion of love that even she (if not most of her critics) can understand is not only foolish, and morally wrong, but dangerous to her very being. She is, as has sometimes been observed, like Dante's Francesca in her subjection to Love.[91] She begins the last part of the narrative section of the work with reference to "gli antichi inganni di Fortuna" which have made her miserable (VIII, 18). But is her misery Fortune's fault or her own? True, Fortune governs all earthly things; but one is not compelled by her ministry to choose the worst and not the best. That choice is our own. If we choose to wear the chains of love in the "laberinto d'Amore," we will live the life of Fiammetta. Her last words in Chapter Eight are in the form of yet another prayer. Still enflamed, she prays to God for "salutevole acqua" against those flames, which may take the form, in her narrow formulation of the possibilities, either of her own death or the happy return of Panfilo. Those two possibilities satisfy only the alternatives of the religion of love, of which Fiammetta has made herself a willing victim, a sacrifice on Cupid's altars.

For Vittore Branca, who is apparently willing to argue that Boccaccio was acquainted with the *De vulgari eloquentia,*[92] an *elegia* is a sad tale concerning unhappy people. Yet, no matter which particular medieval description of the genre we may choose to believe that Boccaccio had in mind,[93] the question remains as to how we are to comprehend his intention in the *Elegia di madonna Fiammetta.* It seems difficult to believe that he hoped that his readers would find his sad lady a morally positive creature. Whatever the strength of his desire to create an elegy, to exhibit his talents in still another genre, it seems foolish not to expect him to have been aware of the irrational quality of his heroine's conduct.

Boccaccio's two "epics" in *ottava rima* were each to be re-elaborated by Geoffrey Chaucer, the *Filostrato* as *Troilus and Criseyde,* the *Teseida* as *The Knight's Tale,* and so are known, if indirectly, to some of those who do not read Italian. The narrative portion of the *Filostrato* begins and ends in epic dress, opening with a brief mention of the armed Greeks who surround Troy (I.7) and concluding with a brief account of Troiolo's death at the hands of Achilles in the field (VIII.25–27).[94] In between these two military scenes there is precious little that deals with arms. The *Filostrato,* as its *incipit* implies, deals nearly exclusively with the matter of love.[95] The passional narrative begins in the Trojan temple of Pallas Athena, where we see the jocund young blade Troiolo giving the girls of Troy a looking over

(I.20). He boasts of his own freedom when he observes another young man's gaze become fixed on a woman (I.21–22). For him love is "follia," a "maladetto foco." He has known the joys of love, but holds them little or nothing when they are compared with the many sighs and sufferings caused by love (I.23).[96] He thanks God (addressed as "Giove, dio vero") for his own freedom from the toils of love and laughs at those who are in love (I.24). But within five stanzas Love's darts, shooting from Criseida's eyes, shall have struck him down (I.29) and replaced prayers of thanksgiving with prayers for mercy, now addressed to Amore rather than Giove (I.38).[97] The sudden change is probably not all that surprising—when we first see him Troiolo is a boastful lounger of Athena's temple, not a follower of wisdom; and he who skirts the toils of love is likely to be snared—especially if he boasts of his ability to resist them. His prayer of thanks to Venus, given once Pandaro assures him that his hopes of Criseida are likely to be rewarded with amorous success, reflects an amorous disposition that was ready to be reawakened easily, despite his own earlier protestations.[98]

The praise of love which we find in the *Filostrato* should probably be understood as being the praise offered by fools and knaves, by those who are blind to their own true interests or only too calculatingly aware of these. Such a judgment is at variance with the general perception of Boccaccio's intention in the work.[99] Perhaps the most challenging passage in the *Filostrato,* as far as this thesis is concerned, comes in Troiolo's hymn of praise to Venus ("O luce etterna"—III.74–89).[100] Had this "hymn"—or its first six stanzas, at any rate—come down to us as a self-contained fourteenth-century poem, it might indeed seem what it seems to many readers, a heartfelt paean of praise.[101] In fact, Troiolo's hymn sounds very much like Venus's hymn to her own powers in the *Fiammetta* (I.17). In both cases those who make benedictions of Venus [102] (as Fiammetta will do in response to the self-praise of the goddess) will shortly learn how fleeting her gifts are. And clearly there are ironic contrasts between the religion of love and more orthodox religion: Troiolo blesses God (III.85.1) for giving the world such a lovely lady, much as the narrator of the *Caccia di Diana* thinks that the creation of his beloved was an act especially pleasing to God Himself.[103] God is recorded in neither Testament as having been interested in creating specially pulchritudinous females who might serve as objects of carnal desire and worship. The sense of ironic inversion is frequent throughout the long speech.[104] The conclusion of this section of the work (III.94.1–2) strikes the undercutting note we hardly need: "Ma poco tempo durò cotal bene,/mercé della Fortuna invidiosa. . . ." What the narrator laments (since he too is a "Filostrato") is precisely what Boethius has offered him (and Troiolo) a cure for—the vicissitudes of this world. It is more than likely that Boccaccio had Boethius's Lady Philosophy in mind as a foil for Criseida.[105] And Troiolo's frequent complaints against Fortuna—e.g., IV.30.2—have an anti-Boethian spirit that bring the *De consolatione* to mind as a corrective model. The same might be said for his finding "consolation" in love (IV.33.6). Boccaccio was surely aware of the Boethian tradition his character chooses to oppose.[106] Once Criseida is exchanged for Antenor Troiolo falls into *tristizia.*[107] He longs to die.[108] Unlike the Fiammetta of the *Elegia,* he manages to accomplish this end. But only after he too attempts unsuccessfully to commit suicide (VII.33–36)—an act which he knows will send his soul to hell (VII.35.5). Boccaccio does not even allow him to find Diomedes—Criseida's new Troiolo—in the ranks of battle. His death receives a single line: "misermente un dì l'uccise Achille" (VIII.27.8), and a commentary of sorts (VIII.28), which attacks "Criseida villana" and laments the death of the noblest Trojan of them all from the love of her. At this point our "autore" enters and tells us (or those of us who are young men) to beware young women like Criseida—they are fickle; indeed, they are beasts, not "donne gentili." One does better to find an older woman (VIII.29–32). The business is amusing. Our "author" will not give over *his* religion of love merely because it ends badly for Troiolo. He wants to have his cake and eat it too. That his view is Boccaccio's own is a notion which, for all its currency, seems dubious. While I have foresworn comparison of Boccaccio and Chaucer, I may beg the reader's indulgence on this single occasion. The Chaucerian narrator of the tale of Troilus rather pointedly keeps his distance from his "hero," whose love not only leads to death but hell:

Swich fyn hath, lo, this Troilus for love!
Swich fyn hath al his grete worthynesse!
Swich fyn hath his estat real above,
Swich fyn his lust, swich fyn hath his noblesse!
Swych fyn hath false worldes brotelnesse!
And thus bigan his lovyng of Criseyde,
As I have told, and in this wise he deyde.

O yonge fresshe folkes, he or she,
In which that love up groweth with youre age,
Repeyreth hom fro worldly vanyte,
And of youre herte up casteth the the visage
To thilke God that after his ymage
Yow made, and thynketh al nys but a faire
This world, that passeth soone as floures faire.[109]

In reading Boccaccio's text, Chaucer may well have believed that Boccaccio, while having told an edifying story, had mistakenly sided with the wrong forces. At any rate his narrator emphatically denounces Troiolo's fault and is in this respect different from the narrator of the *Filostrato,* who does not see it as a fault, but only as a mistake. Boccaccio's narrators, as I shall argue in my fourth chapter, are not to be trusted as spokesmen for their creator.[110]

The *Filostrato* is the least classicizing of Boccaccio's early works. Yet even here Venus, the goddess of carnal love, if not a major "character" in the work, is a major presence.[111] Against her is posed no better version of herself (for example, the matrimonial Venus of the nurse's speech in *Elegia* I.15).[112] There are the hazy presences of Pallas Athena, of Apollo, and of Jove. But she is not specifically opposed by any specific forces. This is not to say that she triumphs in the work as a moral force; rather, that, as in the *Caccia di Diana,* the vast power of the goddess of love is the result of what is granted her by the humans who elect her. The *Filostrato,* like the *Elegia di madonna Fiammetta,* is not a celebration of love, but an analysis of its terrible power. Troiolo was right, if callow, at the beginning, when he thought himself well out of the chains of love; when he was free. That word, as we have several times noted, is perhaps the key word in Boccaccio's negative view of carnal love, which robs us of that precious freedom of choice that makes the next world possible and this world livable.

If the *Filostrato* displayed some of Boccaccio's eagerness to win repute as the Italian inheritor of the epic tradition, the *Teseida* is the result of some fairly feverish labor in that direction. Still, despite the frequent imitation of Virgil and Statius (especially the latter) and the "martial" nature of Books I, II, and VIII, it is the romantic elements which predominate heavily; one can sense Boccaccio's ease and comfort when he leaves the battles of Book II for the amorous "battles" of Book III.[113] For here, as elsewhere, his great *materia* is love.

Book I describes the battle between the forces of Teseo and the Amazons under Ipolita, who are specifically reminded by their queen of their opposition to Cupid ("contro a Cupido avete presa guerra"—I.24.6). They fight to preserve their *libertà* (I.35.3; 88.1), a word which has at least as important a sexual frame of reference as it has a political one. Nor is Teseo particularly interested in things sexual. When he prays it is to Mars (I.58) and Minerva ("dea della sapienza" in Boccaccio's gloss [114]—I.60) that he prays. After the Amazons are defeated, Ipolita declares that they have been so because Venus (it is her first mention in the text of the poem) was justly angry with them and joined her lover Mars in support of the Athenians (I.117). It is then that, the peace treaties signed, Amore enters the action, and wounds Teseo's heart with his golden arrow (I.129). The Amazons, on their side, feel shame for their past hatred of men, and reopen the temple of Citerea, in which, to the accompaniment of prayers to Hymen, nuptials of Teseo and Ipolita, and of many another couple, are celebrated (I.133–35). The virgin sister of Ipolita, Emilia, will accompany the royal pair back to Athens. What is most impressive about the love sponsored by Venus and Cupid [115] here is that it acts upon the previously chaste in such a way that marriage is an immediate result. She is, as Boccaccio's own later gloss will make tacitly plain, celestial in her provenance.

That neither Teseo nor Ipolita is excessively devoted to the carnal flames of Venus is apparent throughout the narrative. At the conclusion of Book II Teseo will return after his victory over Creon and Thebes to give thanksgiving in the Temple of Mars (II.94–95).

As Emilia was the "dividend" of the epic action of the first book, Palemone and Arcita return with Teseo as prisoners of war at the end of the second. While it is true that Boccaccio has spent 237 *ottave* in describing actions that have very little relevance to the romantic plot that will occupy the next ten books, it is not true that the moral atmosphere of these two books goes unused. They offer us an antithesis—Mars vs. Venus—as well as a resolution—marriage of warriors. Once we join the third book we re-enter a familiar world: the sweet springtime of Venus and her son, with all its painful consequence. If the movement of the first two books was from war to reconciliation in marriage, the movement of the next large segment of the work is from love to death.[116] The two prisoners of love, Palemone and Arcita, clearly follow the rules of the religion of love in their parallel and rival responses to the beautiful Emilia. Arcita, the first to see her, thinks that she comes from Paradise (III.12.8), and Palemone agrees that she is surely Venus herself (III.13.3;14.6). No sooner are they in love than their thoughts turn to death (e.g., III.23.8). It is precisely the sort of "loving" behavior we have found in the other works.

Arcita, having secured his release from prison on the strength of Peritoo's friendship and his own (soon falsified) oath that he will never return to Athens, returns disguised [117] in Book IV, and finds a position as a servant to Teseo under the name of Penteo.[118] Overheard in his lament to Fortuna (by now surely a familiar enough trapping of the Boccaccian lover) by Panfilo, another of Teseo's servants, he loses his anonymity when his identity becomes clear to the still imprisoned Palemone. And in the fifth book Palemone contrives his own release, similarly using fraud. The two former friends finally have at one another, in their first and abortive combat, which is interrupted by the advent of Emilia, Teseo, and their attendants. At this point there is little to choose between the two lovers—except, perhaps, that they have prayed (at least on one occasion) to different gods. In Book IV Arcita's prayers were addressed to Apollo, Amore, and Venus.[119] In Book V Palemone prays to Diana (V.30–32). The basic contrast between Apollo and Diana (as Boccaccio's commentary testifies) is merely between sun and moon. Yet it may be significant that Palemone here identifies himself with worship of the goddess to whom Emilia's prayer in Book VIII is addressed. Yet one must hasten to add that Palemone's kinship with Diana is expressed in sexual terms.[120] And later in Book V each of the two lovers will call on Mars, Venus, and Emilia, with identical purpose (victory in combat against the other). In short, the difference between their prayers is merely topographical. The lovers are essentially mirror-images of one another, if not physically (see III.49–50), at least morally.

The crucial moral action of the *Teseida* occurs in Book VII in the form of three competing prayers.[121] The prayers themselves, and the gods to whom they are addressed, occupy one *ottava* less than half of the book's one hundred and forty-five *ottave* (VII.22–93). It would be to them that our attention would naturally turn, whether or not they happened to be accompanied by Boccaccio's own lengthy glosses to the first two of them. In Book V Theseus had decided that a proper joust would be the fitting instrument by which would be determined the disposition of Emilia, and Book VII recounts the final preparations for that event. A sense of the parallels and differences among these is perhaps most readily made apparent in tabular form:

	ARCITA	PALEMONE	EMILIA
prays to	Mars (24)	Venus (43)	Diana (77)
particularly as	lover of Venus (25) [122]	lover of Adonis (43)	"deitate triforme" (80)
for	victory in battle (27)	not victory, but Emilia (46)	peace between the lovers; if that is not possible, to have the one who loves her the most (84–85) [123]
offering in return sacrifice	of Palemone's arms (28)	at all her altars (48)	
temples described	Mars (29–38)	Venus (50–66)	Diana (72, 1) [124]
prayer is granted when	the armor of Mars resounds (40)	Venus concedes (66, 8)	Diana's arrows resound, her bow moves (89)
reaction of gods	Mars and Venus agree to honor both prayers (67, 5–8)		Diana's virgins assure her that she shall marry one of them (89)

That favorite device, the disastrous answered prayer,[125] lies behind Arcita's request of Mars. For he prays only for victory, which he will be granted. Palemone's prayer is to have Emilia, whether he wins in combat or not. Yet, although he is the eventual winner, his intentions, as derived from his prayer, are hardly any more honorable than Arcita's. That is, at least, what Boccaccio's parallel treatments of the two lovers suggest. And this conclusion is more than reinforced by his own commentary to the prayers and to the gods they address.

The fourteenth century in Italy offers us a number of noteworthy examples of poets who wrote specific glosses to their own works. It was, of course, Dante who, with only the precedent of the Provençal *razos,*[126] began the Italian tradition with the self-exegetical prose of the *Vita Nuova* in the last decade of the thirteenth century. The phenomenon was greatly expanded in his *Convivio* and continued in the *Epistola a Cangrande.* As for Petrarch, whose *Invective contra medicum* offer a generic defense of poetry that is strikingly similar to that later found in the fourteenth and fifteenth books of Boccaccio's *Genealogie,* we must be content with *Familiares,* x, 4, which puts forward an allegorical explanation of his own first eclogue for the benefit of his brother Gherardo (and any posterity that would happen to like to read over Gherardo's shoulder—the document is last of all private in character; but the "familiar" letter is probably the most public performance of such as Cicero and Petrarch). In the case of Boccaccio—a born glossator, as is evident in his exposition of Dante's *Inferno*—all that we have for certain is his gloss to the *Teseida.*[127] But having it is to have a guide to the author's intention that is, if little used (perhaps because it tends to disturb—to use an understatement—the usual view of the work), not without its value. A large number of Boccaccio's notes are mythographic, ostensibly clearing up various references for readers in need of such assistance (e.g., "Egeo fu padre di Teseo," "Belo fu re in una parte di Grecia"), while most of them are "philological," in that they explain the literal sense of "difficult" or "learned" locutions (e.g., *achiva:* "cioè greca"; *le case sante:* "cioè i templi"). In only two cases do they offer extended "allegorical" interpretations of the text. But these two cases are worthy of some note, for they are the *chiose* to descriptions of the temples of Mars and Venus in Book VII.[128] Boccaccio's description of the Temple of Mars (VII.29–38) is given with the following justification in the gloss (to 29.4): He has personified Arcita's prayer so that he may describe the Temple of Mars as though it had been seen by human eyes.[129] What the "eyes" of Arcita's prayer see is not ultimately pleasant. The abode of Mars is cold and windy (30), located in a sterile forest (31) that is not unlike the wood of the suicides in *Inferno* XIII.[130] The temple itself is characterized by hardness (*acciaio, ferro, adamante*—32). Its personified inhabitants (*Impeti dementi, cieco Peccare, ogni Omei* [= "ogni maniera de guai" in the gloss], *Ire rosse, Paura pallida* in 33; *Tradimenti, Discordia, Differenza, aspre Minacce, Crudele Intenza, Vertù tristissima* in 34; *allegro Furore, Morte, Stupore*), and the detail that "every altar there is plentiful in blood" in 35 call up feelings of ear and a sense of danger. In short, without aid of a commentary, we might easily understand that one who prays to Mars is hoping for dread things indeed. But the gloss helps us to grasp more clearly Boccaccio's "psychology." There are, he says in the gloss to *ottava* 30, two principle appetites in man, the concupiscible and the irascible.[131] The following text makes the identical natures of the irascible appetite and the Temple of Mars clear ("il tempio de Marte, cioè questo appetito irascibile"). There is much that could be properly said concerning Boccaccio's gloss on the temple. Let me simply state that, with a single exception,[132] everything there is described in terms that leave no doubt about its negative valence. The allegorical exposition has a moralizing tone throughout, even rising on one occasion to the phrase "divine grace"—the first specifically Christian note in gloss or poem.[133]

If the Temple of Mars seems, in this context, if not in all, reasonably enough taken as a vicious place, we might expect to find its antithesis in the Temple of Venus—for such an antithesis is at least as old as the Homer whom Boccaccio had not as yet read—[134] which many of Boccaccio's readers apparently take to be a fine place indeed. After all, does not Palemone, having prayed to Venus, win Emilia? And the place itself, compared with the Temple of Mars, seems much to be preferred. Her temple is situated among great shady pines, and the first presence to greet the "eyes" of Palemone's prayer is *Vaghezza* (the natural desire to possess lovely things, as the gloss interprets—50). In the guiding presence of this eager instinct, we and Palemone's prayer arrive at the necessary garden, leafy, green, flowery, fountained, and especially abundant in myrtle (51—the gloss explains that "la mortine" was, according to the poets, the "albero di

Venere, perciò che il suo odore è incitativo molto"); it is full of singing birds, rabbits, and other little creatures (52), as well as the sound of music (53). There we see Cupid making his arrows, which his daughter *Voluttà* tempers in the water of a fountain; with them are *Ozio* and *Memoria,* who help in the tasks of this foundry of love (54). Let us pause for a moment. This seems a pleasant place indeed. A good deal of the interpretation of medieval literature—one thinks particularly of the *Roman de la Rose* [135]—hinges upon the way in which we interpret the venereal *locus amoenus* in its various manifestations. And one must admit that up to here, in Boccaccio's first four *ottave*—if we choose for the moment not to accede to his own gloss—Venus and her temple seem to offer, if not the summit of earthly bliss, at least something which is greatly preferable to what is offered by the Temple of Mars. But negative details, which seem so without benefit of gloss, begin to appear. We see *Leggiadria* with *Adornezza* and *Affabilitate,* and *Cortesia,* who has (elsewhere, one supposes) disappeared; but then we see *Arti.* These have the power to make men do mad things (55.4–5). And there is *Van Diletto* alone with *Gentilezza* (a suggestive detail in light of Boccaccio's other invectives against claimants of nobility by birth). *Bellezza* passes, admiring herself, in the company of *Piacevolezza* and *Giovanezza;* there are *folle Ardire, Lusinghe,* and *Ruffiania* (56). At least some of these personifications are distinctly unpleasant on anyone's terms. And Boccaccio's treatment of all of them in the gloss is moralistic and negative.

The temple itself is surrounded by dancing barefoot young men and ladies, while sparrows and doves [136] fly overhead (57); at the entrance are found *madonna Pace, Pazienza, Promesse, Arte* (58); within we find *Sospiri, caldi Disiri, Martiri,* [137] and the cruel, wicked *Gelosia* (59). *Priapo* is here (60), and trophies: the broken bows of the maidens of Diana, including that of Callisto; and here are Atalanta's apples, and the arms of the other Atalanta (61). And of course there are stories painted here of the victories of Venus: Semiramis, Pyramus and Thisbe, Hercules (spinning for Iole), Biblis and Caunus (62).[138] But where is Venus? "In più secreta/parte del tempio si sta a diletto" is Boccaccio's punning answer to our unvoiced question (63). On its way in, Palemone's prayer finds *Ricchezza* guarding the door,[139] and then sees Venus nude upon her great bed (64), her lower parts covered by such thin vestments that she is as though entirely naked (65).[140] Bacchus and Ceres sit at either side of her, and by one hand she holds *Lascivia,* in the other, the apple she was awarded by Paris when he judged her to be the most beautiful of the three goddesses (66).

The one hundred and thirty-five lines may seem artificial and labored, traditional in the worst sense of the word. Yet they are clearly here to tell us about Palemone, and, more importantly, about the venereal instinct in general. Whatever we as readers may make of them, and it seems to this reader rather clear what they mean (Venus is as dangerous and destructive as the Mars whom we have just seen), Boccaccio has eased our task considerably. The gloss to these seventeen *ottave* overpowers the poetic text in the Mondadori addition: *ottave* 50 and 51—sixteen lines of poetry—require eleven pages of text in order to accomodate the nearly five thousand words of Boccaccio's essay on Venus. It seems absurd that such an obviously important example of self-exegesis has received so little attention.[141] Most of us who work with the endlessly pleasing and difficult texts of a Dante or a Boccaccio find ourselves, in our less guarded moments, having fantasies of being visited by the shade of Dante (who explains, smiling, that of course our mad construing of the *Veltro* is correct, that that really *is* his image on the bronze door of San Zeno in Verona) or of Boccaccio (who good-naturedly explains the meaning of the sequence of lyrics in the *Decameron*). But here we have Boccaccio speaking to us in his own voice—from the grave, as it were—and we do not choose to listen.

Looking back to his gloss on the Temple of Mars, Boccaccio makes the following brief resumé of his stance as interpreter: "dicendo Marte consistere nello appetito irascibile, così Venere nel concupiscibile." [142] It is well to remind the reader of the definition of the *appetito concupiscibile,* given in the gloss to the Temple of Mars, from which Boccaccio's discussion of the Temple of Venus depends: "per lo quale l'uomo disidera e si rallegra d'avere le cose che, *secondo il suo giudicio, o ragionevole o corrotto ch'egli sia,* sono dilettevoli e piacevoli" (italics added). Whether our judgment is reasonable (rational) or corrupt is, it would seem, of central importance. And Boccaccio's phrase helps the reader prepare himself to form a judgment of the behavior to which he is witness. Our loving or concupiscible selves are free to love either well or badly, either *in bono* or *in malo.* That simple statement is probably a fair one-sentence version of the central notion of Christian morality. Boccaccio's ensuing definition of Venus, like his definition of the concupiscible appetite, is double.[143] His argument comes to the following crucial point:

> La quale Venere è doppia, perciò che l'una si può e dee intendere per ciascuno onesto e licito disiderio, sì come è disiderare d'avere moglie per avere figliuoli, e simili a questo; e di questa Venere non si parla qui. La seconda Venere è quella per la quale ogni lascivia è disiderata, e che volgarmente è chiamata dea d'amore; e di questa disegna qui l'autore il tempio e l'altre cose circustanti ad esso, come nel testo appare.[144]

"E di questa Venere non si parla qui" could depend as a footnote to most of the Venuses we meet in Boccaccio's fiction. It seems clear that one of our tasks as readers is to determine which is which, and to draw further conclusions as a result of that determination.

Whereas much of his gloss on Venus is taken up with the usual morally unaligned recounting of pagan myth (Pyramus and Thisbe have fifty lines of text—Boccaccio was fond of their story), so much of the gloss is pointedly moral that its intent is utterly clear. Only a few high points need detain us. The fountain in which *Voluttà* tempers Cupid's arrows is the "fonte della nostra falsa estimazione, quando per questa dillettazione, nata d'amore e di speranza, giudichiamo che la cosa piaciuta sia da preporre ad ogni altra cosa o temporale o divina." The delusion of carnal love, as we have seen frequently enough, makes lovers judge (and there is another key word, *giudicare,* again), incorrectly, that their beloved is preferable to anything earthly or heavenly. Or take the darkness of the "secret part" of Venus's temple: "Poi dice il luogo essere oscuro; e questo perciò è perché coloro li quali adoperano male, odiano la luce." [145] Or his comment on the personification *Lascivia:* "la quale lascivia intende essere il basciare, il toccare e il cianciare e 'l motteggiare e l'altre sciocchezze che intorno a ciò si fanno." And as for the Judgment of Paris, Venus's apple "vuole dimostrare la stolta elezione di quegli che così fatta vita ad ogni altra prepongono." Now all of these remarks are nothing short of blasphemy in the religion of love. The point perhaps requires no further belaboring. One thinks of Giuseppe Billanovich's words. If the *Corbaccio* is "l'inevitabile, conclusivo *Adversus amorem,*" [146] what is this? I shall have more to say about Boccaccio's sense of himself as Ovidian poet at the close of the fourth chapter. But before we leave this gloss, we had better turn to its reference to Dino del Garbo.

It would be fitting, Boccaccio says, glossing the personifications of *ottave* 55 and 56, to tell how Amore is helped to generate himself in us by these accomplices. But he begs off, claiming that it would be too long a story. Whoever wants to know it, he says, should read Guido Cavalcanti's *Donna mi priega* and the gloss on it made by Maestro Dino del Garbo.[147] We would not have this Latin text except for the copy made of it by Boccaccio himself.[148] Since we have already spent so much time with one commentary in this chapter, it seems hardly fair to ask the reader to do more than to take Boccaccio's advice and read this document. Nevertheless, a few comments seem called for. Aristotelian in spirit (it is probably for this reason that Marsilio Ficino and Pico della Mirandola would feel called upon to do their own Platonizing glosses on the great *canzone*—to rescue it from Dino, as it were), Dino's commentary makes no bones about the carnal nature of love. He begins by referring to the *canzone* as "Ista cantilena, que tractat de amoris passione . . . ," [149] and he never loses sight of the carnality of the phenomenon of love as he conceives Guido to have treated it.[150] In Quaglio's view Boccaccio only became deeply involved with Dino's commentary ca. 1366, when he made the lone surviving copy of the Latin text (preserved in Vaticano Chigiano L. V. 176). He points out that Boccaccio's discussions at *Genealogie,* IX, 4, "De Cupidine 1º Martis filio," and in the *Esposizioni* to *Inferno* V.100 (as was previously noted by Toynbee, Guerri, and Padoan), clearly reflect Dino's words,[151] but argues that in no work between *Teseida* and the late works, from *Comedia ninfe* to *Corbaccio,* is there reference either to Guido's *canzone* or Dino's *glossa.*[152] Branca, however, points out that there are allusions to and echoes of the *canzone* in the earliest of the *Rime* (IX, XI, XIII, XXIV, etc.), in the *Filostrato* (IX, 5, 6, 7, 8) and the *Teseida* (X.55–57).[153] That does not counter all of Quaglio's position, which may be summarized as follows: Boccaccio refers to the gloss as to a "novità"; [154] the references to Guido in several of the *Rime* (which Quaglio believes were composed at the same time as the *Teseida* or even later) have nothing to do with Dino's gloss, "che rimane eccentrico alla concezione amorosa giovanile dello scrittore, cortese-stilnovistica, quasi neoplatonica, ma sempre lontana dalla determinazione filosofica troppo precisa, direi impegnata, con cui il Del Garbo spiega la trattazione del Cavalcanti"; [155] and then he comes to a point that creates some further difficulty: Boccaccio, even if he did cite Dino's gloss in his own gloss to the *Teseida,* makes no meaningful reference to the matter it contains.[156] There are two issues here. One is whether or not Boccaccio knew Dino's gloss very well when he cited it. The second is whether or not he agreed or disagreed (or would have agreed or disagreed) with Dino's view of love. The first question is probably not easily resolved. Having mentioned Dino's gloss, Boccaccio gives us a hasty and summary definition of love, one which seems at least closely related to Dino's: "questo *amore* è una *passione* nata nell'*anima per alcuna cosa piaciuta. . . .*" Cf. ". . . *amor,* ut dictum est, *passio* est quedam *anime* (et passio causatur in anima *ex apprehensione alicuius rei* quam consequitur appetitus). . . ." [157] Four of the five terms are identical, the last only similar.[158] It seems at least reasonable to believe that Boccaccio had some idea of what Dino thought of love, and that if he cited Dino's commentary as his authority he would not want a reader to find divergences between his treatment of love and Dino's. Which brings me to the heart of my dispute with Quaglio. It is possibly true that Boccaccio was not as deeply involved with Dino's gloss as he was later to be, as Quaglio has argued. But Quaglio's second point, that Boccaccio either did not agree or, to be punctilious, would not have agreed with the attitudes expressed in the gloss, needs closer attention.

What Boccaccio found in Dino (even if all of the gloss known to him was the sentence of it which he quotes—an unlikely hypothesis at best), whose scholastic Aristotelianism may or may not have seemed overly philosophical to Boccaccio (whose disinclination toward "philosophy" is much overdrawn), was a moral view of love that was extremely close to his own. The burden of Dino's lengthy commentary is, over and over again, that carnal love has nothing to do with true virtue or true intellect.[159] For him, as for Boccaccio, there are two Venuses—even though that term is only Boccaccio's, the thought is clear in Dino. Quaglio's position is based on a given—precisely the given of almost all interpretations of Boccaccio "minore": that the young Boccaccio defends carnal love, even finds in it the highest form of human activity. If that given is rejected as the false construction that it likely is, Boccaccio's view of Dino del Garbo [160] will be a consistent one, at any period of his work. Not that they possessed minds that showed similar styles of thought, but that Boccaccio's Christian morality found Dino's Aristotelian insistence on the mere and noxious carnality of the venereal ("in quibus actibus est furiositas et intemperantia" [161]) entirely to his liking and purpose.

The apparent opposition Mars-Venus turns out to be, because of the nature of the two worshippers, Arcita and Palemone, a double version of a similar impulse toward self-centered worldly success. The truer opposition in the *deomachia* of Book VII is between Mars-Venus (as defined by the limited aspirations of the two rivals) and Diana. For hers is the culminating temple, which, if described in a single line (72.1, where it is "mondo"—cleansed, in the Levitical sense—and "di bei drappi ornato"), is the *locus* of a better prayer, that of Emilia. If she had at first appeared vain in her feminine love of being praised (e. g., III.30), she is now portrayed as chaste, god-fearing, and humble (in III.29, in a nearly unbearable redoing of *Vita Nuova* XXVI, she is described as being "d'umiltà vestuta"). It is small wonder that a Romantic reader claims that Emilia "finisce per ripugnarci." [162] But we need not be troubled by such responses. Emilia, whether we like her or not, says the sort of things of which Boccaccio's gloss on the two previous temples would have us approve. She prays to Diana by "la tua gran deitate/triforme" (VII.80.2–3). The phrase would seem even more Christian in intent had Boccaccio's gloss not clarified the tripleness.[163] Still, the phrase might reasonably have had Christian overtones for Boccaccio—"triform deity" is probably too close to "Trinity" for it not to have had. Emilia proclaims her continuing virginity and antagonism to Venus (81)—in light of the Venus stretched out on her voluptuous couch some eight lines before, that cannot be all bad. And then she does the "right thing," at least in terms of the rhetoric of obedience to the gods we have elsewhere observed (as in the first book of the *Teseida,* where Ipolita's opposition to the carnal Venus yielded to Teseo in matrimony [I. 134]): She announces herself ready to be put under Juno's law, if such be the plan of the Fates (VII.83).[164] Needless to say, her wish shall be granted, as will be Arcita's and Palemone's. The difference among them is that Emilia is "devout" in her orisons, the two rivals merely self-seeking. They each get what they have sought. In light of their equivalent lack of positive qualities, what makes Palemone worthy of happiness, Arcita, of death? Rather the necessities of plot than anything else, it would seem: Boys meet girl, but only boy gets girl. Arcita, victorious in battle, is unhorsed by the force of Venus, whose agents are, perhaps predictably, the Furies (IX.4). As the winner in battle, the wounded Arcita marries Emila (IX.83)—but the marriage is not consummated before he dies.[165] He dies a better man in a scene full of mutual admiration and forgiveness (X.86–113), and Palemone honors him by having a temple, dedicated to Juno, built to his memory; it contains the story of Arcita's life (which is indeed a summary of Books I–XI of the *Teseida*—XI.71–88). The eleventh book ends with Arcita's epitaph, in which the dead Theban, from the grave, as it were, finally recognizes his fault.[166] That epitaph ends Arcita's war with a retraction. But he has come to know the truth too late.

Book XII is nuptial in character, like the end of Book I. It is Teseo who initiates the movement in this direction, first consoling the grieving Emilia in ways that almost seem to look forward to Claudius's consolation of Hamlet (XII.6), and then doing a similar turn for Palemone, who fears that in loving Emilia he will commit a "villania" against "cortesia" (XII.28). The unwilling lovers (Palemone's reticence is particularly comical—he has spent the middle books of the poem trying to kill Arcita in order to have Emilia) are finally won over by Teseo's sound advice. Palemone prays to Jove (XII.34), and then to Diana and Venus.[167] After Emilia's final dubieties about Diana's enmity are soothed by Teseo (XII.39–43),[168] the marriage may proceed. Diana yields her place to Venus. The occasion is the opening of the Temple of Venus, which is described in practically the same words that accompanied Teseo's marriage to Ipolita.[169] This Venus is clearly not the same goddess to whom Arcita prayed in Book VII. Her temple can only be the temple of a celestial Venus, the Venus who "si può e dee intendere per ciascuno onesto e licito disiderio, sì come è disiderare d'avere moglie per avere figliuoli, e simili a questo." Here, as in the wedding scene of the *Filocolo* (IV. 160, 1), voices call on Hymen and Juno (XII.68.6–8).[170] And the *Teseida* can have its happy matrimonial ending, following in the traces of its own first book. Palemone, under the auspices of this Venus, enjoys seven times in one night (XII.77) what he was ready to die either to have or for not having. He changes his name to Panfilo and brings gifts to "la bella Citerea" as he had promised in Book VII (XII.78). And it is perhaps with this last detail that we may look back toward all that we have witnessed in Boccaccio's treatment of pagan deities. There are two Venuses only in one sense—man may worship the uses of Venus in either of two ways, "secondo il suo giudicio, o ragionevole o corrotto ch'egli sia." The carnal Venus is the object desired by a corrupt judgment, the celestial Venus—as we have seen her in the works discussed in this chapter she is earthy enough in her matrimonial function—the aim of a rational choice.

Pagan Integument and Christian Design

WE NOW TURN to Boccaccio's two most "allegorical" productions, the *Comedia delle ninfe fiorentine* and the *Amorosa Visione.* Included here as preamble is a brief consideration of the *Ninfale fiesolano,* a work which offers less in the way of allegorical mechanism, and which, in its ironic treatment of carnal love, is one of Boccaccio's most delightful efforts in that mode, and thus may serve as a transition between our study of the works which are predominantly ironic—as I would characterize all of the works which we have examined until now—and our consideration of those which are predominantly allegorical. Although it perhaps has more in common with the *Caccia di Diana*—with respect to theme—than with any other of Boccaccio's works,[1] its pastoral setting also tends to associate the *Ninfale* with the *Comedia ninfe,* and the titles of the two works make us see that Boccaccio thought of them as related. And for this reason too it seemed acceptable to treat the *Ninfale* at this juncture.

It is Diana who will here enjoy her largest role in Boccaccio's many fictions that contain or refer to her. In the pre-Christian setting of the work [2] she represents rigid principle, and is first, last, and always the goddess of virginity and the opponent of *lussuria* (7.6). The wooded playground of the nymphs at Fiesole, under the *vicaria* of one Alfinea (16.5-6; 25.2), is more like a nunnery (as nunneries were supposed to be, at any rate) than the setting for a classical hunt.[3] This Diana, despite her evident classical attributes, would seem to have more in common with the hierarchies of conventual orders than the life of the hunt. It is May as she visits her "convent" at Fiesole. She leaves her "nuns" with a pointed warning: If you happen to come across a man, run from him lest he use deceit or force against you; those of you who are seduced I will put to banishment and death (21.4-8). While her words and actions are hardly those that are likely to please a modern audience, it would probably be unwise to assume that Boccaccio intends her values to be mocked. For if she is too rigid (as opposed to the Diana of, for instance, the *Filocolo,* she seems unwilling to join Venus in marital compromise), she has at least the virtue of opposing the licentious values of Venus. As she speaks to her assembled virgins, the young Africo, hidden among the green leaves (28.2), spies upon them, and singles out the as yet unnamed Mensola as the object of his affection.[4] He will indeed use deceit and force against Mensola, and she will indeed suffer banishment and death. Boy meets girl, boy gets girl, Diana turns boy and girl to water. His first instinctive response to Mensola's beauty is to want her as his wife (27.4), a desire that will shortly turn to unadulterated *lussuria,* with no such social commitments in view, once Venus enters the story in Africo's dream (43–48). Had Boccaccio wanted to write the sort of tale that most of his current readers like to believe he wrote, Africo and Mensola would have married, and Diana might then have seemed the sort of bigot she is today considered, while Venus, marital rather than lascivious, would have presided over their union. None of these possibilities is brought into play. And as for Venus, she is familiarly herself, boasting of her conquest of the gods, including Jove (46.8). It is by agency of her son's wounding arrow (48.2) that she reinvigorates Africo's flagging passion for Mensola. (It is worth pointing out that his natural lust—which included a marital instinct—would evidently have spent itself had not Venus intervened—42.1–4.) From that moment on he plays the role of the maddened lover—also familiar enough in Boccaccio's fictions.

Where at first he is a bumbling rustic swain (his honest male statement of love for Mensola sends a flock of nymphs dutifully flying—61–62), he quickly learns deceit, which the text specifically identifies as a lover's art (75), as when he lies to his father, Girafone, about the cause of his distraction.[5] His father is, however, not deceived, and warns the boy by telling him the sad fate of his own father, Mugnone, and the nymph Cialla, both of whom pay for Mugnone's lust in Diana's wrathful metamorphoses (83–95). Like grandfather, like grandson. Africo naturally heeds none of his father's advice. He hunts down the still virtuous Mensola. But she is at least a wavering member of the chaste *brigata.* As she hurls her dart at her pursuer, she is moved simultaneuosly to warn him (111). Her warning cry enflames him all the more (116), and though she has escaped him this time, she will not be safe for long. He complains to Venus and calls on Death (144–48). While he sleeps, Alimena, his mother, having noticed his melancholy,[6] gives him an herbal bath which is, however, unable to cure this disease (159.7–8). Like all of Boccaccio's unsated lovers, he looks terrible. In Boccaccio's witty parody of Narcissus, Africo looks into a fountain and sees himself disfigured by love (171). The mating of the forest animals which surround him serves to increase his own lust (174–76), and he finally prays again to Venus 183–92), having first killed and burned a lamb in sacrifice to her. The "pecorella . . . molto grassa e bella" (180.7–8) which he kills, splits, and burns, is a foreshadowing of the death his love will bring to Mensola. Venus shows her acceptance of his offering and prayer by performing a "miracolo": [7] the burnt halves of the lamb (to Africo they represent himself and Mensola—182.1–2) are joined; however, the creature, reborn and bleating, falls back into the fire to be consumed all over again (193). The touch is a nice one: The bodily resurrection performed by Venus is not long lasting.[8] But the "miracolo" of course heartens Africo, who now presses his suit armed with Venus's best advice, which is that he disguise himself as a nymph (200). The ensuing action, like a great deal else in the *Ninfale,* is richly—if slyly—comic. Africo purloins one of his mother's less-used dresses and, disguised as a nymph in accord with Venus's instructions, goes off to look for Mensola. With his bow and arrow he kills a dangerous boar [9] and is welcomed by the nymphs after Mensola tells them that she has never seen a nymph make so fine a shot. Africo among the nymphs, able to speak to and touch Mensola girl-to-girl (229,7–8), is a brilliantly funny creation, a fourteenth-century "anticipation" of Jack Lemmon's and Tony Curtis's transvestite penetration of the sacred grove of the all-girl orchestra's sleeping car on its way to Florida in the great perverse pastoral of our time, Billy Wilder's *Some Like It Hot.* Despite his girlish appearance,[10] his utterly "male" appetites are incapable of lengthy restraint. When the nymphs decide to bathe [11] Africo reveals his true nature:

> Before he took off all his clothing
> all the nymphs had left the shore;
> then he came forward wearing nothing,
> revealing what went him before.
> All the nymphs drew back in loathing,
> in fear and trembling did deplore,
> shouting loudly "Goodness me,
> can't you see that she's a he?" [12]

Had Boccaccio been acquainted with Aristotle's *Poetics,* we could say that he here burlesques dramatic *anagnorisis.* Without benefit of Aristotle we may still call this a "recognition scene," one that occurs at roughly the numerical center of the work (*ottava* 239 of 473) and which tells us what the "argument" of the *Ninfale* is: sexual pleasure. It offers a fitting emblem for the theme in Africo's phallus.

It is difficult to read the *Ninfale* and remain severe. It is not a work designed for the pleasure of a tight-lipped moralist. Its predominant tone is that of the lascivious wink. The resultant problem, for a modern audience, is that it is all too easy to assume a carnal posture in response, to let Boccaccio's sensuality involve one in the misconstrued fellowship of hygienic carnality. Yet the text does not really allow such a construction. In all that follows—and the inevitable does follow—Boccaccio's text makes it plain that, whatever his titillations were in writing it, love is the world's most dangerous outdoor sport.[13] Africo rapes Mensola, the other nymphs having run for their lives.[14] Mensola wants to kill herself, since Diana will kill her anyway (248).[15] Africo argues her out of her desire to die and slowly kindles the spark of affection in her. The rape in the pool has left him sexually spent, and his only loving resource is verbiage, until he has regained his forces for another assault, first having prepared the way with the usual lover's blandishments and oaths.[16] If Mensola was blameless by any but Diana's harsh standards in her deflowering, she can not be said to be so in her second and sweeter taste of love. This time she is seduced, not raped. The textual process from *ottava* 246 to *ottava* 303 is one of that shows her increasing openness to Africo's desires.[17] And it is this second coupling, the text makes it quite clear, that will be the efficient cause of her death. The all-knowing narrator lets it be known that it is on *this* occasion that she becomes pregnant (306, 311).[18]

The two lovers die of their carnal love, Africo when the fearful Mensola does not return to their trysting place the following day. His suicidal end (361) is fitting to one who had at the outset associated himself with Amore and Fortuna (34, 7–8). Words that might well serve for his epitaph have been previously uttered by his father, as the latter considers Mugnone's mad pursuit of Cialla: "tu correvi dietro alla tua morte" (88.2). As for Mensola, faced by her vengeful goddess, she hides her baby in a thornbush and runs for her life—to no avail. Diana takes her promised vengeance and kills her (412). She and her lover become Tuscan streams in their metamorphoses.[19] But our fabulist's aim can hardly be thought of as being merely or even primarily historico-physical; their tale is a cautionary moral tale.[20] This is made pointedly clear when we observe the sexual history of their offspring, who is named Pruneo (after the thorns, or *pruni,* he is found among—433.7). The last forty *ottave* are hardly great literature, or even very good Boccaccio. But they are there, and one of their features is to show us a Pruneo who is brought up by Girafone and Alimena in continual awareness of the cause of his parents' deaths (435). When Atlas "discovers" Tuscany he too "chases" nymphs—either out of the area or into matrimony (437). One thinks of Theseus among the Amazons in the first book of the *Teseida.* What appealed neither to Africo nor to Mensola, so receptive to Venus, suddenly is present as a possibility which they might have done well to consider. Atlas gives the twenty-five year old Pruneo Tironea in marriage (448). They have ten children (452.3), and live happily and wisely until their deaths in a house built by Pruneo near the church of San

Martino at Maiano (449.1). Even in the shorthand form which Boccaccio chose to use for his conclusion, the moral antitheses to Africo and Mensola are evident.[21] In the *Ninfale fiesolano* praise of Venus is as ironically structured as it was in the works we have previously studied, but the answer to venereal conduct is present in the work. In this respect the *Ninfale* resembles the *Filocolo* and the *Teseida* and differs from the *Filostrato* and the *Elegia di madonna Fiammetta.* And like the *Filocolo* and *Teseida,* the work ends with a marriage, and thus, in this case under a specifically Christian dispensation, resolves the warring claims of Diana and Venus.

The foregoing remarks give short shrift to a work that, for its grace and charm, deserves another kind of consideration. Those of its readers who have previously admired it, while they have had worthwhile things to say about the elegance of the *Ninfale* as literary creation, have also, without exception, dealt with it as a serious treatment of the joys and pains of carnal love, as a kind of fourteenth-century version of Erich Segal's *Love Story.* I do not believe that the *Ninfale* (or any other of the *opere minori in volgare*) is well read in this way. And my concern is less that Boccaccio's moral intentions are obscured by such readings than that his status as artist is deeply undercut when he is treated as praiser of lasciviousness. At the same time, if he is seen as mocking the religion of love in the *Ninfale,* he should be seen to be doing so in the spirit of serious play which we are gradually learning to understand deeply in such later figures as Erasmus. The common mark of Boccaccio and that later illustrious mocker is wit. The folly which they both praise is never hospitable to blind and foolish lust (an activity totally devoid of wit), but to the more human—and sociable—frailty of natural desire for the opposite sex. Such desire, without which the human race would quickly be extinguished, frequently advances its own claims in witty ways, or at least in ways that cause our sympathetic laughter. And yet when these writers turn their attention to aberrant sexual behavior, even then their tone is not one of sarcasm, but of large good humor; one thinks, perhaps, of Isidore of Seville's delightful distinction: not *sarcosmos* ("hostilis inrisio cum amaritudine") but its opposite, *astysmos* ("urbanitas sine iracundia"—*Etymologiarum* I.xxxvii.29–30) is the tone which we find most often and admire the most in their works, even though both Boccaccio and Erasmus could be masters of invective when they chose to be so. Boccaccio's "urbanity without wrath" should allow us to see such as Africo for the foolish lovers that they are within the context of a highly wrought literary world, one in which wit may confront conventional Christian morality without ever quite destroying the mold of that morality.

There may be—to borrow a modern critical term—some tension experienced by a modern reader when he confronts so comfortably ironic a medieval writer. And if Boccaccio's readers were to find that his very irony undercuts the values which oppose the butts of his *astysmos,* one could sympathize with their discomfort. Yet those readers who deal with Boccaccio as though he had not presented such figures as Africo as fools of Love—neither victims nor heroes, but fools—have probably missed the greater pleasures of the collaboration that these beautifully contrived texts hold out to them.

The *Comedia delle ninfe fiorentine,* [22] "read superficially, seems like nothing but a boring pastoral romance." [23] But, with the exception of the *Amorosa Visione,* no early work of Boccaccio has so long been recognized as having a moral intent wrapped in an allegorical covering. Vittore Branca is probably correct when he claims that Boccaccio turned to "quella nuova letteratura vagamente allegorico-didattica" as a result of his return to Florence from Naples. For in the north he found a cultural pose that held such literary enterprise in high repute.[24] At any rate, it may be assumed that no serious reader of the work has failed to observe the allegorical nature of its proceedings, even if some of the interpretations that have been offered border on the bizarre.[25] The modern recognition of an allegorical design in the work begins with Vincenzo Crescini, whose essential finding is as valid today as it was when he made it: the *Comedia ninfe* is a Christian allegory.[26] But many readers have been uncomfortable with such a recognition, and most late nineteenth-century and twentieth-century studies of the work are, as Quaglio says,[27] primarily interested in the "biographical facts" that can be gleaned from it, and thus treat the work more as a *roman à clef* than anything else. And many of those who deal with the text in more literary ways are plainly uncomfortable with this "allegorical" Boccaccio.[28] Others, while uneasily accepting the allegorical premise of the work, simply do not find its stylistic qualities pleasing.[29] Quaglio, the last and best editor of the text, has clearly understood and, in his notes to the text, expressed the author's allegorical equations; he nonetheless presents a view of the work in which Boccaccio's allegorical intentions and sensual instincts fail to blend harmoniously.[30] In short, the *Comedia ninfe* has either been misunderstood or disliked by most of its readers. This is not to say that those who find it labored and mannered are wrong. That is not the point. The result has been to put the work off to one side—often in the company of the *Amorosa Visione.*[31] This allows them to keep their ancient *schema:* Boccaccio, the great poet of Love (Nature, the Renaissance, etc.) from the *Caccia* to the *Decameron,* also happened to write two unBoccaccian allegories. These are understood as abortive attempts to write a "philosophical" poetry which would appeal only to an erudite classicizing audience, and thus in this respect as well, are seen as foreign to Boccaccio's usual intentions.

As I have been attempting to demonstrate, however, the Boccaccio of the other *opere minori* has been proposing moral values in these works that are in no way opposed to the clear Christian principles advanced in his two large-scale allegorical productions, that both ironically (indirectly) and directly (by means of various techniques, ranging from flat statement to allegorical presentation) all of the minor works operate on the same moral matrix, the principal axes of which are the carnal and the celestial Venus. That such is the case in the *Comedia ninfe* has long been recognized.[32] The work exists as a tease—both for the central character in it, Ameto, and for the reader.[33] It falls into three parts, in the first of which Ameto, the rough hunter, is stupefied by the beauty of Lia and the six other nymphs; in the second the seven nymphs tell the stories of their love affairs; in the last Ameto comes fully to understand the Christian truth of all that he has observed. After the narrator's introduction (and once again we postpone our examination of his role in the proceedings) we move to the forests and hills of antique Tuscany, where we find Ameto, *vagabundo giovane* (III.4) returning from a successful hunt. He hears a marvellous new song, thinks the gods have descended to the earth, and traces the source of the melody to the lovely nymph Lia, singing a *canzone*[34] which celebrates her own and Venus's loving nature.[35] Ameto understands everything in the song except the identity and meaning of Amore (V.9), and realizes that he is in love with Lia. He has a debate with himself (he first thinks it presumptuous even to consider the possibility that such a heavenly creature would want anything to do with the likes of him [36]—the mental gesture sharply distinguishes him from all the previous lovers whom we have met in Boccaccio, none of whom seems capable of so humble a thought—but then decides to take a chance on love: what can he lose? [37]) and then offers his prey in sacrifice to his lady (V.34).[38] Some time later he wanders into the Maytime celebration of Venus, at which all the ensuing "action" will take place. He hears the explicitly Christian hymn of the shepherd Teogapen (XI), sees the growing assemblage of beautiful nymphs (XII), hears the rival songs of Alcesto and Acaten in praise of the ascetic and the worldly life (XV), and thinks he is in paradise (XV.6).[39] Interestingly enough, when he admires one of the nymphs he is unable to decide whether she is Venus or Diana (XV.9–10).[40] As we saw in the *Filocolo,* when we find these two goddesses in sympathetic conjunction we are dealing with a love that is other than morally deficient. This section of the work closes with Ameto's prayer for aid in love to Jove and the as yet to him unknown Amore (XVI.8, 22).

To this point we have witnessed nothing but the most chaste sensual responses one can imagine. Ameto's purely sexual instincts toward the nymphs find expression in covertly Christian language. But now Lia proposes that each of the seven nymphs tell the story of her love in honor of this celebration of Venus. These tales, far from being chaste, are often lascivious, even obscene. In each of them the nymph gives her human genealogy, her particular divine dedication, the details of her marriage (generally to an unsatisfactory husband, but in Fiammetta's case to a perfectly serviceable one; Lia is the only one who is not married, and Ameto is, despite the universal affection she proclaims in her first song, apparently her first love), and the change wrought in her by Venus, whom she worships for the adulterous love affair which now contents her.[41] One can readily understand that readers are uneasy with Boccaccio's allegorical pretensions.[42] We are supposed to believe that these purely carnal love affairs, replete with striptease (XVIII.34–35), the flagging phallus of an old man (XXXII. 16), and other such *lascivia*, mean something else. When we find that at least some of the ladies—and some of their husbands—are associated, either by heraldic devices or verbal puns, with actual persons, the sounding of Boccaccio's intent becomes even more difficult.[43] In short, the central portion of the *Comedia ninfe* (XVII–XXXVIII), had it been published as a "picciolo *Decameron*" without the surrounding material, would have passed for another of Boccaccio's "lascivious" works, an *Ars amatoria* with none but carnal intentions. In each of the seven "novelle"—or at least in the first six—we find the same plot: a nymph dedicated to a goddess and who is married (usually unhappily) gladly accepts the rule of intervening Venus and has a happy love affair. It is only this last detail (for, as we have seen, Boccaccio's carnal lovers all end unhappily unless they marry, that is, unless they worship the right Venus) that would allow an analysis like this one to maintain that this putative complete work were an ironic attack upon the religion of love.

The surrounding material is, however, there. And in it, and especially in the concluding mystical apparitions and hymns, Boccaccio wrenches *lussuria* out of its apparent context and transforms it to *caritas*. The fact is that modern readers are not very happy with such literary behavior.[44] A brief remark of E. H. Gombrich goes to the heart of the difficulty. He describes some renaissance allegorical production as follows: "The humanist allegory frequently oscillates between the search for the Orphic arcanum, bordering on primitive magic, and the sophisticated conceit, bordering on parlour games." [45] In our own more than defensible concern for aesthetic integrity (we have at least Aristotle and Aquinas on our side) we tend either to dislike or to misinterpret such works. Yet Boccaccio's intent in the *Comedia ninfe* glances out at us—whether we choose to like the work or not—even in the midst of all the carnality of the "novelle." As the last of the first four nymphs, Acrimonia, tells her tale, Ameto's musings point us upward.[46] His desires for the nymphs, as he listens to them, become more tempered. He puts from himself vain imaginings (XXXI. 1). He longs to see the seven ladies as nude as Paris saw the three goddesses on Ida, but considers that as a "semplice cacciatore" he may expect no such boon, and concludes that it would also be superfluous in light of the inflamed condition caused in him by the sight of their faces alone (XXXI.5–7). His modesty (we have heard him in this vein before—V.19) and his distinction between *viso* and *corpo* show that he is becoming ready to understand.

The Christian design of Boccaccio's pagan integument becomes altogether clear in Lia's hymn to Cybele, who, as the Great Mother, seems to represent either Theology or the Church.[47] Her words reflect the Bible and the Creed,[48] and leave no doubt as to the Christian intent of the work. In the following chapter, perhaps reflecting the feathery omens of *Aeneid* XII.247–256, Boccaccio has seven swans defeat seven storks in airy battle (XL.3–5), thus offering us a clue as to how we are retrospectively to read the carnal seductions of the seven swains by the seven nymphs: they are victories of the Virtues over the Vices. And from classical omen we turn to Exodus 13:21–22—there appears a pillar of fire that blinds Ameto by its brightness (XL.7–8); in nineteen lines of *terza rima* Venus speaks as the Trinity ("Io son luce del ciel unica e trina"—XLI.1), promising heavenly joy to those who will follow. Ameto's response gives us a key to the *Comedia ninfe:* "secondo lo stato parlare estimò colei veramente essere non quella Venere che gli stolti alle loro disordinate concupiscenzie chiamano dea, ma quella dalla quale i veri e giusti e santi amori discendono intra' mortali" (XLII.1).[49] This venereal Trinity may have seemed as blasphemous a literary creation to some fourteenth-century readers as she may seem to some readers today. Nonetheless, one aspect of the fourteenth century that is truly anticipatory of the renaissance is to be found in its Christian mythography, which builds on a long medieval tradition (running from Fulgentius to Bernardus Silvestris) and moves it one step further in order to make pagan myth not only philosophically worthy, but theologically true.

Staring into the living depths of the flame, highly reminiscent of the Dante of *Paradiso* XXXIII,[50] Ameto discerns the "luminoso corpo" of Christ (XLII.3) before the vision becomes too bright for him to behold it any longer, when he must be content with hearing the venereal Trinity (described as "la santa dea") petition her "sorelle" to aid his intellectual ascent to heavenly things (XLIII). The rest of the action of the work need not detain us long. Ameto is duly baptized by the nymphs (XLIV) and leaves the sacred grove with an eternal recognition of what he has seen, a happy man (XLVIII.4). Like the narrator of the *Caccia di Diana* he feels himself changed from brute to human [51]—but the change in him may be taken without reservation as a positive development. The evidence for the change is given without equivocation by Boccaccio: Where the shepherds' songs (XI and XIV) had first merely delighted him, he now realizes how useful they are; [52] similarly the nymphs, who had first pleased his eyes rather than his intellect, now have the reverse effect, and he understands the true significance of the temples and goddesses of which they sang, and of the loves they told, and is ashamed of the concupiscent thoughts he had had; now he understands what the lovers signified as well.[53] The passage exists as a sort of commentary to the entire work, and makes its Christian intent absolutely explicit. If, in the furrow of Alban Forcione, we wanted to call the *Filocolo* Boccaccio's "Christian romance," the *Comedia ninfe* is his Christian eclogue.[54] It may well be that its frequent detractors are correct about its lack of literary merit, although this would not be my position if I chose to debate its aesthetic success or failure. But one of the reasons for their negative judgment is that they had decided to dislike the work for being what Boccaccio wanted it to be, a celebration of the "veri e giusti e santi amori" (XLII. 1), that transform a carnal understanding into a celestial one.

While, as medieval dream visions go, the *Amorosa Visione* is not terribly long (some 4400 lines), it admittedly has its *longueurs,* at least for the modern reader. In its own time and far into the renaissance it was enthusiastically received.[55] There are probably two main elements in the work which help to explain its popularity: Boccaccio here presented the morally "correct" vision of earthly and heavenly love, and he did so in the "humanist" format that became increasingly precious in the years between 1350 and 1600.[56] Thus, while to most modern readers such lengthy recapitulations of classical matter as the major portions of two *canti* which Boccaccio devotes to the story of Achilles' loves (XXIII–XXIV) are ineffective when compared with Dante's two lines (*Inferno* V.65–66) on the same subject, we must at least try to understand Boccaccio's cultivation of a "humanist" style, one in which the world of classical antiquity is a magical presence. To tell these tales again, and to tell them in the vernacular that has only since the time of Dante been seen as a worthy vehicle for a major literary effort, is a task which Boccaccio seizes with perhaps some *parvenu* zeal and certainly with great genuine emotion. And, at least when compared with the *Comedia ninfe,* the *Amorosa Visione* is a work filled with deeply felt gestures to the literary past. We may tend to forget the missionary character of Boccaccio's vernacular work; the task he took on himself was not a small one.

The *Amorosa Visione* is, according to Landau, Boccaccio's "opera più bizzarra." [57] One must accede to this judgment, even from the point of view of this study, at least when one tries to make sense of the conclusion of the work, which is fairly dizzying. Since the analyses offered of the *Caccia di Diana* and the *Corbaccio* in the first chapter, I have avoided discussion of the narrator's role in the text he narrates in order to preserve that subject for discussion in the chapter which follows this one. That tactic would be close to impossible here, since the narrator is the central character of the *Amorosa Visione,* whereas, in the last six works we have examined—with the exception of the *Elegia di madonna Fiammetta* [58]—his presence was confined to the cornice. But before we encounter him we must observe the existence of what may well be the most imposing piece of scrimshaw in the history of literature: Boccaccio's acrostic sonnets and their relationship to the text of the entire work.[59] These stand at the head of the work. Each letter in the sonnets is the first letter of the corresponding *terzina* in the body of the text. It is fascinating to imagine the labor of composition thereby required. Branca has pointed out that the first letters of the three sonnets are, respectively, M, I, O.[60] Has Boccaccio also in this way "signed" his strange creation? It seems likely.

The acrostic sonnets are in the form of a dedication to a *donna gentile* (sonn. I.2). Seeing her one day, the narrator was moved to treat of her, "parlando brievemente" (sonn. I.8—the intention is hardly carried out). He now sends the work to her, naming her ("madama Maria"—sonn. I.11), and also using a form of her *senhal:* "cara Fiamma" (sonn. I.15); and then Boccaccio refers, the only time in all his fictions, to himself by name: "que' che vi manda questa Visione/Giovanni è di Boccaccio da Certaldo" (sonn. I.16–17).[61] There is no clearer statement in all of his writings that he was personally enamored of a lady named Maria, code name Fiamma or Fiammetta. Yet that does not require that we accept the relationship as historical or consider it as other than the further elaboration of the already elaborate fictional "autobiography" that winds its way through the *opere minori.* For in defense of those readers who have seen these works as "autobiographical," one must agree that it is Boccaccio himself who continually raises the issue, not least of all by having his narrator speak as the author.[62] The rest of the dedication is conventional enough. The poet-lover hopes for "pity" from his lady (sonn. II. 16), and in the third sonnet addresses us, his lover/readers who burn within Love's flame (sonn. III.3–4). If we take fruit or delight from the work we are to thank his lady, to whose beauty he is subject (sonn. III. 13–16); we will recognize her by her resemblance to Amore (sonn. III. 17–18).[63] To conclude, Boccaccio reaches the height of playful false modesty while remaining in the conventional modest pose of the religion of love: we are asked to give *her* (rather than him) the laurel (sonn. III.23). In short, all of the trappings of the carnal lover are here put on, before our very eyes, by Boccaccio himself. What then allows us to believe that the Boccaccio who wrote the passage had any other convictions than the ones expressed in it? The thousands of pages of earlier criticism which argue that these were exactly Boccaccio's sentiments cannot merely be brushed aside. What I shall hope to demonstrate, both in the light of previous arguments and from evidence within the *Amorosa Visione,* is that "Boccaccio's" values and actions run counter to those presented by the work in which he, the lover-poet, is a character. Let us turn to the best source of evidence we have, the text of the poem.[64]

The *Amorosa Visione* opens with its author's statement of intention, which is to narrate the content of a dream vision sent him, "wounded" by his lady's eyes, by Amore (I. 1–6; Cupido in *A*).[65] In his dream, wandering along the edge of the sea, he is accosted by a *donna lucente* (I.26).[66] This lady will serve as his guide for the next fifty *canti.*[67] Who or what she is or represents is one of the more vexed questions of Boccaccio studies. Vittore Branca suggests that it is perhaps not necessary to fix her identity, and, claiming that Boccaccio's usual habit of mind is to make allegorical identities readily apparent, suggests that she is only generically identifiable as a heavenly guide, that she represents "l'aspirazione alla virtù che è in ogni anima." [68] Yet the lady has a clear iconographic identification, or, to be more precise, two clear iconographic associations: she is regal [69] and venereal. In short, and only to resurrect the nearly century-old and generally disregarded or else discarded thesis of A. Gaspary, she is likely to represent the celestial Venus.[70] Her venereal attributes are as follows: she is dressed in purple (I.39) [71] and she holds a golden apple (I.41). We remember the Venus hidden in the secret part of her own temple in the *Teseida*. In her hands she holds Lascivia and the apple given her by Paris (VII.66 and gloss). That the *guida*'s golden apple is the one Venus was given by Paris is made all the more likely by the description of the Judgment in the valley of Ida, including of course the "pomo d'oro" (XXVII.14), which occupies the first thirty-three lines of the twenty-seventh canto. It seems unnecessary to look further for the just iconographical reference when we find it in Boccaccio's own text.[72] But her identification with Venus is tempered by Boccaccio—if she wears purple (or violet, a softer hue of purple), she is not nude; if she carries her golden apple in her left hand, she carries a royal sceptre (and not the personification of lust, Lascivia, which she held there in the *Teseida*) in the better one. It would seem likely that Boccaccio would want the celestial Venus to be present in this work as she was in the similarly allegorical *Comedia ninfe*. And we can note that her dilineation of her relationship with the narrator is similar to that offered by Lia to Ameto, as it is to the self-description offered by Trinity/Venus in that work.[73] Further, the comparison of her gait to Juno's (I.43–44—only in the *B* text) may not be as aimless or spontaneous as Branca supposes,[74] but may be an attempt to associate Venus with the better aspect of herself, the Juno who presides in her temple when a marriage is performed there.[75] Even the narrator—who will prove to be one of the slowest and most perverse learners since the dreamer-protagonist of the *Roman de la Rose,* a work with which the *Amorosa Visione* has many affinities [76]—refers to her as *donna celeste.* She is not one who merely seems to have descended from heaven, as are all the mortally beautiful girls who look like angels, but one who has really come down. Her celestial nature, coupled with her iconography, make it seem fairly certain that Gaspary had solved Boccaccio's riddle.[77] (For purposes of my argument she need be no more than the agent of the celestial Venus, comparable in this sense to the "messo di Diana" of the *Caccia;* whether she "is" the celestial Venus or not makes little difference—as long as she is identified with her.) The identity of the guide, it need hardly be added, is of some importance in any attempt to deal with the allegorical meaning of the *Amorosa Visione.*

If the attitudes and behaviors of the character "Boccaccio" will be the frequent cause of his guide's rebukes (as we shall shortly find), what of the attitudes and expressions of Boccaccio the narrator? To put this question another way, is it possible that while the values of the celestial Venus, with all her associations with Christian morality, inform the allegorical significance of the work, the moral attitudes of the lover-poet who narrates the work are to be examined critically rather than taken at face value? If the hypothesis implied in that question has any weight, the lover-poet's invocation (which, like Dante's in *Inferno,* occurs only at the beginning of the second canto of the work) should express the wrong values. That is, within the context of the previous point, if the *guida* represents the celestial Venus, the narrator should seek aid from the carnal Venus. His eighteen-line invocation, filled with echoes of Dante, is addressed to the "santa dea" (II.4—"Citerea" in *A*).[78] Which Venus does he address? If *this* is a higher philosophical principle, as Branca believes,[79] Gaspary's and my own identification of the *guida* and the good Venus seems at the very best unlikely, and at the worst impossible. However, if the narrator calls on the carnal Venus, we have a most appealing configuration, in which the two competing aspects of the goddess of love are present in antithetic stances within fifty lines of one another. And this possibility seems, in light of our previous studies in Boccaccio's text (for example, the *Teseida*'s gloss on the two Venuses, but also the several cases of their antithetic conjunction already examined), more than possible, even likely. If, on the other hand, the narrator correctly understands the relationship between the *guida* and the goddess to whom he appeals, my hypothesis makes no sense whatsoever. For his view (II.13–18) is that the *guida* will lead him to the goddess, who will then take him where he wants to go.[80] A parallel is found in Dante's *Commedia,* where Virgil cedes his place to Beatrice. But this does *not* happen in the *Amorosa Visione.* The *guida* never retreats from the work in favor of another.[81] If in the concluding *canti* our poet-lover for the moment moves away from her and toward another, it is in carnal desire for his beloved, not in awe of a celestial figure. Yet the work concludes with him in the presence of the *guida,* not of that other lady. In short, the narrator's request will not be granted, for his expectations at the outset are simply incorrect. That may perhaps become more evident when we compare his invocation with its model in the *Comedia ninfe,* the narrator's prayer to Venus at the beginning of that work.[82] Remembering who it was who speaks in that invocation, the narrator, *not* Ameto, we should reflect that he too, like the narrator of the *Amorosa Visione,* will remain mired in a sexual vision of love. For him Ameto's "resurrection" seems desirable because Ameto is among such pretty women (XLIX. 1–66)—that is, at the end of the work the narrator is at most the equal of the sexually inspired Ameto of its beginning. Where the rustic hunter has learned the meaning of the allegory he has experienced (XLVI.3), the literate narrator has not. He "deallegorizes" the nymphs back into Florentine pin-up girls. His invocation offers a clear indication of his carnal nature at the outset. He prays to Citerea (II.8), Cupido (II.28), and to his lady ("E tu, più ch'altra bella criatura"—II.43). If the celestial Venus is triform ("Io son luce del cielo unica e trina"—XLI. 1; "per lo tuo santo e ineffabile nome triforme"—XLIV.6), so too is this one—but she is the antithesis of the celestial Venus. It would take too long to work through the ninety-one lines of the narrator's invocation in the *Comedia ninfe.* However, I may say this much: They are inspired totally by the religion of love. For Branca to argue for the "philosophic" nature of the invocation of the *Amorosa Visione* on the basis of its resemblance to the invocation of the *Comedia ninfe* is to argue from a false premise, and helps to overturn his assertion.

The language of the two religions, as has frequently been noticed, is necessarily similar, since the vocabulary of the later one was modelled on the vocabulary of the former. One thinks of but a few of their common key words—*salute, beatitudine, amore, grazia,* even *fiamma*—and understands that only context can tell us which one we confront.[83] The inspiration sought from Venus (either carnal or celestial) is sought to glorify either of two kinds of love, unless we have a context which allows us to make a choice among the possibilities.

What has already been said, and what will be said, about the *Amorosa Visione* offers a possible context. But something in the passage itself perhaps offers a better: the reference to Orpheus.[84] And once again, in a study which has fairly frequently been concerned with the ways in which, for Boccaccio, so many things may be taken either *in bono* or *in malo,* we are compelled to examine positive and negative valences. Boccaccio's Orpheus is a complex figure, usually represented in one of two guises, either as the lover-poet or as the theological poet. In Boccaccio's many allusions to him he will own either of these two identities, but not both of them together. As the lover-poet he uses the instrument of his art to the end of all-too-human sexual endeavor.[85] As the *poeta-theologus* (a concept which plays such an important part in the fourteenth-century argument about the relationship of poetry to truth [86]) he stands for higher moral principles. This double view of Orpheus meets us in Boccaccio's lengthy gloss occasioned by *Inferno* IV. 140–41, where the poets Orpheus and Linus are interwoven with the philosophers Cicero and Seneca. Boccaccio's reaction to Orpheus is to divide him into two, first retailing the story of the sad lover of Eurydice, "secondo che i poeti scrivono," and then, "lasciando le fizioni poetiche da parte," declaring that the historical Orpheus was one of the first Greek priests who began to know the true God; from the "parole esquisite" that he composed came the name *poet.*[87] With two exceptions, that we may leave to one side for the moment, the Orfeo whom we find in the *Filocolo, Teseida, Comedia ninfe,* and *Amorosa Visione* is the singer of love, not the *poeta-theologus* of the *Esposizioni.* And while there Boccaccio's description of him includes Ovid's tale of the sad, chaste Orpheus who, for consoling other like-minded males, is torn apart by the Maenads (*Metamorphoses* X), this matter also does not enter his treatment of Orpheus in these four works.[88] What is Boccaccio's attitude toward Orpheus in them? As opposed to Dante, who seems to have turned away from what would have been only a natural exploitation of his own topographical similarities to Orpheus in the *Commedia,*[89] Boccaccio frequently uses Orpheus as a prototype of himself, or, to put that more precisely, as the prototype of the Orphic lover-poet who is presented in his fictions. Let us see.

In the *Filocolo* (IV.45, 7) Caleon, ineffectively defending carnal love against Fiammetta's attack on it in favor of *amore onesto,* calls Orfeo as his witness. The passage is hardly tepid and comes indeed as the crowning example in Caleon's defense of Amore. His final words are, if unintentionally so, ironic enough (inspired by Amore, Orfeo's *cetera* sounded so powerfully that he "meritò di riavere la perduta moglie"—we surely remember that Orfeo ended up losing her all the same); but Fiammetta herself takes up Caleon's claim on behalf of Orfeo (46, 11) and says some fairly harsh things about Amore and, by implication, Orfeo. Of course, she says, Orfeo's guitar sounded sweetly—Amore's subjects are given tongues of such sweetness and so many flatteries that they can move stones—and if stones, how much more easily inconstant hearts? Orfeo's guitar, or, by metonymy, the singer himself, is here seen as a "suggetto" of Amore, and a flatterer. This is the only *locus* in these four works in which Orfeo is overtly attacked.[90] But this is one of the few *loci* in which he is not summoned up by a speaker who is himself a subject of Amore,[91] as he is when Idalogos tells his auditors (V.8, 29) that he first gave himself to Orfeo (poetry) and then to bowmanship (love)—it is probably not by chance that the two characters in the work, Caleon and Idalogos, who are most closely identified with Boccaccio's "autobiography," that is, the two love-struck sufferers, identify themselves with Orfeo.

In the *Teseida* there are only two references to Orpheus. Emilia thinks unhappily of the battle going on between Palemone and Arcita over her and thinks enviously of Orfeo, who was so adept in humble prayer that he got his Euridice back (VIII.103). Of course she is eventually wrong, as Boccaccio's gloss to the passage makes plain ("non potendosi più tenere, si volse indietro e guatolla, e subitamente la perdé"). It is at the wedding of Emilia and Palemone that the Orfeo of the Augustinian tradition [92] makes his appearance. Where the Orpheus of the opposed tradition is "banished" from the mystical wedding of Filocolo and Biancifiore, the "historical" Orpheus, *poeta-theologus,* is fittingly referred to in the temple dedicated to the celestial Venus, in the company of Hymen and Juno (XII.68.6 & 8): The instruments which accompany the wedding ceremony call to mind Orfeo, Museo, and Lino (XII.72). In the *Comedia ninfe,* the work that is closest in time and spirit to the *Amorosa Visione,* we find considerable concern with Orpheus. Ameto, doubting that Lia could find him, "un semplice cacciatore," pleasing, says that he has not the bodily form of Adonis, the riches of Midas, the "cetera d'Orfeo" (v. 18). Perhaps the lack is meant to have positive implications. Perhaps it is merely an innocent detail.[93] But the invocation of the work begins precisely with Orfeo, as the narrator sings his praise of Citerea in the name of the power of love that moved Orfeo.[94] Once again Orfeo is spoken of as winning back Euridice (ll. 3–4), though such crucial words as "forse" and "a condizione" warn all but headlong readers that the victory was neither all so sweet nor long-lived. If Orfeo's love for Euridice is to be understood as beneficent in Boccaccio's eyes, it can only be so if we are content to contort his context. It is more likely to be the case that Orfeo, as lover-poet, is always treated ironically. Such is surely the case in the *Amorosa Visione,* to which we can at last return. The use of Orfeo here (II.8–9) tells us what kind of poet-lover narrates the work. His name may be Giovanni Boccaccio, but he is the same putative *auctor* who wrote the *Comedia ninfe,* who there referred to himself (I. 12) as "non poeta, ma piuttosto amante," and, as this poet does, prays to the wrong Venus. Orfeo is seen, nearly halfway through the poem, as one of the many in the long rout depicted in the triumph of Venus (XXIII.4–30). When the narrator sees him his heart takes joy, and he imagines that Orfeo's words are his own. The identification is so closely and affectionately made that only the perception of an ironic structure in this and others of Boccaccio's works keeps one from falling victim to Vittore Branca's enthusiasm.[95] This Orfeo is seen as reunited with his Euridice and proclaims himself happy in his love for her. While it is striking, as Branca has pointed out,[96] that there is no reference to his winning over of Pluto, what is more striking is the lack of any indication that Orfeo will lose his Euridice a second time. But, as we have seen, the omission of this crucial detail is a common phenomenon in those characters who take Orfeo as a positive *exemplum* of the lover. And when we consider the model for this and other scenes in the triumph of Amore—Dante's *Inferno*—we see the larger dimension of the scene, for we gain the sense that Orfeo and Euridice are together in Hell in the afterlife. The "lunga stagion con gioia" which he desires to share with her *will* be eternal. It is in this sense that he will not lose her again: They are Boccaccio's version of Paolo and Francesca.[97]

If we see Orfeo in the triumph of Amore, we have already seen him earlier in the poem. There are, literally, two Orpheuses in the *Amorosa Visione.* This one is the lover-poet; in the fourth canto, in the triumph of sapience, we find the *poeta-theologus,* as in Dante, accompanied by Linus (IV.70–72).[98] It is rather pointedly the case that our narrator identifies fully with the lover-poet, but merely mentions the better Orpheus as being present. In a sense, Orpheus, as he is treated in the *opere minori,* offers us an epitome of Boccaccio's mythographic technique in these works, which, in my view, is highly conscious and ironic. There are those who will disagree, preferring to believe that the enthusiasms expressed for Orfeo the lover-poet are Boccaccio's own. This discussion may help to define the grounds for our disagreement. It has been to that end that I have spent so much time with Orpheus. Like the Ovid whom we will encounter in the next chapter, he is an alter ego (or, if I may invoke the aid of a poor Freudian pun, he is the alter id) of Giovanni Boccaccio. And like that Ovid, he has his moral side as well. But we have not gotten past the opening lines of the second canto of the *Amorosa Visione,* to which I return, promising an effort at brevity.

Confronted with a rather obvious adaptation of the biblical straight and narrow path (with elements of the purgatorial gate of the ninth canto of Dante's *Purgatorio* thrown in for good measure),[99] the narrator chooses instead, and against the urgings of his guide, a portal from which issue festive sounds and which stands invitingly wide and open at his left. The moral stage business is clear enough: He does not yet wish to be led on up, preferring, like Dante's Ulysses, to gain experience of this world (II.35–45). And the metaphor that lies behind this moment in the poem would have been clear enough to fourteenth-century readers. It is the Y of Pythagoras,[100] the fork in the moral road. Here, and throughout the *Amorosa Visione,* the pilgrim will make the wrong choice, despite the *guida*'s clear explanations and warnings.[101] Boccaccio's language here and in the following canto makes the nature of the choice absolutely plain: "il bene eterno" (II.57) or "cose vane" (III.8) are his two possibilities. The narrator's devotion to the latter is, and will remain, unswerving. Having made up his mind to reject his guide's advice, he is aided in his rebellion by two youths, one wearing red, the other, white, who issue from the open gate and offer totally perverse advice.[102] He of course accepts it, though it is vigorously countered by the guide. She seizes the narrator's right hand, the two youths, the left.[103] The guide realizes that she is at least temporarily beaten, laments the fact, but promises not to leave her charge, awaiting another opportunity to lead him in better directions (III.76–80). The irony (as well as the humor) of the entire situation becomes even more apparent in the opening *terzina* of Canto VI, which presents the guide as *following* the narrator in his leftward journey. I shall not discuss the visits to the four "temples" in which are depicted, in ways that strongly affected Petrarch and Chaucer, the triumphs of Sapienza (IV–VI), Gloria (VI–XII), Ricchezza (XII–XIV), and Amore (XV–XXX).[104] That the last of these is not so happy an experience is made plain by the inserted moralizing "commentary" that begins Canto XXI (ll. 1–12), which warns against the dangers of love, which so often leads to death. And if this "internal" warning is insufficient, we have the response of the *guida* once the four triumphs are completed. When the narrator tells her how valuable the experience has been that resulted from his choice of the wrong path, her answer is in the form of a rebuke,[105] which finds itself repeated a few lines farther on in condensed form, relying strictly on the words of Dante, when he responds to Beatrice's rebuke in *Purgatorio* XXXI.[106] At the end of the canto the guide only now reassumes her leadership and is followed by the narrator and the two youths who had helped to lead him astray. Under her Boethian guidance they learn the hard truths of Fortuna (XXXIV–XXXVII), a discourse which results (finally!) in a momentary conversion of the narrator (XXXVII.30–42). It will last exactly twenty-three lines, or until he perceives, standing to his left, a lovely garden. "Let us go in," he exclaims (XXXVII.67). We are as though back in canto II, with the left branch of the Pythagorean Y to be traversed all over again. Boccaccio's carnal lovers are a disheartening prospect to anyone who teaches or preaches for a living.

The love-garden, like the setting of the *Caccia di Diana,* is morally charged but morally neutral: the response of the onlooker creates its moral effect. Indeed, he finds there an allegorical presentation of the three loves (*onesto, per diletto, per utilità*) which we found put forward in *Filocolo,* IV, 44.[107] And things are as we might have suspected. The narrator chooses the second one (represented, in allegorical trappings, by a bull—XXXIX.72), and is of course duly and uselessly chastised by the *guida* (XXXIX.77–88). In the fortieth canto the narrator finally breaks away from his guide. Unlike the Dante of the *Inferno,* who can progressively be left more and more to his own devices as his will grows firmer,[108] the Boccaccio of the *Amorosa Visione* becomes less and less reliable, more and more volatile. The closer he comes to truth and morality, the less he wants them. Here he tells the *guida* that he would like to let his salvation wait, for he feels the flame of love in his heart (XL.7–10). Her disdain is apparent (XL.18), but within the space of ten *terzine* he is on his knees worshipping the beauty of "la bella lombarda." [109] Whatever her identity, all we need understand of her is that she represents carnal beauty in the eye of her beholder, as will the bevy of beauties he will examine in the cantos that immediately follow. In short, both he and his perceptions of them are precisely similar to the untutored Ameto and his first perceptions of the nymphs in the *Comedia ninfe.*[110] Unlike Ameto, he will not get beyond a physical appreciation of their beauty.

That the two youths have taken him where they have promised ("Vien dietro a noi, se vuoli il tuo disire"—III.54), to the pleasures of the flesh, seems assured by their Virgil-like disappearance in this "sixth triumph" (they are missing from the action after XLII.2). It is here that, his guide left behind, he will finally find his Maria d'Aquino (XLIII.37–63).[111] We have seen her before in the triumph of love (XV.45f., XXIX.49–51), first in the presence of Amore, and then as the narrator gazes back on her countenance at the conclusion of the triumph. If she was seen standing next to Cupid then, she should have been associated with carnality. But it is possible that she stands next to him as an alternative, rather than as one who is under his sway.[112] Her speech, or the speech which her gestures seem to impart (XVI.1–27), insists upon her celestial nature at its beginning and its end,[113] and she claims provenance from God, not from the god of Love.[114] In short, despite the narrator's carnal appreciation of her beauty, it asks to be taken as truly celestial—as is Lia's in the *Comedia ninfe.* The problem is that the narrator, unlike Ameto, cannot see her in her true light. When he sees her in the garden of delight she is again associated with heaven,[115] and now her cognomen and name are adduced in ways that may offer us better than biographical clues—she is descended from the family of St. Thomas, and her name is that of the Virgin (XLIII.46–59). Our attention has so long been fixed on the "biographical" problem in the text that we have tended to overlook the iconographical one. A lady descended from the line of Thomas and associated with the Virgin is not a likely object of carnal love. But that is precisely what she is to the narrator.

The conclusion of the *Amorosa Visione* is difficult to follow and to understand and perhaps makes no sense whatsoever unless we recognize the Christian identity of "Fiammetta" and the failure of "Boccaccio" to perceive her true nature. Otherwise at least two important elements of the action that transpires here make no sense: How can Maria, who has asked for and received the narrator's total allegiance (XLIV.70–85) tell him to return to his *guida* (XLVI.70–88), and how can the *guida,* having met Maria, recognize her as her "sister," and put the narrator under *her* guidance (XLVIII.4–51)? Boccaccio has not contradicted himself only if Maria is a heavenly lady, only if she is like the Lia of the *Comedia ninfe.* In Canto XLVII, when the narrator returns to the *guida* full of shame, she quite rightly upbraids him for his perversity. She knows full well what his desires toward women are. But when she discovers that his beloved is Maria, all is changed. The only mistake she makes is to believe that he is ready for celestial love. She leaves him alone with his love for moments of repose before the demanding climb upwards (XLVIII.58–60). What follows is predictable. The moment Maria falls asleep he sees his chance. He takes her in his arms, kissing her a thousand times (XLIX.26—the motif is a familiar one, but brings to mind especially *Filocolo,* IV, 118, 5, where Filocolo kisses the sleeping Biancifiore; the difference is that there the lover will wish to desist in order to marry his love before consummating his physical desire). His purpose seems unabashedly carnal, despite Branca's protestation of an allegorical significance here, which would equate physical satisfaction and moral perfection.[116] However, is it not a fact that the lover does not gain such satisfaction? At the moment he is about to have sexual intercourse with Maria his dream breaks (XLIX.45), making the conclusion of the *Amorosa Visione* the greatest anti-climax in the medieval literature of love.[117] If Branca were right, the narrator would surely (like the swains in the allegorical love stories told by the seven nymphs in the *Comedia ninfe*) have his carnal victory, which would "really" be a spiritual one. Once he is awake, however, his own view of what he has lost is entirely physical (XLIX.46–88).[118]

The last canto of the work contains one of its most surprising moments. Once he is awake, once his dream is finished, the narrator finds himself confronting his guide.[119] How or why a dream character may extrude in this way into the frame narrative is not explained. One has some sense, at least, that Boccaccio may be playing rather coquettishly with the tradition of the dream vision. What has upset some readers even more is that the *guida* now proposes to lead him back to his sensual pleasure.[120] At least that is indeed what she seems to promise to do. However, if she and Maria are related as sisters, each of whom wishes to bring the narrator to salvation, this solution is impossible. That it is not the case is at least hinted at, most conclusively in the final detail of the narrative portion of the work, which informs us that the narrator will, in this next attempt at an ascent, follow her through the "portella stretta" (L.50). In this way (and in this way alone) does it seem logical to argue for an "allegorical" reading of the ending of the work, one that makes the *Amorosa Visione* into something like a prefiguration of Petrarch's "Ascent of Mount Ventoux" (*Fam.* IV.1), a record of a non-conversion. To put this another way, the *Amorosa Visione* is a *Comedia ninfe* without an Ameto, a work in which the central character in the drama of redemption resolutely refuses to be redeemed. Such a reading would seem to veer toward the position of those readers who have seen even the *Amorosa Visione* as a celebration of carnal love. What it does in fact do is suggest that the work is a complicated blending of an allegorical presentation of orthodox Christian morality and an ironic treatment of its central character, who refuses to accept that truth in the name of his lower morality, which is entirely worldly and primarily sexual. We might reflect that in the *Amorosa Visione* we have returned to the basic situation of the *Caccia di Diana*. Like the nymphs of that work, "Giovanni di Boccaccio da Certaldo" has looked upon the true way but chooses the carnal Venus instead. If this interpretation has any merit, it would suggest that the world of Boccaccio's fictions, while maintaining the moral orthodoxies of their time, is fully aware of the tension between those orthodoxies and the way in which most people actually live their lives. This is not to suggest that it calls into question the truths of those orthodoxies, but to suggest that it knows they are growing fainter in human perception, that it is a world created by a man who has looked honestly at life, and seen what a botch we humans make of it. Boccaccio, a bastard and a maker of bastards, living a life at the margins of the marital life his celestial Venus nourishes and protects, knew fully the extent of the rulership of the carnal Venus. He does not celebrate her sway, but he does document it.

It is only the narrator of a *second Amorosa Visione* who would look upon different sights, coming back to his Maria along a different path (that of *amore onesto*). Then he, like Ameto, would no longer desire her carnally, but would understand her and his own true nature. If that is what eventually is supposed to happen, the narrator, who is eager to be off on this second voyage, still anchored firmly to concupiscence, has at this time only one compelling desire for wanting to be off—he wants to get back to that garden where the pretty lady is. The *congedo* of the work has a usual form; it is a dedication to his lady. The thoughts which it expresses seem entirely carnal. The writer does not care if his rimes or his meaning do not please others as long as they please her.[121] And what is his aim in pleasing her? It is the consistent aim of Boccaccio's narrators, as we shall observe in the following chapter: to move his lady to sexual compliance.[122] The allegory of the *Amorosa Visione,* for all its cumbersomeness, "works." [123] It is only the central figure in the piece, the lover-poet "Giovanni di Boccaccio da Certaldo" of the first acrostic sonnet, who does not understand it. But if he had difficulty, think of all the difficulty we readers of the piece have had as a result.

The three works which we have examined in this chapter have any number of topographical differences, yet their blend of allegory and irony, of pagan and Christian, associates them not only with one another,[124] but with all the literary production of Boccaccio. From the difficulties presented by the nature of the narrator of the *Amorosa Visione* we now turn to the problem of the narrator's role in all Boccaccio's fiction.

The Book as *Galeotto*

IN THE FIRST three chapters I have tried to demonstrate the ways in which nine of Boccaccio's works should be read—or at least may be read—as consistent ironic attacks upon the celebration of the earthly Venus, as consistent if concealed praise of the celestial Venus. In these discussions, which have confined themselves in the main to the narrative portions of the works, I have paid small attention to their narrators. Yet, if my interpretive position has any merit, it will clearly need to account for, insofar as this may be accomplished, the role of the narrator in Boccaccio's shaping of the significance of his fiction. Since the narrator is the source of the attitudes we find expressed in the works, we would like to know something about *his* attitudes. To whom have we been listening in these nine works? One thing seems certain: if we have the *Corbaccio* in mind, that voice seems totally different from the voice we have heard in the other eight.[1] Since that seems a supportable claim, do we conceive of "two Boccacci"? [2] Or do we wonder whether the narrative voice we hear in these works is Boccaccio's at all? That is, do we perhaps wonder whether we should not think of the narrator in each of the works as being the first "character" whom we encounter in the work, someone to whom we must attend critically rather than assuming that his attitudes are those of Boccaccio? Such a hypothesis is unlikely only if we accept the traditional view (one that continues to the present day) that Boccaccio, like the Ibrida of the *Comedia ninfe,* is himself a "lover-poet." What if he is not? What if his identification is—throughout his literary career—with the Ovid of the *Remedia amoris* rather than with the amatory Ovid? [3] For such an ironic handling of his presence in his own fiction he found an antecedent in his beloved Dante, who, as character, is intellectually and morally less than himself as retrospective poet. And he found, depending on his interpretation of these works, similar precedents in the *Roman de la Rose* and, more importantly, perhaps, in the *Ars amandi* of Andreas Capellanus.[4] Whatever his sources for such a treatment of his narrator, the works themselves seem open to such an understanding. The problem may be stated simply: If *all* the *opere minori,* whether directly or indirectly, champion good love and castigate bad, why is the narrator of the works himself an unhappy lover who follows Cupid, and who apparently learns nothing from the very tale he tells us? There are several possibilities here: (1) The works are *not* anti-venereal; (2) they are, but Boccaccio, a poet and not an intellectual, is a bit confused in his own purposes, or only holds to them intermittently; (3) the narrator is himself a foolish lover, a target of Boccaccio's ironic attack upon the religion of love. Since I have spent a good deal of time asserting that the works have a Christian moral framework, I shall not re-enter those lists here. The second objection, which would have it that poets cannot "think" as well as critics, is offered only by the sort of critic who cannot think very well himself or does not like to consider poems as more than a jumble of rhetorical parts, an assemblage of tropes having no overall design, or only vague pretensions toward "significance." Whatever its merit in dealing with certain kinds of contemporary art, it has no historical footing among the theories of poetic signification which are so frequently advanced in the middle ages, not least effectively by Boccaccio himself. And so, among these possibilities, I—if not my readers—am drawn ineluctably to the third position. To those who reject the findings of the first three chapters of this study—if they have come this far—I can only suggest that they would be illogical if they found much of value in what follows. To those who find the preceding arguments either plausible or just, this further point may seem excessive. Boccaccio, they might point out, not a little alarmed, is, after all, not Henry James. Let us turn to our texts.

And let us begin by observing that all of Boccaccio's vernacular fictions contain framing elements which present, if not the narrator's absolute identity, the nature of his condition and his hope or desire in writing the text. On one occasion the narrator's absolute identity does seem to be given. The first dedicatory sonnet of the *Amorosa Visione* tells us that the writer of the work is "Giovanni di Boccaccio da Certaldo." When I discussed this ascription in the last chapter, I raised a question. Can we accept this "signature" uncritically? That is, must we assume that the attitudes put forth by the author/narrator "Boccaccio" are those of Giovanni Boccaccio? One good reason for hesitating at this brink is that, as I have attempted to demonstrate, this "author" seems to be at some variance not only with the values expressed (and fervently urged upon him by his celestial *guida*), but with those expressed by the work as a whole. Another, which we are about to examine in some detail, is that "Giovanni di Boccaccio da Certaldo" sounds exactly like all the other narrators. And they, as I shall try to show, seem clearly to be at odds with the moral intent of the works which they narrate. But before we begin an examination of the morphology of the narrator's frame, we might confront an allied problem that perhaps holds out a clue to Boccaccio's intentions.

Who is "Fiammetta"? Is she an actual being or a fictional one? The answer seems plain enough—she is a literary lady and not a historical one.[5] It is worth spending a few minutes with her in order to grasp how fully true this is, for it is a fact with important implications for this argument. For a lady who is supposed to be Boccaccio's "Beatrice," she has a strangely variegated career in his works. To begin with, she is not named or otherwise referred to in four of them, the *Caccia,*[6] *Filostrato, Ninfale fiesolano,* or *Corbaccio.* While one may argue that her absence from the first two is the result of their having been written prior either to Boccaccio's encounter of the "real" Fiammetta or to his invention of the literary one, that does not account for her absence from the *Ninfale,* unless one follows P. G. Ricci, and claims an early date for the composition of that work.[7] As for the *Cor-*

baccio, although one is not surprised to find Fiammetta absent from its blistering attack on the religion of love, it is also true that in his later lyrics (see discussion below) Boccaccio does refer to her as being in Paradise, and so could have easily, had he chosen to do so, incorporated Fiammetta in that work as a foil to the widow. He chose not to. While her absence from these four works, one of which, the *Filostrato,* is even dedicated to a different lady ("Filomena"), is in no way intended as conclusive evidence that she did not actually exist (there are far better grounds for such an argument), it does put Boccaccio's treatment of her into some perspective: Fiammetta's reign in his heart was either intermittent or limited, depending on how we date the works that do not contain her.

A far more interesting situation meets our attention when we examine the works in which she does appear. In three of these she is the object of the author's dedicatory amorousness (*Filocolo, Teseida, Amorosa Visione*). In four of them, including two of these, she appears as a morally positive lady within the fiction (*Filocolo, Comedia ninfe, Amorosa Visione, Decameron*). In these four works, despite the narrator's (or a character's) sexual desires for her, she seems to represent or at least defend more charitable views of love. There are further complications. For instance, is the "Maria" of *Filocolo,* I, i, 15, meant to correspond to the Fiammetta of the *questioni d'amore* in the fourth book of the work? [8] This is altogether possible, but certainly far from clear, though "biographical" critics tend to assume a strict equivalence between the two, perhaps because the *Amorosa Visione* equates "Maria" and "Fiamma" in the opening acrostic sonnet. But even in that work the question exists as to the reasons for Boccaccio's not having called her "Fiammetta" when he does so in the *Filocolo, Comedia ninfe,* and *Decameron.* As for Fiammetta in the *Comedia ninfe,* she tells her own fabulous history (XXXV) in ways that have encouraged the biography-hunters and which more or less dovetail with the pieces we find in Caleon's sad tale of love for Fiammetta in the *Filocolo.* But if she is the same lady, why does she not submit to Caleon in the earlier work, while she gladly does so in the *Comedia ninfe?* The allegorical nature of the later piece helps to explain why. But an ungainly literal contradiction remains. Such details have not failed to sharpen the ingenuity of those who are determined to find an autobiographical key to the *opere minori.* And then there is the Fiammetta of the *Decameron,* who, like her of the *Amorosa Visione* (except that she has not even a minimal connection with the supposed life story of "Fiammetta") seems to live, in the midst of carnality, chastely. The entire question is not a simple one, but only the "biographical" critic is forced to solve it. And it becomes perhaps insoluble when we consider the Fiammetta of the *Elegia* which bears her name. Here we have a most carnal lady, not a champion of *amore onesto.* She is seduced most easily by one Panfilo (*not* Caleon), who seems pretty clearly *not* to be related to the most religious-minded teller of tales in the *Decameron,* who also bears that name, nor even to Palemone, who ends up taking it on in the *Teseida.* And as for that work, we have in it the dedication to Fiammetta which begins it—and nothing more of her after that. In fact, were one to remove her name from the dedication, where it stands only in the title, all reference to her, with the exception of the *senhal* "fiamma" in the concluding sonnet, would be lacking. Insofar as she "exists" in the dedication, she seems carnal indeed, roughly a copy of the Filomena of the dedication of the *Filostrato.*

I have raised the spectre of so much contradictory evidence not in the hope of clearing up the "Fiammetta mystery," but in the hope of demonstrating how garbled it is if Boccaccio is to be taken as having made her out of the whole cloth of life. One could add that it seems to have been purposely garbled by a Boccaccio who is fond of such games as these, with their insistence on the separation of life and art. Sometimes present, sometimes not; sometimes carnal, at others spiritual; sometimes called "Fiammetta," at others "Maria," once both (or nearly so)—this lady seems clearly to be a literary contrivance whose presence and significance vary with the intent of the various works that contain her.[9] Even Petrarch's Laura seems a pillar of historicity by comparison. And I have raised this issue, even in this brief and incomplete form, primarily because it bears upon the larger issue raised here. If "Fiammetta" is so largely artificial, so much the result of a self-conscious literary game, what of her celebrant? Is he "Giovanni Boccaccio" or is he himself a literary creation, a prototypical lover-poet? The second answer seems far more likely to be the better one—perhaps even the correct one. To support this contention

I shall attempt to establish a morphology of the figure of the narrator in these fictions, to which task I now turn.

Living for the most part only at the margins of the fictions which they narrate, these creations of Boccaccio have a number of attitudes and purposes in common. I shall examine some of these, under the following rubrics: (1) the narrator as subject of Amore, (2) his complaints against Fortuna, (3) the object of his dedication and his purpose, (4) his *congedo* and its version of the book's eventual aim, (5) his desire that his book reach the hands of his lady. In all cases I shall limit my investigation to the narrator's frames, those sections that begin and end all the works. Some of these are clearly set apart, others (one thinks especially of the *Caccia*), if not formally distinct, are rhetorically separate. In all cases we hear the voice of the narrator speaking directly to us. While it has been my previous practice to steer clear of the vast bulk of the *Decameron,* I shall here allow myself this much intrusion—into the outer edges of that work. To include it in this discussion has at least one interesting effect. Where the predominant view in Boccaccio studies tends to see the *Decameron* as Boccaccio's defense of the natural and thus of carnal love, that is, as it tends to see all the work of his youth (and the traditional view of Boccaccio tends to keep him a "youth" until the age of forty), a comparative analysis of the components of the narrators' frames associates that frame in the *Decameron* with those found in the *Fiammetta* and the *Corbaccio,* that is, with those narrators who warn against the dangers of carnal love.

(1) *The narrator as Love's subject.* With the exception of the narrators of the *Elegia di madonna Fiammetta,* the *Decameron,* and the *Corbaccio,* all the narrators proclaim themselves to be subject to Love, or at least to love. They may speak of their subjection to Amore, to his power through the *donna,* or to the lady herself. The word they use is almost always some form of *suggetto,* and if not that, then at least of *servo.*[10] It is small wonder that Boccaccio's readers think that his works are celebrations of Amore's reign over humankind—his narrators are celebrants (or, as in the last three works named above, former

celebrants) in that religion.[11] That the narrator is under the sway of Love might warn the reader that his testimony is suspect—especially in light of the anti-cupidinous sentiments expressed in the very works which they narrate. Either he is wrong or they are. The importance of this common element is thrown into sharp relief by the narrator's frame of the *Elegia di madonna Fiammetta.* For here our narrator is attacking the dangers of love, and thus presents herself not as subject but as victim, and offers her sad tale as an *exemplum* of what all should flee. Still, as we shall shortly discover, she is not in fact free from Love's yoke and holds a position midway between that of the previous narrators and that of the narrators of the *Decameron* and the *Corbaccio.* In the *Decameron* we are addressed by a former lover. I have elsewhere discussed the striking similarities between the *proemio* of the *Decameron* and the opening words of the *Corbaccio.* Rather than repeat my findings here, I merely refer to them.[12] In both these works the narrator has been recently freed from the bonds of love and attempts to use the experience, gained so dearly, to aid others who are not yet so fortunate. The only ambivalent or at least perplexing note struck in either the *proemio* or *conclusione* occurs in the last sentence of the former, when the narrator informs his audience of ladies that they may thank Amore for freeing him from his chains—a locution which grants the otherwise absent god of Love a power which is elsewhere denied in the *proemio.* Likewise, in the *Elegia,* at the beginning of her *congedo* (IX, 1), Fiammetta speaks of the laws of Amore. She, as I shall shortly point out, is not free of her bonds, despite her diatribes against Amore. It is only in the *Corbaccio* that Amore has been totally banished from the narrator's frame, where he is replaced (as he is in the *Decameron*) by God, as Venus would there seem to have been replaced by the Virgin.

(2) *The narrator's complaints against Fortuna.* While this element is absent from the narrator's frame in the *Caccia,* the *Amorosa Visione,* and the *Ninfale fiesolano,* it is prominent in some of the other works. Apart from the tempered remark of the narrator of the *Filocolo,*[13] Boccaccio's narrators tend to rant at Fortuna.[14] When we hear them do so, we probably should not think that they voice Boccaccio's own opinion.[15] The narrators, like the lovers whose sad tales they tell, are

merely doing what the lovelorn in Boccaccio (and in other medieval works as well) liked to do—give vent to their unhappiness in terms of Fortuna's culpability, rather than their own. It is likely that Boccaccio had Boethius's lessons in mind in all or most of these passages.[16] It is not, to return to Branca's argument, Boccaccio who did not have Boethius in mind, it is his morally deficient narrators who rather pointedly fail to draw necessary conclusions from the apparent adversity of Fortuna.[17] The narrator of the *Decameron,* like the narrator of the *Corbaccio,* speaks of consolation and fortune within several lines of text.[18] They are not prey—in this respect at least—to the same confusions as were their earlier counterparts. The complaint against Fortune, though not as widely present as the poet-lover's insistence on his subjection to Amore, is widespread enough in the narrator's frames to make Boccaccio's intentions clear: most of his narrators speak as lovers, not as wise men.

(3) *The narrator's dedication and his purpose.* Boccaccio's dedications as well as his ascriptions of the cause of a given work (or its "muse") all concern ladies. A brief topographical survey is perhaps called for here. In the *Caccia,* which has no formal dedication, the narrator hopes that every subject of Amore will pray for him, so that he will long remain in love and will do honor to his lady (XVIII.37–42). The dedications of the *Filostrato* and the *Teseida* are very much alike, with the major difference that the former is directed to Filomena, the latter to Fiammetta. In each case the narrator announces that he will give vent to his own love for his lady behind the screen of the fictive identity of a lover drawn from "una istoria antica."[19] In the *Filostrato* there is the added hyperbole which makes Filomena the author's muse (I.2.8).[20] The *Filocolo* is written at Maria's request, which he treats as a command (I, 1, 25–28), and to please her (V, 97, 7).[21] It is also addressed to young men and women, both to assuage the pains of the men and give them grounds for hope and to help the women learn the benefits of loving one man steadfastly (I, 2, 1–5).[22] The *Comedia ninfe,* despite its patent dedication to Niccolò di Bartolo del Buono (L, 3), remains within the usual amorous scope of Boccaccio's narrators;[23] the work is addressed to lovers, offering hope to those who are unhappy, delight to those who,

happy, possess "i cari beni" (I, 13–14), and if it is dedicated to Niccolò, its "movente cagione" is the narrator's *bella donna* (L, 2). The *Amorosa Visione,* dedicated to Maria/Fiamma in the first acrostic sonnet, is offered to her again at its conclusion (L, 61–75). The *Ninfale fiesolano* is not technically "dedicated" to anyone; its purpose is to honor Amore and his *donna* (3), and it is addressed to young men and women who are in love. Both the *Elegia* and the *Decameron* are, if without formal dedication, respectively addressed to "innamorate donne" (IX, 1) and "quelle che amano" (*Proemio,* 13)—and have similar purposes. Fiammetta hopes that her sad story will help those ladies who are happier in love than she (effectively *all* loving ladies, since she claims absolute unhappiness as her own) by warning them against fickle males in her *congedo;* the narrator of the *Decameron* offers delight and "utile consiglio" in his *novelle,* from which the ladies may learn what they should flee, and what they should follow (*Proemio,* 14).[24] The narrator of the *Corbaccio* takes, as usual, a harder line. His work is "dedicated" to the honor and glory of the Virgin, and has the purpose of offering *ulilità* and *consolazione* to its readers (5); in the final paragraph of the work he mentions that he has young people especially in mind. Once again we can see that these last three works are set off from the first—and probably earlier—six. A discussion of the difference between the two groups awaits us.

(4) *The narrator's congedo and his eventual hope.* After the *congedo*-less *Caccia di Diana* Boccaccio concludes four of his works with highly articulated and formal addresses to his book put into the mouth of his narrator. The *Filostrato, Filocolo, Teseida,* and *Ninfale fiesolano* all contain elaborate metaphoric equivalences of the concluded work and a weary ship that has finally entered its port.[25] And all these *congedi* express the hopes that the book (usually after a brief repose) will make its way to his lady.[26] Perhaps tiring of this formula, Boccaccio abandons the metaphor of the arriving ship in the *Comedia ninfe.* He has finished; let Venus have her incense, *la bella donna* her deserved laurel (L, 1). And let Niccolò keep the work until it may reach his *donna* (L, 7). Such an "implicit congedo" is also found in the *Amorosa Visione,*[27] where the writer's hope is that his *visione* will please his *donna* (L, 58–62). Fiammetta's *congedo* to the

Elegia reflects the earlier metaphorical equivalence book/ship in a new way: she abandons her book to the waves of the stormy sea, comparing it to a ship without rudder or sail. This self-conscious playing with the figure of speech serves Boccaccio's purpose well. Fiammetta, in the last lines of her narrative, which conclude Chapter VIII, prays that God will answer her own or her auditors' prayers by putting out her passional fire by means either of her death or of the happy return of Panfilo. As her own "voyage" has not yet been concluded, so she in her *congedo* speaks to a work that cannot yet be concluded in the properly inconclusive terms. The "port" she hopes for is a sympathetic reader. Rather than take leave of his book, the writer of the *Decameron,* in the final paragraph of the *Conclusione,* takes leave of the "nobilissime giovani" to whom the book is dedicated, thanking them for their prayers, God for his Grace; his pen and tired hand may now take their repose. The author of the *Corbaccio* does address his "piccola mia operetta" in the final paragraph of that work and sounds very much like his colleague of the *Decameron:* He too has found peace for his writing hand and instructs his book to try to be of use to those, especially the young, who, in the dangerous territory of love, are most in need of a guide. And his thoughts, too, turn upward, in this case to the Virgin.

(5) *The book in the lady's hands.* Perhaps this trope is the most striking of the five we have observed. The *Caccia, Comedia ninfe,* and *Amorosa Visione,* possibly because they all lack a *congedo,* do not give it literal expression, and in the *Ninfale fiesolano* it is present only by clear implication. However, in the *Filostrato, Filocolo, Teseida,* and *Elegia* we find it present: the book is to find its way to his lady's hands, with the purpose of (re)kindling her sexual passion for the narrator.[28] (In the *Elegia* we see once more how unsuccessful Fiammetta's attempt to escape from Amore has been—even after warning all those ladies against love she longs for her impossible Panfilo). But these four works only make forcefully explicit what is clearly implicit in the four first mentioned. In the *Caccia* the narrator lies in wait, hoping to have his *salute* from the *bella donna* (XVIII.58). If the book is not meant to be the agency of that *salute* it would seem to be only because Boccaccio had not yet developed the *topos.* In the *Comedia ninfe* the

narrator's final thought is of the book reaching his lady (L, 7), while the purpose of the *Amorosa Visione* is clearly amatory.[29] This is also the case in the *Ninfale.*[30] The whole business is turned upside down in the last paragraph of the *Corbaccio:* the narrator wants his little work "di non venire alle mani delle malvage femine," especially not those of the widow. The wittiness of the passage is lost if one has not in mind the *topos* of "the book in the lady's hands."

A book that is intended to kindle passion in a lady's heart is a familiar enough literary object. It even has a name: "Galeotto fu 'l libro e chi lo scrisse," proclaims Francesca. Boccaccio's narrators—with the emphatic exception of the *Corbaccio*'s reformed lover—are, or at least aspire to be, writers of "Galeotti." And the *Decameron,* if it contains no overt reference to "the book in the hands," is subtitled "Prencipe Galeotto." It is a detail that causes no little consternation to critics of all persuasions. Since Barbi discredited Massèra's judgment that the subtitle could not have been put forward by Boccaccio himself for "ragioni intrinseche di decoro e d'amor proprio," [31] almost all readers have been compelled to accept it as genuine. But many had previously accepted it as such, even when it seemed painful to do so. Hauvette thought that the "lecteur rigide, qu'avait choqué l'immoralité de certaines nouvelles" was none other than Boccaccio himself—albeit in his old age.[32] Neither Barbi nor anyone else would accept this particular "two Boccaccio" theory—the notion of the sickly Boccaccio catching up with at least several of his numerous MSS, by now scattered about Italy and points north, in order to scribble in the subtitle at the *incipit* and *explicit* really does seem fanciful. If then we must accept the genuineness of the subtitle (and my own brief notice of the presence of a "Galeotto motif" in the early works surely lends further, if unneeded, support for doing so), we need to attempt to determine Boccaccio's purpose in calling his book "maître enjôleur" or "maître suborneur." [33] The obvious tack to take is to explain away the negative indications and find that to call a book "Galeotto" is to say positive things about its contents. This unlikely task was first undertaken by H. Morf.[34] His arguments are a bit strange, if they are interesting.[35] Their two main elements, that Boccaccio sees Galeotto as positive in *Inferno* V and treats him positively elsewhere in his writings, are worth considering. Branca, in his note to Galeotto's appearance in the train of the Arthurian love pageant in the *Amorosa Visione,*[36] claims that he is "per il Boccaccio, come per Dante, non {la figura} d'un turpe mezzano, ma di un cavalleresco messo d'amore. Con questo sentimento, molto probabilmente, il Boccaccio volle che il nome del cavaliere . . . andasse innanzi al suo capolavoro."[37] An interesting detail in Canto XI of the *Amorosa Visione* is that it is divided into two groups, Arthurians, mainly lovers (1–54), and Carolingians, all fighters (55–88). The amatory world of romance, so appealing to the narrator of the poem, may not be as innocent as Branca finds it, especially if Boccaccio read *Inferno* V in the 1340's as he would in the 1370's. But from this evidence it is difficult to make a convincing argument on either side of the question. Giorgio Padoan's findings here are worth having at some length.[38] Padoan, who begins by correctly opposing Branca's judgment of Galeotto's valence in Dante, nonetheless follows Barbi's positive sense of the *mezzano* in Boccaccio (as does Branca). His argument runs as follows: If in Dante Galeotto is used to condemn "la letteratura erotico-cavalleresca," in Boccaccio's subtitle "svanisce ogni sottinteso polemico"; indeed, Boccaccio seems to like being a "Galeotto," "cioè mezzano, nell'accezione di cavalleresco messo d'amore." In this evaluation Boccaccio follows, according to Padoan, Francesca (but not Dante) and Pandaro (*Filostrato* III.6.1: "Io son per te divenuto mezzano"—but the very sense of Pandaro's locution makes the word a dirty one; what he has done was obviously to lower himself) and thus associates himself with a literature that is worldly, indifferent to religion—like that, Padoan continues, of the "romanzi francesi e dei *fabliaux,*" as opposed to the moral rigor of the *Commedia.* Nor is there, Padoan claims, any "sottinteso polemico" in the scene in which Florio and Biancifiore are served by the *Ars amatoria,* their "Galeotto" (*Filocolo,* I, 45, 6). He concludes: "Il Boccaccio non coglie insomma l'intimo ed appassionato messaggio della *Commedia,* che egli interpreta assai superficialmente, colpito più dalla novità delle storie, dallo stile vigoroso, dalla potenza drammatica che dal contenuto più profondo." This last is a curious comment from the man who has so proficiently edited Boccaccio's *Esposizioni.* While it is true that the "official" view holds that Boccaccio, while using Dante's text in such a way as to indicate that he knew a great deal of it by heart even in his youth, did not really "understand" Dante, a critic of Padoan's stature might have been expected to do better by this problem. But in his arguments, and in those of many others, what continually disturbs is a sensation of overstatement being put to the service of a wrong argument. In this particular case we are observing highly intelligent scholars trying to decide whether Boccaccio thought being a pander was a good or a bad thing. It is really not a difficult question to answer. It is made into one in order to protect a bad hypothesis—that Boccaccio thinks carnal love is a perfectly honorable pursuit for a civilized person. Reality, in the form of Boccaccio's gloss to Francesca's "Galeotto fu 'l libro," does force Padoan to modify his position slightly. In his gloss to the gloss he claims that the commentator, "piegato dagli anni e dalla crisi religiosa," only *now* takes a harder line toward Galeotto.[39] Any sort of a reading of Boccaccio's commentary to *Inferno* V gives one the sure sense that in it Boccaccio understood clearly and without hesitation Dante's moral purpose there. He characterizes "i romanzi franceschi" (see *Corbaccio,* 441: the widow's paternosters are "i romanzi franceschi e le canzoni latine [Italian versions thereof], ne' quali ella legge di Lancelotto e di Ginevra e di Tristano e d'Isotta") as "cose, per quel ch'io creda, più composte a beneplacito che secondo la verità." [40] If they are untrue, they are also immoral—the allegorical exposition of Dante's fifth canto is plain enough on that score—in that they are associated with adultery ("adulterium: alterius ventrem terere [sic]," philosophizes Boccaccio, *Esposizioni, Inf.* V., *esp. all.,* 68). In short, it seems unlikely that Boccaccio's later writings, either the *Corbaccio* or the *Esposizioni,* give aid and comfort to a "pro-Galeotto" reading. Quite the contrary. And here we may allow ourselves to wonder why so few *studiosi* (can we really think of any?) have at least experimented with the late works to see if they might help explain the earlier ones. Even a poet like William Butler Yeats, who is cut up by his critics into so many neat segments, tends to be examined for the continuing themes and attitudes that run through the length of his work. Boccaccio, on the other hand, is seen as "young" and pagan, "old" and Christian. While they are surely elements that are found only in one or the other, there are a great many more that move from one end of his work to the other. But as long as that convenient contrivance, his "conversion" to Christianity sometime after he wrote the *Decameron,* is within reach, we may be fairly sure someone will put it between an early text and a late one so that the similarities between them will not be observed. What does a study of the early works that touch on our current topic of investigation suggest to as Boccaccio's attitudes there? Let us return for a moment to Padoan's "mezzano-cavalleresco messo d'amore." I have suggested that Pandaro's very phrase makes it plain that being a pimp is a dirty business. Now let us look at the lines that follow his declaration (*Filostrato* III.6.1–4): "Io son per te divenuto mezzano,/per te gittato ho 'n terra il mio onore,/per te ho io corrotto il petto sano/di mia sorella. . . ." Now whatever we may personally choose to think about Pandaro's motives, nobility, friendship for Troiolo, etc., etc., one thing is inescapable: He himself states that his role is a dishonorable one. And that is all that we are and should be interested in for purposes of this discussion. What we want to know is what Boccaccio thought of panders, in order to ascertain whether the subtitle of the *Decameron* has a positive or a negative moral valence. If the word *mezzano* has a negative valence in the *Filostrato,* the concept of the Galeotto has a similar valence, as I have previously argued, in the *Filocolo.* Florio's and Biancifiore's reading of the *Ars amatoria* and their subsequent worship of Venus and her son are nearly fatal to the two lovers, who are united happily only after they correct their carnal affections under the sign of the better Venus. As for the eleventh canto of the *Amorosa Visione,* its evidence may be read in either direction. But the presence of Lancelot, Guinevere, Tristan, and Isolde with Galeotto is at least likely to attach that passage also to Boccaccio's "sottinteso polemico" against the religion of love. Padoan, here and elsewhere, and like many of Boccaccio's readers, tends to take the narrator straight. What he praises, Boccaccio praises. That may not be the best way to read these texts.

Boccaccio's subtitle for the *Decameron* is clearly of some importance.[41] To argue that "Prencipe Galeotto" is removed from his usual signification is to fly against the wind of logic.[42] If Galeotto was a pander, a book that is a Galeotto is a book that leads to lust. Hauvette's formula is absolutely just on this occasion. The question that still afflicts us is why Boccaccio should have called the book that. The "naturalists" have less difficulty here than the rest of us. If the book celebrates "natural" love, what better title? If Boccaccio is a suborner of the Church, what better title? But if Boccaccio is a Christian moralist, how did he dare put that scabrous name to the *incipit* and *explicit* of the great work? Here Giuseppe Mazzotta's view of the *Decameron* is of the greatest interest. If the work demonstrates the dangers of literature, the subtitle is precisely right.[43] The book *is* a Galeotto in that it is certain to inspire lustful thoughts in its readers—as it so frequently does in the tellers themselves.[44] One can hardly consider the *fortuna* of the *Decameron* without considering the millions of its readers who have been moved by it to carnality, if not *con alteris,* then at least *con se ipsis.*[45] Boccaccio is fully aware—and not only in the celebrated epistle to Mainardo Cavalcanti [46]—of the sexual nature of so much of his material. This does not necessarily mean, as Mazzotta would have us believe, that the *Decameron* is, in Boccaccio's own mind, a symptom of the moral plague that is sweeping through Europe, but more likely that the author is warning us, as he has done throughout his career, of the terrible power of sexual love. And thus here too an ironic reading seems the most appropriate one. In a single gesture Boccaccio accommodates those *morditori* who have complained of the sexual nature of so much of his material in the *Decameron* and continues his own favorite pose, that of the lascivious narrator. If these motives seem at all likely, they do not solve the problem, but do at least help keep us from the more patent absurdities of "positive" readings of the subtitle itself. The subtitle of the *Decameron* peers out at us like the skull and crossbones on the bottle of dangerous medicament that must be taken in full consciousness and so lead to life and not death: Reader, beware; here is a book that has the power to move you to lust.

That does not mean that such is its purpose. The narrator/author of the *Decameron* frame spends almost all his time with us, in the *Proemio* and the *Conclusione,* striking the attitudes of a Christian moralist. The one time that he seems most clearly to correspond to the sense which the "naturalist" takes of his purpose occurs in his interruption at the beginning of the Fourth Day. The "part of a *novella*" that is the tale of the Christian moralist Filippo Balducci and his irretrievably natural son underscores the problematical quality of the treatment of love which we find in the *Decameron*. And at first glance the broken tale (if it really is "incomplete") seems to affirm the "naturalist" hypothesis: Raise your son in Christian love and truth, denying him the knowledge of the temptations of the flesh, and his natural instincts will assert themselves the first time he sets his eyes upon a woman. In the *novellina* God loses to Nature—or so it may seem. Filippo Balducci, like Cervantes' "Man in the Green Coat" is dedicated to a closely ordered morality which is incapable of dealing with complications of the simplest kind. It is *he* who is the "loser" in the tale. For Boccaccio he would seem to represent the monastic escapee from the welter of life. He is, within the logical program of the Introduction to the Fourth Day, associated precisely with Boccaccio's "monkish" detractors, while Boccaccio associates himself with the woman-loving son, as he makes it clear that the love of women is the given of his being,[47] the very ground of complication on which the Christian life—at least for himself and those of us who are like him—must be lived. This is precisely what he tells us in his peroration to the ladies (IV, *Introduzione,* 41–42): He, and all who love women, do so naturally; opposing nature's laws requires too great strength, and, if attempted, is often attempted in vain, or with the greatest harm; therefore, let those who feel no sympathy for his passional nature leave him to his own devices. It is the request of a man of the world and is aimed at monkish souls, who are seen both as envious and as hypocritical. The crux of his argument is not that we should seek Love, or even love, but that our having to live with it should draw compassion for those who suffer its afflictions (we should remember that such compassion is the motive force of the *Decameron* itself—*Proemio,* 2). The sensual world we find in the *Decameron* does not represent a celebration of lust. It is a threshing floor. The narrator of the work, unlike those earlier narrators who praise Amore, and unlike the Christian misogynist of the *Corbaccio,* who despises him, lives in the moral center of the tempest of this world, drawn and repulsed by love, struggling toward the moral life and perhaps a distant heaven. It is no accident that he presides over Boccaccio's most complex and human work.

In offering this brief morphology of the narrators of these ten fictions, I have hoped to show the common themes and attitudes that collect around them.[48] But what is perhaps most important to see is the differences among them. Those of the first seven works, the *Caccia, Filostrato, Filocolo, Teseida, Comedia ninfe, Amorosa Visione, Ninfale fiesolano,* are all lovers.[49] Fiammetta, the teller of the *Elegia,* is a disenchanted lover who has not yet escaped from the toils of Amore; the *Decameron*'s narrator/author seems almost entirely free of the toils of love ("ora che libero dir mi posso"—*Proemio,* 7), while the misogynist of the *Corbaccio* is defiantly so. In these last three works the narrator's express intent is to turn us away from love,[50] while in the first seven it is to celebrate the Amore to whom he himself is subject. And this much of a morphology would seem to suggest that the traditional view—the "young" Boccaccio was himself a lover, while the more mature author turned from love to Christian morality—is the correct one. But if we are to accept this implication, we must accept a very different view of the *Decameron,* one that is greatly different from that usually proposed.[51] Those who argue for a "naturalist" Boccaccio in the *Decameron* [52] are then forced to argue—as some do—that we cannot take the "author's" remarks seriously. Similarly, we must try to decide whether or not our view of an ironic Boccaccio with respect to his narrators in the first seven works is authorized by their contexts or not. There are two logically acceptable views of the phenomenon. If we are to take the evidence offered by the attitudes of the narrators at all seriously, either Boccaccio experienced a "conversion" roughly about the time he met Petrarch (in 1350—or even earlier if we wish to consider the *Elegia* as bearing the "first signs" of a "conversion")—and hence a good deal earlier than is generally supposed—or else he was only accomplishing ironically in the earlier narrative frames what he chose to accomplish more openly in the later ones. The question is not a simple one to resolve and has drawn a cry of anguish for our critical uncertainties from a figure as imposing as Guiseppe Billanovich.[53] It is an issue to which I shall devote some attention in my Conclusion. The point that can be made here is that either of these two alternatives points to a single interpretive *datum:* Boccaccio's work—all of Boccaccio's work—involves the central opposition of the Lord of Love and Christian morality. If in the earlier works he was on the side of Love (and this is surely not my own interpretation) he was so with full knowledge of the other God he was opposing. If he was not one of Love's celebrants, his *alter ego,* the narrator of each of those works may not be taken as other than a negative version of himself, a "lover-poet" who must be seen ironically. My own view of the matter is that there is no real difference in the moral attitudes of the Boccaccio of the *Caccia* and the *Corbaccio,* that all that changes, and I address myself to the question of his treatment of his narrators in particular, is the ironic tactic which controls the work. Why Boccaccio should have given over his "unknowing narrator" in favor of the moralizer of the *Decameron* and the *Corbaccio* is not something that is easily known. We may speculate that in his own day his ironic intent baffled too many readers, that as a result, in the *Fiammetta,* Boccaccio began to experiment with an anti-venereal narrator. But this is merest speculation. And we must not allow ourselves to forget that ironists have a way of keeping critics off their scent. One is reminded of Boccaccio's own gloss to the *Teseida* (III.35.7).[54] There Boccaccio the commentator seems as subject to Love as Boccaccio the narrator or Palemone and Arcita. Limentani's characterization of this moment—which he sees as highly coquettish—is probably basically just.[55] And the Boccaccio we see, in such a moment, is an *eiron* even at the margins of his fictions, a comedic commentator who admits that he too is *preso d'Amore.*

That phrase, or versions of it, has fairly extensive currency in his *Rime,*[56] a series of lyrics which may reasonably be joined to this discussion of the narrator, and which, for various reasons, I have only infrequently approached until now. For there too we have a large and apparently consecutive series of works that present a speaker who is subject to Amore, followed by a smaller number of works, also apparently consecutive, which celebrate a higher love. In this sense at least the *Rime* offer us an epitome of the career of Boccaccio's narrators in the ten fictions we have here considered. But if they do so, we must proceed with extreme caution here, for the *Rime* are fraught with every kind of critical difficulty. As Branca has demonstrated, at either end of Boccaccio's long career as lyric poet[57] there lies a severely self-critical act: the putative burning of some of the earliest works, the failure to collect and form the roughly one hundred and fifty poems into a *canzoniere.*[58] And the reason which Branca offers for such behavior is most likely the right one: Boccaccio was aware of his inferiority in the lyric to Petrarch.[59] But if Boccaccio never published a *canzoniere,* it is at least likely that he contemplated doing so, and that such an intention may be reflected in such collections as the one hundred and one sonnets found in Codex F^1.[60] While it seems impossible, or most unlikely, that we shall ever have more than fragmentary evidence as to what Boccaccio's *canzoniere* would have ultimately comprised, it is as least plausible to speculate that it would have resembled Petrarch's. And while Massèra's edition of the *Rime* has been justly criticized for ordering the components according to his sense of the "historical" progress of Boccaccio's love affair with Fiammetta,[61] it is also likely that Boccaccio's eventual *canzoniere* would have moved from *innamoramento* to the "death" of Fiammetta and beyond. Dante's *Vita Nuova* and Petrarch's *Canzoniere* made such a format nearly inevitable for Boccaccio. And so if Massèra's critical methods seem woefully "positivistic," [62] his end result may actually be reasonably close to what Boccaccio might himself have chosen to do by way of ordering his poems into a whole.

Yet the problems, even in the realm of speculation, are enormous here. Even some of the one hundred and twenty-six lyrics which Branca attributes surely to Boccaccio are only problematically his.[63] In short, and avoiding any discussion of the "rime dubbie" (matters are in enough disarray without adding another difficulty to this brief discussion), any argument one may choose to make about the *Rime* may be only hypothetical and venturesome.[64] We may try to establish a "*canzoniere*" for Boccaccio, but only while knowing that it is a task that he himself consciously decided not to undertake. But among the components that we have we may try to construct a possible *canzoniere* along the following lines:

I. "In Vita"

The poet beholds the lady and is caught	(II) [65]
The first Baian group: his enamorment	(III–VII)
The poet's song inadequate to her beauty	(VIII)
The power of her beauty: his subjection	(IX–XIV)
The celestial nature of his lady	(XV–XVII)
Poems in praise of his subjection	(XVIII–XXIII)
Mixed with joy, the pain of loving	(XXIV–XXVI)

The sadness of love	(XXVII–XLIII)
He desires to be free of her power	(XLIV)
Fiammetta's answer [66]	(XLV)
Maledictions of love—but he is still caught [67]	(XLVI–LII)
He longs for *pietà*	(LIV) [68]
She greets him; he is glad to be in love	(LV)
He is at Love's mercy [69]	(LVI–LVII)
She seems to give him hope	(LVIII)
His pain was worth it: he has had her	(LIX)
But she has gone to Baia: jealousy	(LX–LXII)
The joys of love at Misenus [70]	(LXIII–LXIV)
More Baia poems: jealousy	(LXV–LXVIII; LXXXII) [71]
Complaint against Love	(LXXIII–LXXIV)
She has betrayed him	(LXXV–LXXVII) [72]
Desire to repent his carnal love	(LXXXIII–LXXXIX) [73]
Poetry calls him; he does not come	(XC)
Poetry calls him; he follows	(XCI) [74]

II. "In Morte"

The heavenly Fiammetta [75]: he longs to join her	(XCII–CVI)
The vanity of poetry	(CVII–CIX)
Praise of God	(CX–CXVI)
Praise of the Virgin	(CXVII–CXIX) [76]
On the death of Petrarch	(CXXVI)

While Massèra's "positivistic" organization of the *Rime* may seem to be based on a false principle of scholarship, what is apparent in the individual poems and groups of poems, whenever various of them were composed, is a series of subjects which might easily have been used to construct the sort of "autobiography" of a lover-poet that Boccaccio would have found indispensable in the formation of a *canzoniere* along the lines set down by Dante and Petrarch.[77] In fact, one might argue that the various subjects for lyrics we find in the *Rime* would almost guarantee that Boccaccio, over a long span of his life, at the very least toyed with the notion of putting together a *canzoniere.* Had he done so, it too would have undoubtedly furnished the "biographical" critics apparent ammunition. And it too would have served to show that Boccaccio's life in love moved from pagan celebrations of Amore to Christian reconciliation—or so it would have seemed to most of Boccaccio's readers. And it too would have seemed to me rather to demonstrate that Boccaccio's concern was to attack carnal love in the name of a higher Christian love—that the "true" Fiammetta was his necessary goal from the beginning, his carnal love a delusion. The question, both in the *Rime* (and here I speak of individual poems that seem to celebrate Amore) and in the earlier *opere minori,* involves Boccaccio's attitude toward his poet-lover.[78] It is at least plausible that the early lyrics too are the result of an ironic view of carnal love. Boccaccio's *canzoniere* would probably have been the record of a conversion that is absent from the experience of all the early narrators (only the narrator of the *Corbaccio* has experienced a complete and specific conversion, although the narrator of the *Decameron* frame is close behind him, as is, in severely flawed ways, the lady "author" of the *Elegia*). But, as I have argued earlier, any such construction of the *Rime* is dubious at best, no matter how attractive it may seem.

If Boccaccio's books are "Galeotti," their author is "Ovid." The presence of Ovid in Boccaccio outdistances all classical rivals and falls short only of that of Dante. Boccaccio's allegiance to the texts of his classical *auctor primus* is readily apparent. Ovid is everywhere and is clearly celebrated as being *primus inter pares* as early as the *Filocolo.*[79] But it is not Ovid's presence in the texts of the *opere minori* that I wish to discuss, but his existence as Boccaccio's alter ego. If for Boccaccio Dante was the Italian Virgil, he was to be the new Ovid. A more than plausible place to begin is offered by Boccaccio's biography of Ovid in the *Esposizioni.*[80] What should probably long ago have struck readers of this document, a blend of extrapolations from the autobiographical passages in Ovid's own works and existing medieval constructions (themselves largely dependent on the former), is that in Boccaccio's description Ovid's early life is so closely parallel to his own that he could have regarded it as a model. I am not suggesting that Boccaccio modified the life of Ovid, as it came down to him, in order to make it correspond to his own. All we can surely say is that the parallels between the two lives are striking. And if I were to suggest anything on the basis of that evidence more than that Boccaccio must have looked on Ovid's biography as well as his *œuvre* as being extremely close to his own, it would be that Boccaccio had constructed details of his own "vita" in accord with what he found in Ovid's. For there is another striking similarity between the two poets. Both of their *"vitae"* are primarily known to us through their fictions. That is, Boccaccio may well have been imitating Ovid when he chose to include his own "autobiography" as a lover as a subject in his fictions.

The first half of Boccaccio's three-page *vita Ovidii* [81] reveals the following resemblances:

1) Ovid's birthplace is cited as described in *De tristibus:*"Sulmo michi patria est." See Boccaccio's epitaph, which he composed for himself and which contains the phrase "Patria Certaldum . . . fuit."

2) In his youth Ovid, like Boccaccio, showed an *ingegno* which was "marvellously inclined to learning."

3) His relationship with his father is remarkably like Boccaccio's, such as he has presented the matter. His father forces him to study law (he has an older brother who also does so), but Ovid prefers poetry. His father upbraids him: "Sepe pater dixit: studium quid inutile temptas?" (*De tristibus* IV. 10.26). Ovid's response is reminiscent of Boccaccio: "Per la qual cosa, eziandio contro al piacer del padre, si diede tutto alla poesia" (and see, again, his epitaph: "studium fuit alma poesis").

4) As Boccaccio left the city of his youth, Florence, and settled in a royal center, Naples, so had Ovid moved from Sulmona to Rome. Each enjoys the patronage of "Augustus"—for Boccaccio he is King Robert. Ovid, says Boccaccio, is made a member of the "ordine equestre"—what today, in Boccaccio's words, we call "cavalleria." Here, if not exact, the parallel exists in Boccaccio as *corteggiano.*

5) Ovid was a lover—of boys, to be sure—but a lover. And he is a "lover-poet": his early works speak only of "suoi inamoramenti e di sue lascivie usate con una giovane amata da lui, la quale egli nomina Corinna." The parallel is fairly striking.

6) In his description of *De fastis* Boccaccio's phrase "come appo noi fanno i nostri calendari" perhaps underlines the closeness of the rest of the *vita* to Boccaccio's own. For here, in describing a work unlike any that Boccaccio had composed, he offers that much by way of a contemporary equivalent. For the rest, he himself serves as a contemporary equivalent.

7) Ovid also wrote *De arte amandi,* "dove egli insegna e a' giovani ed alle fanciulle amare; e oltre a questo, ne fece un altro, il quale intitolò *De' remedi,* dove egli s'ingegna d'insegnare disamorare."

This is the basic matter of Boccaccio's *vita* of the young Ovid, of *Ovidio minore,* as it were. The figure whom we find here is Boccaccian enough to make us think that Boccaccio himself would have been struck and pleased by the resemblances. And it is pleasing for me to conclude by noting that the *Remedia amoris* is here seen joined with the *Ars,* and if as a retraction, as a retraction written as a companion piece and, most importantly, in Ovid's youth.

What is most striking about both poets is that each is, by his own confession, a carnal lover. At any rate that is what Boccaccio's text would lead us to believe about the two authors. And each author has a complicated relationship to the guilty activity he owns as his own. He both celebrates his passions and condemns them. While in Ovid the distinction is neat (*Ars amatoria* vs. *Remedia amoris*), in Boccaccio it only seems to be so (early works vs. late works). That is, as I have argued on other grounds, the tradition of the *Remedia* operates in Boccaccio simultaneously with that of the *Ars* as a continual correction to the bad doctrines of love. In short, Boccaccio, from the very first of his poems, regards himself as "the new Ovid" in a positive sense only. When he presents love in the tradition of the *Ars,* he does so in order to condemn it.

His view of Ovid's relationship to his own amatory verse is a more complex issue. While he knows that one of the two reasons for which Augustus sent Ovid into exile was the *Ars* (*Esposizioni, Inf.* IV, *esp. litt.,* 124): "La seconda cagione dice che fu l'avere composto il libro *De arte amandi,* il quale pareva molto dover adoperare contro a' buoni costumi de' giovani e delle donne di Roma," and while he elsewhere seems to hold Ovid culpable for being exactly what he twice proclaims himself to be in the *Ars,* a poet of lascivious love,[82] it is possible that he at least at times looked upon the *Ars amatoria* as mocking carnal love. This is a question which I prefer to raise rather than attempt to answer. Without entering into a discussion of Ovid's actual intent, I can suggest that, both from the text of the *Ars,* which is urbane and cynical, and, more importantly, from some medieval appreciations of the text, that the effect of Ovid's book—whatever the sins of the writer or his intent—was or could easily be comprehended as being anti-venereal.[83] It all depends upon the way in which one reads the text. Still, the best evidence would seem to indicate that Boccaccio, whatever his own methods of being the "new Ovid," looked upon the amatory verse of the original Ovid as indeed lascivious and culpable.[84] This would indicate that Boccaccio did not read the *Ars* and the *Amores,* as he might have, as ramifications of the *Remedia.* But if that is true, it in no way requires that when we find the *Ars* or the *Amores* in Boccaccio's texts we are to take him as embracing their moral precepts. The "conversion" of the young Florio and Biancifiore to Amore by agency of their reading of the *Ars* (*Filocolo,* I, 45, 6) is surely not an indication of Boccaccio's support, as I have previously argued. Throughout his literary career Boccaccio seems to identify himself with Ovid. The question is, with what Ovid and to what aim? That is, when a lascivious narrator identifies himself with Ovid, are we to take him as voicing Boccaccio's sentiments? Or should we see Boccaccio as using his narrator and Ovid to mock carnal love? The entire problem, to which I have already given my sense of a solution, assumes sharp focus in the Introduction to the Fourth Day of the *Decameron* (3), when the author refers to the text of the first three "Days" (which has apparently caused so much adverse criticism for its sensuality) as being "senza titolo." Though the fact has apparently escaped most readers of the *Decameron,* that is the "title" of Ovid's *Amores*—"the book without a name." [85] One wonders what the first three "Days" of the *Decameron* looked like as they circulated ca. 1350. Were they really without an *incipit?* If they carried one, as is at least possible, Boccaccio's readers could not have missed his point. To say that a book is "senza titolo"—whether it has one or not—is to suggest what the eventual subtitle will announce:

the book is a Galeotto, and should be read with that caution in mind, as is the case with the *Amores,* that other "libro senza titolo."

Boccaccio's sense of Ovid involves both identification and distance. He is the "new Ovid" in that he thinks of himself as the prime vernacular writer in the matter of love, but he wants simultaneously to keep himself separate from Ovidian sentiments that are only carnal. That judgment, it should be acknowledged, is offered tentatively. This question, like so much with which we have had to deal in Boccaccio, is made extremely difficult by the existence of a varied medieval view of Ovid and is further complicated—again like so much else with which we have attempted to deal—by Boccaccio's own use of irony. Indeed, the entire question of Boccaccio's sense of Ovid centers in this last, and is a question which I have rather tried to pose than answer in these few pages, while also indicating what I would hope a likely answer would be. It is a question which should be given concerted attention, but which to date has remained mainly peripheral to Boccaccio criticism.

In this chapter I have argued, not for the first time in this study, but with reference to different forms of evidence, for an ironic Boccaccio. I am aware, now as before, that such a view is likely to find unsympathetic response among those who see Boccaccio's vernacular fictions as being offered in praise of carnal love. I must also admit that such an interpretation rests on textual evidence that is sometimes less than immediately clear. All I hope to accomplish is to reopen a question that has long been closed and to suggest that these works need to be examined against a medieval matrix of value. That is, if they are to be perceived as being pagan in spirit, they must be seen as being specifically and consciously anti-Christian. Or they may be perceived at least roughly as I perceive them. That they constitute some sort of loosely conscious blending of the two positions—and this has been the best sense in which they have previously been taken—seems, in the light of the evidence of the texts themselves, totally untenable.

Conclusion

How seriously are we to take the Christianity of Boccaccio's *opere minori in volgare?* [1] Perhaps we can agree (perhaps some of us can agree) that all these works, so long understood as celebrating the power of Venus, the joys of carnal love, are in fact anchored in a far more traditional and medieval view of lust as a sin which rational beings should shun and which leads to the death of the body and of the soul. Yet Boccaccio's texts, as we have seen so frequently, fairly swarm with carnal affections and, perhaps even more alarmingly, present positive moralizations in a tone that is often far from serious. This discussion will attempt to respond to this question with particular reference to what has often been called Boccaccio's "crisis." To approach the problem we should begin with some general sense of the relevance of this study to other problems in "erotic" medieval literature, for the ramifications of our subject spread wide. And in this freer discussion, I hope that the reader will not begrudge me the absence of a great deal of documentation.

There is perhaps no more central and far-reaching problem confronting students of medieval literary texts, from about 1050 on, than the role of carnal love in these texts. To illustrate the difficulty of the problem as simply as possible, while avoiding the subsidiary branch that resulted from Gaston Paris' invention/discovery of "amour courtois" in the nineteenth century, we may simply offer a partial list of major figures who would necessarily be involved in any "solution" of the problem: Chrétien de Troyes, Andreas Capellanus, Bernardus Silvestris, Guillaume de Conches, Alain de Lille, Guillaume de Lorris, Jean de Meun, Cino da Pistoia, Guido Guinizelli, Guido Cavalcanti, Dante Alighieri, Juan Ruiz, Francesco Petrarca, Giovanni Boccaccio, Geoffrey Chaucer. It is probably true that no single theory or perception can or could "resolve" the question for all of these. I might suggest in passing that to find a citation of Ovid's *Ars amatoria* in the work of any one of them is probably enough of an occasion on which to base an argument among any number of scholars as to that particular writer's response to the *Ars.* Now let us imagine that we deal with the same citation in two texts. Now with various citations in several. It does not take long to find oneself facing a large measure of chaos. The problem is not a simple one, and though one may hope that it will come to be dealt with better in the future, its depth and difficulty will long be with us. And so will our modern-day Averroists, Neoplatonists, Aristotelians, "Naturalists," Augustinians, and so on. Criticism of the literature of the middle ages has almost as many "rules" as existed then.

All constructed monoliths tend to violate the truths of particulars. For example, the degree of Christian morality expressed by the various writers listed above varies widely. Any attempt to see all of them as being equally concerned with even as major a text as *De doctrina christiana* is doomed to being wrong. At the same time, those who would find a common insistence on the positive "naturalness" of love in all these works would be even more certainly incorrect. As a result, there is probably more to be preferred in an Augustinian monolith than in a "naturalist" one. For the "Augustinians" have one rather impressive fact on their side—Christian culture (here I leave questions of devotion, even of belief, to one side) was the predominant and common literary heritage of all these writers. While we cannot know much about the personal piety of each or perhaps of any of them, and while we must surely be aware that even medieval Christianity, at times and in various "schools," accepted unto itself (or at least absorbed with difficulty) such antithetical philosophies as Neoplatonism, Averroist "materialism," and even something that looks very much like atheism (in Guido Cavalcanti—or in his reputation—and in Frederick II), we have to acknowledge that the Bible, the Fathers, and the culture of a troubled but spiritually unchallenged Church formed the basic intellectual tradition of all the writers we have named. The culture of medieval Europe was Christian. This is to say nothing new, if something necessary.

However, merely to know that medieval writers knew a lot of things as though by instinct which we either do not know or know a little (after years of study) is to have but a slim advantage. There have always been writers who preferred to keep their intentions or meanings less than obvious, whether out of the gnomic pose, out of a less directed and more simple enjoyment of obscurity, or even from incompetence. Even philosophers and theologians—who apparently purpose to make themselves clear—are hard enough to understand, if they happen to be Aristotle, for instance, or St. Paul. T. S. Eliot's Sweeney, noting that he had to use words when he talked to us, made the order of the difficulty plain. Even clear minds are encumbered by the encrustations of culture that make vocabulary the delight of the poet and the bane of his critic. It is not surprising that so many intelligent people are impatient with those of us who are purveyors of "interpretation," inheritors of that long medieval (not to mention classical) tradition of thwarting an author's intention by imposing a meaning on his work which happens to suit our purpose.

And certainly this interpretation of Boccaccio is open to just such a charge. It is able to answer back. And its answer is that the "revised standard version" of Boccaccio, the one that has replaced the "standard biographical" reading of the *opere minori in volgare* (we may settle on a term that has appeared in these pages from time to time and call it "naturalism"), is itself an imposition that suits one kind of modern purpose. This is not to argue that Boccaccio thought he was a bishop, or even that he thought of his works as even minimally increasing the number of pious thoughts between Naples and Florence, but to claim that the *mythos* that informed them was the Christian one.

If the *opere minori in volgare* may be usefully, even "correctly," understood to reflect Christian moral values, their intended effect may still be understood variously. Four possibilities may be advanced:

(1) Boccaccio's Christianity is mainly *pro forma,* while in fact the author expected his audience to share with him a boisterous joy in the carnal.

(2) Boccaccio wrote for a carnal-minded courtly audience (and then a carnal-minded bourgeois audience), yet wanted to protect himself from the Church (or an occasional pious nobleman), and thus made sure to "put in" enough in the way of Christian trappings in order to keep everyone happy.[2]

(3) Boccaccio, though indeed a Christian in his intellectual convictions, was primarily interested in pleasing an audience that sought in literature qualities that have little to do with morality, and thus, while leaving traces of his Christianity everywhere in his work, does not belabor his moral intention, but even leaves it to one side.

(4) Boccaccio wrote for that part of his audience that was as alive as was he to the ludicrous claims of the religion of love, and his intent was to mock that "religion" by showing its falseness in its own terms and in its opposition to Christian morality.

These four possibilities exist only within a context that recognizes a major Christian referentiality in the *opere minori in volgare,* and while they may not exhaust all eventual possibilities, they do reflect, on an ascending scale of moral purpose, the more likely ones. In this scale, Boccaccio moves from pretended Christian (who is actually a pagan) to non-committed writer to hesitant and hidden Christian to confirmed Christian (it is worth reminding the reader that I refer not to his life but to his works). It is clear from what has gone before that the fourth option is my own, and it would hold that Boccaccio's Christianity is serious enough. Yet there remains the possibility that Boccaccio the Christian ironist ended by ironizing even his own position. Irony has a propensity to avoid rest. Such a view would find that in works like the *Ninfale fiesolano, Comedia ninfe,* and *Corbaccio,* the Christian morality which we find is either so forced as to seem itself ironic or so blatantly hectoring as to be itself an object of scorn. And it is that sort of argument that this study must be willing to entertain, no matter how little it finds the basic notion to correspond to what it finds in the texts. What it is unwilling to entertain is a notion which puts forward "Jolly John of Certaldo"—the mindless pagan comedian—or his "serious" counterpart, Boccaccio the "naturalist hero," who does battle to liberate mankind from medieval oppression and who singlehandedly brings the "renaissance" to Italy and the world. When Boccaccio's name is mentioned it is still, despite the cogency and distinction of such studies as Branca's *Boccaccio medievale,* used largely in either or in both of these senses. The intent of Boccaccio's work may be seen to lie between the following poles: the championing of sexual freedom and sexual abstinence; celebration of the pagan and rejection of the pagan; total identification with poetry and total rejection of poetry. For him there is a carnal love that is blessed—in matrimony; there is a use of pagan matter in conjunction with Christianity; there is a poetry that conforms to a Christian vision of humanity.

The debate about Boccaccio's Christianity has a long—if not entirely interesting—history.[3] The more commonly accepted view has it that Boccaccio was a "pagan," was "converted" by Gioacchino Ciani, the *messo* of the recently deceased Pietro Petroni in 1362, and changed his personal, or at least his literary, life as a result.[4] Petrarch's response (*Seniles,* I, 5) to Boccaccio's (lost) epistolary description of the penitential disturbance wrought in him by the warning of the dead Carthusian is the only documentary evidence that we possess concerning what transpired in Boccaccio's soul. Branca's cautious response to this fragmentary evidence is to suggest that, however genuinely terrified Boccaccio might have been at the time, he quickly enough took up his literary work again, and he sees the warnings of the Beato Petroni in the proper perspective of fourteenth-century attacks upon poetry (and poets) made by various religious.[5]

Petrarch's letter, however, has had the effect of creating a pseudo-fact: a "conversion" which has been made to serve as the watershed of Boccaccio's life. Before it lie his "carnal" fictions,[6] after it, his Christian Latin works. The *schema* is a neat one and almost certainly wrong. The most alert and careful attempt to construct, if not a "conversion," a *crisi* in Boccaccio's later years is that of Giorgio Padoan.[7] As I have suggested earlier, the most appealing part of

Padoan's argument joins Millard Meiss in seeing the second half of the fourteenth century in Italy as a depressed era, having a large effect on and reflection in the arts of the time.[8] It is fair to say that some of the stern Christian gestures of the Latin works probably do reflect a sterner Boccaccio. But one must also remember the gaiety of the *Decameron,* which Boccaccio continued to revise well into his old age, as late as 1370–71.[9] Whether or not he thought that Mainardo Cavalcanti's female co-familiars would have considered him a dirty old man for having written it,[10] he obviously did not consider himself one. In short, there seems at least enough evidence to suggest that there was no dramatic "conversion" in 1362, that there was in fact no specific *crisi* either. What did happen was that Boccaccio grew old in a world that was, perhaps even more than is generally the case, a more difficult place to have hopes in.

If there is a notable change, if not in Boccaccio's message, then in the style of presentation of that message, it occurs mainly in his choice of a language in which he would write. After the *Decameron,* with the sole exception of the *Corbaccio,* all of Boccaccio's major work (with the further exceptions of his *opere dantesche* and some letters) is in Latin. The last twenty years of Boccaccio's life are devoted to what the manuals are pleased to refer to as "pre-humanism," but which looks very much like the real thing. If there was, if not a *crisi* but a turning point in Boccaccio's literary life, it was most likely to have occurred during his first meetings with Petrarch in 1350–51.[11] Petrarch may be looked upon as the generating spirit of a great deal of Boccaccio's activity in his last quarter century of life: the *Genealogie, De casibus virorum illustrium, De mulieribus claris, De montibus,* and his Eclogues all date from this period, and probably should be considered to reflect Petrarch's announced hostility to the vernacular in his search for a "humanist" style.[12] But while Petrarch won a large measure of Boccaccio's allegiance, there was the other and vernacular part of him which continued in the vulgar tongue with the heavily Dantesque *Corbaccio* and the works on Dante themselves. Joined to this linguistic change, either as its cause or its effect, is the change in tone we find in so many of the late works, the main feature of which is the relative absence both of irony and gaiety, replaced by a heavier voice, one endowed with the earnest tonality of the preacher.

Yet the life that the dead Petroni wished to turn Boccaccio from, we should remember, was not merely that of the *opere minori in volgare,* but, if anything specific, that of the humanist life in books. Petroni's attack apparently caused him momentarily to want to give away his library, to which anxiety Petrarch responds that he would gladly give all those books a home himself (*Seniles,* I, 5). That is, Petroni wanted Boccaccio (and Petrarch) to desist from *all* literary activity—he did not, as the "conversionary" critics have done—distinguish between two Boccacci, or two kinds of secular literature. His point, and it is a valid point, is that *all* secular literature is a turning away from the purely Christian life. For Boccaccio there apparently was a momentary hesitation at the brink, but then the decision came, perhaps spurred on by Petrarch's response, to continue his life in literature. Boccaccio's late works, far from serving as proof that he had succumbed to Petroni's warning, indeed prove just the opposite.

And for him, we may conclude, the early works were not in need of any particular defense because his generic defense of poetry, the *Genealogie* upon which he labored for some twenty years and which he looked upon as his *magnum opus,* was more than an adequate defense of them as well. If there are moments in the *Decameron* which seem to have caused pointed criticism (and in the letter to Mainardo it is these he acknowledges, not, for example, the sexual exploits of the seven nymphs in the *Comedia ninfe*), they are seen, in the work itself (IV, *Introduzione;* X, *Conclusione*) as violating propriety, but not morality. The early works, we may speculate, are not specifically defended by the old Boccaccio because he did not believe that they required a defense. As far as he was concerned, there was no need to defend them from the charge that they opposed Christian morality for the simple reason that they did not do so.

The Christian morality of Boccaccio's *opere minori in volgare* is not tinged with metaphysics, or even very much with thoughts of the next world. While in his *Esposizioni sopra la Comedia di Dante* there is an expectable and necessary concern with the afterworld, Boccaccio even there prefers to center his attention on the moral choices which man faces in this life. While he seems clearly aware that unmoderated sexual appetite leads to the second death as well, he seems much more concerned with its effects in this world, in which it lays waste man's physical being, takes away his freedom, is anti-social, and leads to physical death. In this respect he is a great precursor of the sixteenth century, of Christians like Erasmus, who are particularly devoted to moral philosophy. He is rarely studied with a view to this dimension of his work, but that is probably its central force. In his close studies of carnality, of the religion of love and its myriad adherents, he has left a record which endures, but is rarely studied in the light I have here proposed for it. I must conclude. For, as Boccaccio says,[13] "De concupiscibili autem amore satis supra dictum est."

Pergo 24 December 1974–Roma 8 May 1975

Notes

Introduction

1. For some of the works, especially the *Ninfale fiesolano,* severe problems surround attempts to establish a date of composition. Indications of the difficulties involving the *Ninfale,* the *Caccia di Diana,* and the *Corbaccio*—the three works that continue to cause the most discussion with reference to dating—will be found at the appropriate juncture in the text. The tentative order and dating which are offered here are just that and depend largely upon Vittore Branca's version of the same, which assimilates most previous scholarship, in the "Profilo biografico," *Tutte le opere di Giovanni Boccaccio,* Vol. I (Verona: Mondadori, 1967), although they also reflect the dates suggested by various editors of particular texts. Figures denoting the line lengths of works in verse do not include *proemi,* introductory sonnets, rubrics, etc.

2. It would be difficult to know where to end a bibliographical listing of the works on Boccaccio that uphold this basic view. For an early example that suggests its one-for-one "positivism" one might consult R. Renier, *La Vita Nuova e la Fiammetta* (Torino and Roma, 1879), pp. 217–341. It is probably Baldelli, *Vita di Giovanni Boccaccio* (Firenze, 1886), who deserves the credit or blame for making the first absolute modern equivalence of Boccaccio's life and art. But a far more impressive figure is V. Crescini, an extremely able scholar who argues a bad hypothesis well, especially in his influential *Con-*

tributo agli studi sul Boccaccio (Torino, 1887). A less impressive but thoroughly pleasant continuer of the tradition is A. Della Torre, *La giovinezza di Giovanni Boccaccio* (Città di Castello, 1905). A. F. Massèra did a great deal of work in Boccaccio studies, some of which will be referred to within. His "Le più antiche biografie del Boccaccio," *Zeitschrift für romanische Philologie,* 27 (1903), 298–338, might detain us here. Discussing the *vitae* of Filippo Villani, Domenico Bandini, Secco Polenton, and Giannozzo Manetti (which were written between 1375 and 1450—the four texts are published by Massèra in this article), he notes without surprise the fact that these early biographers do not deal at all or only in passing with Boccaccio's vernacular work. The silence of his near contemporaries on the relation of these works to Boccaccio's life might have served as an early warning to precisely such as Massèra, who is one of the prime purveyors of the "biographical" approach. English readers will find E. Hutton, *Giovanni Boccaccio: A Biographical Study* (London and New York: 1910) the best book-length presentation in English of this approach. For excellence of research and argument perhaps not even Crescini is as impressive as F. Torraca. His two studies, *Per la biografia di Giovanni Boccaccio* (Milano, 1912) and *Giovanni Boccaccio a Napoli* (Napoli, 1915), are the most scholarly and interesting expositions of a highly dubious point of view. But the work which put the keystone into the arch of this extraordinarily unmedieval edifice was the work of H. Hauvette, *Boccace* (Paris, 1914), which was greeted in Italy with loud applause and some chagrin (that a Frenchman had had the last word—if a few months late—during the great centennial year). Adding insult to unfelt injury, Hauvette's dedication reads as follows: "A la Mémoire de la parisienne inconnue qui donna le jour à l'auteur du *Décaméron.*" Since no one but the least enlightened Francophile will still maintain that Boccaccio was likely to have been born in Paris (see Branca, "Profilo biografico," pp. 7–8, for discussion and bibliography), Hauvette's appalling jingoism, with its overtone of a Frankish smirk, intimating that only French brains would have animated a Boccaccio, now reads as flatulantly as it should. As the culmination of a century of "biographical" criticism, Hauvette's book became the "authorized version" of Boccaccio's life and works, until Branca and Billanovich began shredding the oddly woven fabric. It is now in tatters. On another similar problem—Botticelli's supposed infatuation with Simonetta Vespucci—see E. H. Gombrich, "Botticelli's Mythologies: A Study in the Neoplatonic Symbolism of His Circle," *JWCI,* 8 (1945), 10: "The appeal of these interpretations, and their heated defence in the absence of any tangible evidence, provides an object lesson in the romantic approach to the past, which regards history, not as an incomplete record of an unlimited number of lives and happenings, but rather as a well-ordered pageant in which all of the favorite highlights and episodes turn up at their cue." The remark speaks to Botticelli, but makes a welcome transplant in Boccaccio studies.

3. And see Branca's extremely important article, "Schemi letterari e schemi autobiografici nell'opera del Boccaccio," *Bibliofilia,* 49 (1947), 1–40, which summarizes its own main point as follows: "Le costruzioni biografiche hanno . . . fatto chiudere gli occhi di fronte all'evidenza artistica . . ." (p. 6). For discussion of autobiography as literary creation ("erotic pseudo-biography" is the author's phrase), with reference not to Boccaccio but to his fourteenth-century continental contemporaries, see G. B. Gybbon-Monypenny, "Autobiography in the *Libro de buen amor* in the Light of Some Literary Comparisons," *Bulletin of Hispanic Studies,* 34 (1957), 63–78, as well as his "Guillaume de Machaut's Erotic 'Autobiography': Precedents for the Form of the *Voir-Dit,*" in W. Rothwell et al., eds., *Studies in Medieval Literature and Languages in Memory of Frederick Whitehead* (Manchester, 1973), pp. 133–52. For a later work (ca. 1527) that should also be regarded as "erotic pseudo-biography," see Francisco Delicado, *Retrato de la loçana andaluza,* ed. Bruno Damiani and Giovanni Allegra (Madrid, 1975), and the study by Bruno Damiani, *Francisco Delicado* (New York, 1974).

4. For a careful review of the history of changing critical attitudes toward the *Decameron* see V. Branca, *Linee di una storia della critica al "Decameron"* (Milano-Genova-Roma-Napoli, 1939), pp. 1–72. Since no such comparable documentation exists for the *opere minori* as a group, Branca's study is useful for our purposes as well.

5. It is so understood by those readers who themselves approve of the notion as well as by those who thoroughly disapprove. Documentation of this point will be offered frequently, within. For a similar situation, see Shakespeare's *Venus and Adonis,* which, as R. Putney has pointed out, is disparaged on either of two grounds: for being too lacivious or for not being lascivious enough. The Venus of that work, like the carnal Venus of Boccaccio, is more clearly seen as being ridiculed and attacked than praised. A more dogmatic reader would simply insist that no other reasonable possibility exists. See Putney's "*Venus and Adonis:* Amour with Humor," *Philological Quarterly,* 20 (1941), 533–48. And for another study of Shakespeare's early work that deals with the mythographic background in ways that are compatible with my own views, see R. P. Miller, "The Myth of Mars's Hot Minion in *Venus and Adonis,*" *ELH,* 26 (1959), 470–81. It is perhaps proper at this point to

reflect that almost all the criticism of medieval and renaissance works concerning love that has influenced current views of those works was written during the Romantic era, a period which may be taken to run from ca. 1785 to the present, with a felicitous counter-movement beginning to make some headway only within the past generation. However, the notion that we are not really supposed to respond to literary works mainly in direct proportion to their effect on our own pulses may be said to be only inching forward.

6. Ed. F. Castets (Paris: Maisonneuve, 1881), p. 3: "Fa che m' adori, chèd i' son tu' deo;/Ed ogn' altra credenza metti a parte,/Nè non creder nè Lucha, nè Matteo,/Nè Marco, nè Giovanni" (V.11–14).

7. The *Corbaccio* is an exception, as Venus is mentioned only once in the work and is not a character in it (see discussion in chapter 1, below).

8. See the "bibliografia essenziale" in Giorgio Padoan's edition of the *Esposizioni sopra la Comedia di Dante,* Vol. VI of *Tutte le opere di Giovanni Boccaccio* (Verona: Mondadori, 1965), pp. 728–30, and see notes to the texts in the various Mondadori texts, esp. Vol. III, pp. 857–58. While there are several article-length studies of this major subject, a full examination would certainly seem to be called for. Since this year's centennial observances have already been the occasion of two oral presentations on this subject (by Francesco Mazzoni and Robert Durling) and promise a third (by Franco Fido) one hopes that this major area of inquiry will soon be better served in print.

1. The Flames of Two Loves

1. Branca's study, "Per l'attribuzione della 'Caccia di Diana' a Giovanni Boccaccio," was first published in *Annali della R. Scuola Normale Superiore di Pisa,* S. II, 7 (1938) and is reprinted in his *Tradizione delle opere del Boccaccio* (Roma, 1958), pp. 121–43. This remains, and is likely to remain, the authoritative treatment of the manuscript tradition and of the Boccaccian nature of the work (the second subject is given a brilliant exposition on pp. 129–40). For a record of the degree of Branca's impressive success among the *studiosi,* most of whom had previously denied authenticity, see the following essay (pp. 145–98) in *Tradizione delle opere del Boccaccio,* "Nuove note sulla 'Caccia di Diana,' " p. 147n. This later study begins by adding a few details to the earlier one, then offers an impressive piece of historical scholarship, in which the author attempts to identify fifty-eight maidens of the hunt in their

courtly Neapolitan reality (pp. 168–90). The result of these researches are available in shorter form in Branca's notes to the *Caccia* in *Opere,* I, especially to Cantos I, IX, and X.

2. See "Per l'attribuzione . . . ," pp. 140–41; "Nuove note . . . ," pp. 190–92, counters the methods of the previous study and, admits that it had been too "biographical" in its attempt to establish a date (see Branca's notes to the *Caccia* in the Laterza edition of *Le Rime, L'Amorosa Visione, La Caccia di Diana* [Bari, 1939], pp. 379–80). In Branca's "Introduzione" to the *Caccia* (*Opere,* I, 3) a secure *ante quem* is given as 1338–39, while the likelihood of an earlier dating is still argued for. See n. 10, below, for Giuseppe Billanovich's dating of 1337?–38?

3. The formula is, of course, 3t + 1, in order to accommodate the necessary closing rime of the *terza rima.* Only the third canto violates this rule. It has an additional *terzina,* thus 61 lines. Boccaccio, in the *Amorosa Visione,* was forced by his opening acrostic sonnets to violate the usual canto length on several occasions. One wonders why he apparently chose to do so here.

4.

Nel tempo adorno che l'erbette nove
rivestono ogni prato e l'aere chiaro
ride per la dolcezza che 'l ciel move,
sol pensando mi stava che riparo
potessi fare ai colpi che forando
mi gian d'amor il cuor con duolo amaro.
(11.1–6)

5. See E. R. Curtius, *European Literature and the Latin Middle Ages* (New York, 1963), pp. 515–18, for a brief survey of this general subject.

6. A consideration of the "narrator's frame" occupies the fourth chapter of this study.

7.

quando mi parve udir venir chiamando
un spirito gentil volando forte . . .
(11.7–8)

This cautionary distancing of the allegorical vision from literal truth is formulaic in precisely similar ways in, for instance, Dante, Petrarch, Chaucer. See R. Hollander, "*Vita Nuova:* Dante's Perceptions of Beatrice," *Dante*

Studies, 92 (1974), esp. p. 14. And see Boccaccio's insistence on the formula a few lines later: "E, se non m'ingannò 'l vero ascoltare / che far mi parve . . ." (ll. 16–17). A similar phenomenon is observable in the *Corbaccio* (see n.62, below). For a concise review of major "sogni mirabili" in medieval literature, see V. Branca, " 'L'Amorosa Visione,' (Origini, significati, fortuna)," *Annali della R. Scuola Normale Superiore di Pisa,* S. II, 40 (1942), 268n.–69n.

8. While Boccaccio's second group of ladies (Cantos IX and X) contains the numerologically less promising twenty-five, this first group possibly has an overtone of one of Dante's favorite numbers. The *Caccia* is possibly related to Dante in other numerological ways as well: eighteen cantos is the sum of two nines, and it is likely Boccaccio sought to legitimize his numeration by reflecting Dante's mystical nine. As for the verse form, the *terza rima,* which clearly reflects Dante's importance to Boccaccio, it is related to numerological preoccupations in Dante and may also be so in Boccaccio. His numerology is an interesting and not overworked topic. Janet Levarie Smarr, in a thesis recently completed at Princeton University, has some interesting things to say about the numerological arrangements both of the *questioni d'amore* in the *Filocolo* (for which see Victoria Kirkham, "Reckoning with Boccaccio's *questioni d'amore,*" *MLN,* 89 [1974], 51) and of tellers and tales in the *Decameron.* For a consideration of Boccaccio's numerology, see Cesare Segre, "Strutture e registri nella 'Fiammetta,' " *Strumenti critici,* 6, No. 18 (1972), 141–43.

9. See V. Branca, "Nuove note sulla 'Caccia di Diana,' " pp. 168–90.

10. See Branca's long note, *Opere,* I, 689–90, with its appropriate bibliographical indications. If there is a major "riddle" to the *Caccia,* it is the identity of this lady. Branca claims that any successful attempt at making a precise historical identification is most unlikely. This position is eminently sensible, especially since it is probable that not even the "Fiammetta" of the later works has the slightest historical authenticity. But Branca's conclusion draws away from the possibility that this lady is the same fictional lady that Boccaccio will later call "Fiammetta," even though in the "Introduzione" to the *Caccia,* p. 4, he himself calls attention to the two passages which come close to the later *senhal:* IV.11–12; XIII.29–30 (in the latter her eyes are like "due fiammette"). These two passages signify to Giuseppe Billanovich that the *senhal* is already before us in embryo—*Restauri boccacceschi* (Roma, 1945), p. 89. See Guido Di Pino, *La polemica del Boccaccio* (Firenze, 1953), pp.

59n.–60n., for a similar argument. While it is true that the *Caccia* would be the only work to celebrate "Fiammetta" which does not explicitly call her by that name, there may be some merit to Billanovich's side of the argument, especially since it does more to "de-historicize" Fiammetta. See *Restauri boccacceschi,* p. 87: "Quando il giovanissimo Boccaccio (1337?38?) immagina la *Caccia di Diana,* Fiammetta è in gran parte formata." At the same time it should be pointed out that there is no positive evidence of any kind which explicitly links this lady to the later Fiammetta. Nor is the question of any real moment if that lady is as thoroughly fictitious a character as she probably is. The complex problem of the "identity" of Fiammetta is taken up in the fourth chapter.

11. Ma quella donna cui Amore onora
più ch'altra per la sua somma virtute,
che tutte l'altre accresce e rinvigora,
fu l'ultima chiamata, e per salute
dell'altre, quasi com'una guardiana,
avanti gio per guidarle tute
(11.46–51)

12. . . . (né nomò lei,
perché a suo nome laude più sovrana
si converria, che dir qui non potrei).
(11.53–55)

Branca's note to the passage calls attention to the similar gesture made at the conclusion of the *Vita Nuova.*

13. For the classical and medieval tradition of "il contrasto fra Diana e Venere," as well as for the traditions of the *altercatio,* the *tournoiments de dames,* and the *caccia* itself, see Branca, "Introduzione," *Opere,* I, 5–9.

14. Even if we attend to one of Boccaccio's very best readers this is the case. Billanovich, in his review of Branca's edition of the *Rime, Amorosa Visione,* and *Caccia* (Bari, 1939), *GSLI,* 116 (1940), begins by affirming, against Hauvette's judgment in *Boccace* (Paris, 1914), pp. 139n.–40n., that the *Caccia* is authentic Boccaccio: "è infatti un poemetto di facile lettura, attraente perchè il racconto vi si anima con rapide e frequenti invenzioni che agitano le figure e variano il panorama. Certamente è solo movimento esterno: resta la complessiva monotonia della situazione e lo squilibrio di una

conclusione un po' goffa e un po' meccanica, poichè obbedendo a una ingenua pretesa di sublimazione culturale vi si abbandonano le vive realistiche scene di caccia per finire nel macchinoso mitologico degli ultimi canti" (p. 135). To find Boccaccio's hunting scenes "realistic" (should we so describe the unicorn hunted by Fior Curial's group in Canto VII?) and the "allegorical" ending "goffa," or clumsy, is the result of a reading that depends on values other than those Boccaccio reflects in the work. Such is also the case—or so one might claim—in Branca's view of the conclusion of the work, which he does not take very seriously: "Ma nella *Caccia* l'elemento allegorico o allusivo era una gratuita puntata finale, un espediente esterno per concludere" ("Profilo biografico," p. 59n.). See "Introduzione" to the *Comedia ninfe, Opere,* II, 671, for Quaglio's earlier characterization of the conclusion of the *Caccia:* "una gratuita puntata finale, un puro espediente risolutivo, sempre leggero nel ritmo."

15. Ll. 1–21. Branca, *Opere,* I, 691, points out that these lines are "una opaca ma diretta anticipazione" of the "Valle delle donne" of *Decameron* VI, concl., 19f., and draws our attention to similar Boccaccian landscapes in the *Amorosa Visione* (XXXIX–XL), *Rime* (LXI), *Comedia ninfe* (IV. 13–15), *Ninfale fiesolano* (234f.).

16. See the discussions of Diana's function in the *Filocolo* and *Ninfale fiesolano* in chapters 2 and 3 below. In *Filocolo* I, 1, 23, Diana's followers, here clearly meant to be taken as nuns, cultivate "tiepidi fuochi divotamente."

17. The color is usually given to Venus in other works. See chapter 3, n. 71.

18. As Branca observes, *Opere,* I, 691, "Volgono a mezzogiorno (cfr. anche IV, 1f.) proprio le donne fedeli ad Amore, che poi susciteranno la rivolta a Diana: secondo la tradizione delle raffigurazioni delle vere e schiette amanti nella trattatistica e nella poesia d'amore, da Andrea Cappellano all'*Amorosa Visione* (XXXIX)." His remark requires slight adjustment, in that it is "la bella donna" who will raise the rebellion against Diana; she is then joined by *all* the ladies (see XVII, esp. 13). If the southern compass point has a long literary tradition which invokes Venus, does not the eastern one have a similar tradition which invokes Jesus Christ? If at this point that seems too bold a proposition to apply to the *Caccia,* perhaps it will later not seem so. The east, as source of the rising sun, was frequently identified with Jesus. In Dante see St. Thomas's derivation of the name of St. Francis's birthplace

("Ascesi") in *Paradiso* XI.53. And see H. F. Dunbar, *Symbolism in Medieval Thought and Its Consummation in the Divine Comedy* (New Haven, 1929), passim. I would argue that Diana's identification with the east, that of the "bella donna" with the south, is in each case significant. In the moral directionality of the compass east and south are opposite directions. It is perhaps for this reason that Boccaccio begins with the party that heads south, and concludes with the one heading east. In the ensuing action, east is first, south, second, as we move around the compass from a different starting point.

19. "L'azione é un pretesto per rendere un galante e cortese omaggio alle più famose bellezze napoletane del tempo"—V. Branca, "Giovanni Boccaccio," *Letteratura Italiana, I Maggiori* (Milano, 1956), p. 194n.

20. Again one is forced to think of Dante, this time of the unrecorded (and perhaps unwritten) *sirventese* in praise of the sixty most beautiful ladies of Florence referred to in *Vita Nuova* VI (see Branca, "Profilo biografico," p. 41). Whether or not the numbers agree, the genre does. Among its several purposes, the *Caccia* is also Boccaccio's *sirventese* for the ladies of the court of Naples. Still, the numerology is tempting. Both works involve sixty ladies (in the *Caccia* we have the fifty-eight named ladies of the court, the "bella donna," and one presiding goddess—first Diana, then Venus), or approximately so. And in each the poet's lady occupies a numerologically arresting position; though not first, she is best, at number nine and number thirty-three, respectively. See Boccaccio's later *sirventese,* contained in the *ternario* "Contento quasi" (*Rime* LXIX.31–60) and the article of A. F. Massèra, "Il serventese boccaccesco delle belle donne," *Miscellanea storica della Valdelsa,* 21 (1913), 55–67.

21. XVI.25–31. Boccaccio's reasons for setting Zizzola d'Anna apart (her sisters or co-familiars, Alessandra and Covella, are named at I.33, and X.22, respectively) are not at all clear. But for Branca to characterize her status as the only lady *not* called to the hunt by Diana (that this is the case is clear from XVI.26–27) as likely being "una di quelle incongruenze che caratterizzano quest'*opera prima*" (*Opere,* I, 703) is perhaps too impatient a response. It would seem at least as likely that Boccaccio had some purpose in mind in setting Zizzola apart. For instance, he may have intended to say something to or about her (e.g., as a possibility, that she is naturally chaste, or that she actually liked to hunt) that only she and perhaps the courtly audience of the work would have understood.

22. In Canto II she gave the directional charge to the four hunting parties, in III some hunting advice to her own party, and in XVI she called off the hunt.

23. "io vo' che voi sacrificio d'elle
facciate a Giove, re dell'alto regno,
ed a onor di me, che esser deggio
reverita da voi in modo degno.
Così vi priego e così vi richieggio
quanto più posso, onde non siate lente,
acciò che nel mio coro aggiate seggio."
(XVI.39–45)

24. . . . "E' non sarà così niente!
Infino a qui, sì come avete detto
e comandato a noi qui adunate,
così abbiam seguito con effetto.
Or non vogliam più vostra deitate
seguir, però ch'accese d'altro foco
abbiamo i petti e l'anime infiammate."
(XVI.48–54)

25. It is perhaps not a coincidence that Ovid's *Remedia amoris* (199–210) recommends hunting as a means of escaping the clutches of lust. For discussion of several paradigms of the hunt as metaphor of the pursuit of the beloved, see Marcelle Thiébaux, *The Stag of Love: The Chase in Medieval Literature* (Ithaca, N.Y., 1974), esp. pp. 89–228. And for the stylized character of actual medieval hunts see her earlier study, "The Mediaeval Chase," *Speculum,* 42 (1967), 260–74.

26. Branca cites without comment *Purgatorio* XXXI.65: "Con li occhi a terra stannosi, ascoltando." Once Diana is lost from view the ladies "chinaron gli occhi tacite aspettando" (XVII.3). The situation in the Earthly Paradise was certainly familiar to Boccaccio: Dante is being upbraided by Beatrice for his "fault." The situational parallels are clear enough, and it is likely that in Boccaccio's view Dante and the ladies were guilty of similar divagations from a better love.

27. The equation begins in Boccaccio's work (it has a long medieval tradition; see Dante's "o sommo Giove"—*Purgatorio* VI.118) in what is very likely

the first literary exercise he ever composed, the so-called "Allegoria mitologica," which he preserved in the notebook now known as the Zibaldone [Mediceo] Laurenziano (Plut. XXIX, 8), and which was published in facsimile by Guido Biagi (Firenze, 1915). It was printed by A. F. Massèra, in Boccaccio's *Opere latine minori* (Bari, 1928), pp. 231–37. And see a neighbor of this piece in the same miscellany (it occupies 60^{r}, the "Allegoria" 61^{r}–62^{r}), the "Elegia di Costanza," published by Branca as "Il più antico carme del Boccaccio" in *Tradizione delle opere del Boccaccio* (Roma, 1958), pp. 204–07 (first published in *Convivium,* N.S., 1 [1954]). In that work the buried girl makes the following request of her lover: "Et pro me Iovi porriges ore preces" (l. 5). These two little Latin works are of some interest, making plain Boccaccio's early preoccupation with allegorized Christianization of pagan myth and with sexual passion (the *Elegia* is surprisingly carnal-minded), the two great themes of all his later work. This is the only place in the text of the *Caccia* that Jove is mentioned. The seriousness of Diana's request probably underscores the Christian intent of the passage. For the "Elegia" see G. Velli, "Sull' 'Elegia di Costanza,' " *Studi sul Boccaccio,* 4 (1967), 241–54.

28.

"O santa Dea, poich'è nostro disire,
per la virtù del nostro sacrificio
non isdegnar le nostri voci udire,
ma pietosa al two giocondo officio
per merito de' nostri preghi umili
ricevi noi e per tuo beneficio.
Caccia de' petti nostri i pensier vili,
e per la tua virtù fa eccellenti
gli animi nostri e' cor larghi e gentili.
Deh, fa sentire a noi quanto piacenti
sieno gli effetti tuoi, e facci ancora,
alcuno amando, gli animi contenti."
(XVII. 16–27)

If the work is called the *Caccia di Diana,* l. 22 ("Caccia de' petti nostri . . .") gives the title, whether Boccaccio intended to do so or not, an ironic undertone: the hunt held under Diana's auspices becomes the occasion for her being driven out by Venus. What the *donne* now consider "pensier vili" is very likely to be the "tiepido foco" (II.22) that Diana tried to inspire in their "casti petti." In the religion of love there is no thought more vile than chastity.

29. Branca's note, *Opere,* I, 704, while referring (among other possible sources) to the *nuvoletta* on which Beatrice ascends to heaven in Dante's wild imagining of her death (*Vita Nuova* XXIII), does not express or hint at the likely antithetical relationship between the two scenes. The chaste Beatrice is going up to God. She is nothing if not anti-venereal. Boccaccio's Venus comes down to earth, beautiful in her flesh, and promises her "converts" sexual pleasure with men.

30. . . . "Io son colei
da cui, pregando voi, ciascuno aspetta
grazia; e prometto a voi, per gli alti dei,
che ciascheduna avrà la dimandata,
ch'è degna di seguire i passi miei."
(XVII.32–36)

31. The "miracles" performed by Venus are a theme to which Boccaccio will return in the *Ninfale fiesolano.*

32. Branca's comment on the penultimate line of this canto, which looks back to the bathing scene, offers his sense of the meaning of this action: ". . . la purificazione dei 'giovinetti gai e belli' nel 'fiumicello' ricorda quelle dantesche nel 'fiumicello' del Lete" (*Opere,* I, 704). That the purification of the *giovinetti* is purely physical would seem clear (each one is "fresco come un giglio"—l. 46—an expression which Branca identifies as an "espressione popolaresca passata al linguaggio più convenzionale del Boccaccio: cf. *Filostrato* II.71: 'fresco più che giglio d'orto' "—ibid.). The first bathing scene in the *Caccia* involves chaste nymphs (the motif will return in various of the *opere in volgare,* never so strikingly as in the *Ninfale fiesolano*), the second, lovers who wish to be anything but chaste. The different color of the vestments each group is adorned with underlines the change in moral atmosphere, the matronly purple yielding to the more amorous vermilion (but see the later discussion of purple as the color of Venus in many of the later works, chapter 3, n. 71). And if Dante's Earthly Paradise lies behind Boccaccio's final treatment of his garden, it probably does so as a corrective moral framework to the lascivious uses that the place encompasses here.

33. . . . "State
per mio comando e per util consiglio
suggetti a queste donne, e loro amate

fin che meriterete aver vittoria
del vostro affanno insieme con pietate."
(XVII.47–51)

Her concluding word, "pietate," is, like the word "mercede," frequently used in Boccaccio's poetry to denote the bestowing of sexual favors by the lady upon her lover. It is what the narrator will be left longing for in the concluding four lines of the poem.

34. It is likely that Venus' lasting presence, in the *petti* of all the ladies, is intentionally a negation of Diana's role, which is one that "il tiepido foco/ne' casti petti tien" (II.22–23).

35. Boccaccio was fond of Actaeon, referring to him four times in the *Comedia ninfe* (III.18; XVIII.18; XXIV.5; XXXI.8–9), thrice in the *Teseida* (V.57, 6; VII.79, 5; XI.34, 2), and twice in the *Filocolo* (V, 19, 1; 21, 3).

36. Branca's notes to the concluding section of the canto, *Opere,* I, 705, present a number of parallels between this text and similar phrases devoted to praise of the beloved *donna* in others of the *opere volgari.*

37. Ond'io priego ciascun divotamente,
che subbietto è, com'io, a quel signore
che ingentilisce ciascuna vil mente,
ched e' prieghin per me che nell'amore
di questa donna lungamente io sia,
e che io d'onoralla aggia valore;
ché simile orazion sempre mai fia
fatta per me in servigio di quelli
che allegro possiede o che disia;
e per coloro ancor che son ribelli
con le lor donne, acciò ch'egli abbian pace
e che angoscia più non li flagelli.
(XVIII.37–48)

38. Within the rules of the "court of love" the narrator's last intention is, if generous in spirit, blasphemous. In the *Corbaccio* the narrator, before he is enlightened, will think the hell he encounters in his dream the place of punishment for none but these.

39. Although Branca does not spend a great deal of time on the larger meaning of the work, he does clearly hold to this second view: The events of the conclusion of the *Caccia* "non sono che la traduzione mitizzata di un'affermazione ripetuta in tutti i toni nelle sue prime opere: 'i giovani devono attendere ad amare, e amore li educherà alla gentilezza e alla virtù' " (*Tradizione delle opere del Boccaccio,* p. 130). And see the similar view expressed in his "Introduzione" to the *Caccia, Opere,* I, 5: ". . . il Boccaccio vuole esprimere in questa, che con tutta probabilità è la sua 'opera prima,' la vittoria e la supremazia dell'Amore su ogni altro valore e su ogni altra attività umana." In a similar vein, see Carlo Muscetta, "Giovanni Boccaccio e i novellieri," *Storia della Letteratura Italiana,* II, *Il Trecento* (Milano, 1965), p. 324: "La potenza redentrice dell'amore è infatti esaltata in questa piccola 'commodìa' erotica. . . ." A. E. Quaglio, in his note to *Filocolo* IV, 46, 20—the conclusion of Fiammetta's diatribe against carnal love—*Opere,* I, 876, connects the ending of the *Caccia* to this moment in the *Filocolo* and passages in the *Comedia ninfe* (esp. XL and XLIf.) in which Venus "simboleggia il Dio e l'amore cristiano." This reading, which is polar to my own, has the merit of being one of the sole passages, however brief, to deal seriously with Cantos XVII and XVIII (Quaglio had apparently revised his former opinion of the conclusion of the *Caccia*—see n. 14, above). As for the wide divergence in interpretation, I would hold that the Venere of the *Caccia* is entirely carnal in her operation, and certainly in the eyes of her worshippers, that she operates *against* Diana (rather than with her, as is the case in the *Filocolo*—see discussion in the following chapter). In short, one might better gloss the victory of Venus over Diana as Boccaccio himself glosses it in his *chiose* to the *Teseida* (*Opere,* II, 467): "Solevano adunque quelle vergini le quali seguivano Diana andare con gli archi alle caccie; e già ne furono assai vinte da Amore, le quali, lasciato di seguire Diana, seguirono Venere; in testimonianza delle quali vittorie, pone qui l'autore vedersi nelli templi di Venere appiccati gli archi di quelle che vinte furono." It is amusing to imagine that in the Temple of Venus in the *Teseida* the reader sees displayed the weapons of the *donzelle* of the *Caccia* who so happily disport themselves at the work's conclusion. In this context the victory of Venus should be seen as a defeat for her celebrants.

40. When Boccaccio portrays them as antagonists, they seem to represent only lascivious love and chastity, respectively. When Venus signifies a higher love, she and Diana are not necessarily enemies. See discussion of the *Filocolo,* which returns to this point, in the following chapter.

41. Two of these concern the dating of the work and the meaning of its title. For brief reviews of the status of each question, with bibliography, see the recent edition of the *Corbaccio* by Tauno Nurmela, *Annales Academiae Scientiarum Fennicae* (Helsinki, 1968), pp. 18–21 and 16–17, respectively; citations of the text, below, follow Nurmela's numeration.

Until recently there was general acceptance of Hauvette's dating of 1354–55 (*Boccace*, p. 330). Giorgio Padoan, "Sulla datazione del 'Corbaccio,' " *Lettere Italiane*, 15 (1963), 1–27, 199–201, has succeeded in convincing many scholars (including Branca, see "Profilo biografico," p. 140) that it was written much later (1365–66). Since one of Padoan's major grounds of argument is that it was written in a spirit entirely different from that of the earlier "amatory" works, the present study would tend to call that much of his argument into question. Nurmela, while applauding Padoan's effort (and sharing his view of the *Corbaccio*'s relationship to the earlier works), would still like to keep the question open (p. 20), and disagrees with Padoan's interpretation of what is perhaps the key passage in the dispute: "fuori delle fasce già sono degli anni quaranta e già son venticinque cominciatoli a conoscere" (179), which for Padoan refers to the sixty-five years that have already elapsed in the world's last age, and sets a date, therefore, of 1365 (p. 7), while to Nurmela the two numbers refer to Boccaccio's current age and the twenty-five years he has had experience of the world (p. 156)—i.e., he finds Hauvette's basic argument—if not all its particulars—sound.

As for the title, Nurmela offers a brief survey of the leading contenders (pp. 16–17): Hauvette's "oiseau de mauvais augure," V. M. Jeffery's Greek etymologizing (Boccaccio was only finding a fancy way of saying "labyrinth of love"), J. Bourciez's derivation from the Spanish *corbacho* (and thus the work is dark, or obscure, i.e., Boccaccio means the work to be taken as an enigma), Aldo Rossi's resuscitation of F. Torraca's "brutto corvo" (=Amore, derived strikingly from Richard de Fornival's *Li Bestiaires d'Amours*, where *corbeaus* resembles Amour because it eats the eyes and brains of the dead), and Padoan's "brutto corvo" as "uccello di malaugurio" (=the widow). Nurmela shares Padoan's desire to keep the interpretation as simple as possible, but prefers to think that the crow is the book rather than the widow. To these considerations I add the following: A more than likely source of Boccaccio's ornithological title is to be found in Ovid's *Ibis*, the work of the exile which, modelled on Callimachus' poem against Apollonius of Rhodes, vitriolically gives the bird to an unknown enemy. If this is so, and, given Boccaccio's large awareness of almost all of Ovid's work (see discussion at the conclusion of the fourth chapter, below), it is likely to be so, the *Corbaccio* of the title would seem to refer to the book rather than to its victim. In the text itself, however, the mysogynist *guida* claims that virtuous women who deserve praise are as likely to be found as "cigni neri" (Boccaccio apparently did not know that such in fact existed) or "corbi bianchi" (269), and will later refer to his wife (the object of the narrator's frustrated attentions) as first seeming a "colomba," and then shortly changing from a dove to a serpent (293). See M. Cottino-Jones, "The *Corbaccio:* Notes for a Mythical Perspective of Moral Alternatives," *Forum Italicum,* 4 (1970), 490–509, for a similar discussion of the imagistic equivalence of the widow and the crow. This small "network" of images, playing upon white and black, associates birds and women; since the widow is the worst among women, and the very opposite of a dove (Padoan has pointed out that in the text—143—the widow is dressed in black), she may well be thought of as a "corbaccia," if not a "corbaccio." For it is the masculine gender of Boccaccio's ugly bird which offers the main evidence against Padoan's interpretation. Thus it seems likely that the title should refer both to the book—an ugly and satirical vehicle of the author's scorn—*and* to the widow. It is likely that, as in Ovid's poem, which represents Callimachus's enemy as bearing the name Ibis ("Nunc quo Battiades inimicum devovet Ibin"—l. 55), the title of the book and the name of its intended object are one. Boccaccio refers to the *Ibis* (a work which he himself copied in his own hand—see Padoan's note, *Opere,* VI, 829) in the *Esposizioni sopra la Comedia di Dante* (*Inf.* IV, *esp. litt.,* 122) as *"In Ibin,"* thus reinforcing the notion that his own title, insofar as it reflects Ovid's, points in the direction of the object of his attack, as is the case in any number of medieval treatises, from those of the earliest Fathers onwards, which bear the name of the person they attack. This solution, while accomodating that of Nurmela, sides predominantly with Padoan and has the merit of solving the problem of the masculine gender of the title ("book" having the masculine gender in Italian) and the feminine gender of the widow. For an "ornithological" source in Phaedrus, *Liber fabularum* I.3, see A. K. Cassell, "The Crow of the Fable and the *Corbaccio:* A Suggestion for the Title," *MLN,* 85 (1970), 83–91. For an entirely conjectual suggestion of a possible relation between the title and Boccaccio's sense of the anti-venereal stance of Dino del Garbo, see chapter 2, n. 160. I may also observe, if with some trepidation, that the nine letters of the noun of the title only fail by a single letter of forming an anagram of Boccaccio's name.

42. G. I. Lopriore, "Osservazioni sul 'Corbaccio,' " *La Rassegna,* 6 (1956), 483–89, sees Boccaccio as having barely avoided composing a conventional misogynist diatribe by having clothed the work in its fictive garment, and

complains that over half the text is actually only such a diatribe (p. 485). One may, however, argue that the diatribe functions as a support to elements in the frame rather than seeing that frame as the mere pretext for a diatribe. See M. Cottino-Jones in this vein, art. cit. in the preceding note, p. 490. It is principally from the frame that we get our sense that Boccaccio is in the *Corbaccio* reviewing the matter of his earlier vernacular fiction.

43. It is probably fair to say that the narrator of the *Corbaccio* is more closely identified with the actuality of Boccaccio's life than any other Boccaccian narrator (even than the "Giovanni di Boccaccio da Certaldo" of the *Amorosa Visione*—see discussion in chapter 3, below). One thinks especially of the narrator's devotion to poetry and philosophy (188–92). Yet this does not necessarily imply that the work is "confessional" in any specific way, as many have believed. See esp. H. Hauvette, "Une confession de Boccace: 'Il Corbaccio,' " *Bulletin italien,* 1 (1901), 3–21, reprinted in his *Etudes sur Boccace* (Torino, 1968), pp. 45–63.

44. In Dante the word had come to have overtones of moral or theological concerns, which may be reflected here. See R. Hollander, "*Vita Nuova:* Dante's Perceptions of Beatrice," *Dante Studies,* 92 (1974), 9–10.

45. ". . . una spezial grazia: non per mio merito, ma per sola benignità di Colei che, impetrandola da Colui che vuole quello che Ella medesima, nuovamente mi fu conceduta" (3).

46. There are, on the other hand, frequent similarities between the positions taken by the narrators of the *Decameron* and the *Corbaccio.* Both have recently been freed from their imprisonment in love by a *consolatore*—the unnamed friend of the *Decameron* with "le sue laudevoli consolazioni" (*proemio,* 4) and the *pensiero,* "credo da celeste lume mandato" (12) that brings down "divina consolazione nelle menti de' mortali" (47). Each narrator was about to die because of his amorous disposition (*pr.* 4; *Corb.* 9). Each thanks God for His mercy (*pr.* 5; *Corb.* 4), and now wishes to express his gratitude for "benefici ricevuti" (*pr.* 6; *Corb.* 1) so as not to seem "ingrato" (*pr.* 7; *Corb.* 1). Each hopes that his work will offer *utilità* to its intended readership (*pr.* 8; *Corb.* 4). Where that readership is feminine in one case and masculine in another, both the love-struck ladies for whom the narrator of the *Decameron* feels the compassion of fellowship and the formerly love-struck narrator of the *Corbaccio* are seen as being or having been confined to their quarters by their maladies ("nel piccolo circuito delle loro camere racchiuse dimorano"—*pr.*

10; "ritrovandom'io solo nella mia camera"—*Corb.* 6). And both works have as their aims solace and utility: "diletto delle sollazzevoli cose in quelle [novelle] mostrate e utile consiglio potranno pigliare" (*pr.* 14); "utilità e consolazione dell' anime" (*Corb.* 5). The difference in tone between the *Decameron*'s "diletto delle sollazzevoli cose" and the *Corbaccio*'s "consolazione" helps to express the difference in tonality between the two works as wholes. But their *utilità* would seem to be intended to be of a similar nature. One wonders why the close similarity between these two prologues has heretofore not received significant attention. (It was only while making the final revisions of this manuscript that I was able to see a copy of Anthony Cassell's translation of the *Corbaccio* [Urbana, Ill., 1975]. His introduction and notes to the text frequently touch on issues addressed here. His first note (p. 80), for instance, discusses the contrast in tone between the two *proemi*—but not their similarities.)

47. It has a near defender in Lopriore, "Osservazioni sul 'Corbaccio,' " p. 485, who claims that the satire of the *Corbaccio* is directed against *femmine* and not against *donne.* See n. 73, below. A. K. Cassell, "An Abandoned Canvas: Structural and Moral Conflict in the *Corbaccio,*" *MLN,* 89 (1974), 60–70, while opposing the "conversion theory" (see n. 49, below), calls into question Boccaccio's seriousness in the *Corbaccio,* e.g., "The ultimate message of the work, intentionally or unintentionally, parodies the seriousness which the tradition of otherworldly visions usually evinces" (p. 62). His grounds for this judgment are, however, at least questionable. For while he intelligently points to Boccaccio's reliance upon both Aristotle's and St. Thomas's discussions of *odium,* he assumes that what the narrator gives vent to here is "un disordinato appetito di vendetta" (*Esposizioni, Inf.* VII, *esp. all.,* 111) rather than the just hatred of that which should be hated, which is sanctioned by Aristotle and by Thomas (as Cassell's citations make unmistakably clear), and which kind of hatred is also referred to—and praised—in the *Esposizioni* (e.g., *Inf.* VIII, *esp. litt.,* 48: ". . . e quelli cotali, che questa virtù hanno, . . . s'adirano per quelle cose e contro a quelle persone, contro alle quali è convenevole d'adirarsi, e ancora come si conviene e quando e quanto tempo; e questi, che questo fanno, . . . sono commendabili"—for which judgment Boccaccio cites the authority of Aristotle). See Boccaccio's earlier distinction between two kinds of wrath in the gloss to the *Teseida* referred to in Ch. ii, n. 132, below. In short, if the narrator's hatred is of this second kind, Cassell's entire argument falls to the ground. And it would seem at least likely that the kind of hatred which Boccaccio has in mind is not only the "righteous indignation" of Aristotle, the Bible, and St.

Thomas, but also the specific remedy for carnal love referred to in the fourth chapter of Arnaldus of Villanova's tractate *De amore heroico* (pp. 1523–30 in the Basel, 1585 printing of his *Opera omnia*), where love's melancholy—in which state lovers incur the danger of dying—is said to be cured by removing the lover's hope of having his beloved. Such negative thoughts are described as having the effect of "ducentium rem disideratam in odium." For Arnaldus's definition of passionate love, see chapter 2, n. 83. And for a view of the *Corbaccio* that is similar to Cassell's in that its author holds that the satire turns back upon itself, see J. P. Barricelli, "Satire of Satire: Boccaccio's *Corbaccio*," *Italian Quarterly*, 18, No. 72 (1975), 95–111. The most scholarly recent treatment of the *Corbaccio* is by F. Bruni, "Dal 'De vetula' al 'Corbaccio': l'idea d'amore e i due tempi dell' intellettuale," *Medioevo romanzo*, 1 (1974), 161–216. I confess that I am not convinced by the author's main point, the direct dependence of the *Corbaccio* on the pseudo-Ovidian *De vetula*, but the article represents a considerable and helpful review of the scholarly problems which surround the text.

48. See Nurmela, pp. 7–15, 190–93, for a review of interpretations of the work and bibliography.

49. Lopriore, p. 484, considers the work aberrant from Boccaccio's usual championing of love, citing Petrarch's *Fam.* XVIII. 15, of 20 December 1355, as evidence that the work was written in Boccaccio's "periodo di turbamento e scoramento," and reveals "il fanatismo d'un neo-convertito." This view is similar to that expressed by Nurmela, p. 9: ". . . il libro costuisce la prova d'un orientamento culturale, morale e religioso radicalmente diverso da quello che aveva ispirato tutte le opere volgari precedenti del poeta." For a discussion of Boccaccio's "conversion," see my Conclusion.

50. This three-page interlude mediates between the opening "proemio" and the ensuing dream vision. In Nurmela's numeration the passage runs from 6 to 53.

51. One should probably think of Dante's definition of love, itself probably largely derived from Cavalcanti's more philosophically complex definition in "Donna me prega": "Donna me prega, perch'eo voglio dire/d'un accidente che sovente è fero/ed è sì altero ch'è chiamato amore. . . ." Dante's "Amore non è per sé sì come sustanzia, ma è uno accidente in sustanzia" (*Vita Nuova* XXV. 1) is, like Guido's, Aristotelian enough in phraseology, but seems more directed to questions of poetic license than to philosophico-moral issues.

Dino del Garbo's commentary, ed. G. Favati, in Guido Cavalcanti, *Rime* (Milano-Napoli, 1957), 359–78, sounds very much like a source of Boccaccio's words here. Dino characterizes "Donna me prega" as "ista cantilena, que tractat de amoris passione . . ." (p. 359), and begins his comment on Guido's definition of love: "Dicitur autem hec passio accidens, primo quia non est substantia per se stans, sed est alteri adherens sicut subiecto, ut appetitus anime, simili modo sicut anime passiones, que sunt ira, tristitia, timor et similia" (p. 360). See discussion of Dino in the following chapter.

52. The narrator's situation seems likely to offer a burlesque of the endless and sometimes suicidal sufferings of the Fiammetta of the *Elegia*.

53. That he has chosen hanging, as the text will later make explicit, perhaps reflects upon that Florentine mode of suicide as it is recorded in *Inferno* XIII; Boccaccio's own commentary on Dante's refusal to name the nameless suicide described therein concludes with the following harsh words: "o vero, per ciò che in que' tempi, quasi come una maladizione mandata da Dio, nella città nostra più se ne impiccarono, acciò che ciascun possa aporlo a qual più gli piace di que' molti" (*Esposizioni, Inf.* XIII, *esp. litt.,* 113). The sin that the narrator was preparing himself to commit is not one that Boccaccio took lightly. It seems difficult to believe that he felt less scorn for Troiolo, Fiammetta, and the other suicidal heroes and heroines of the earlier works.

54. For the phraseology, at least, see Dante's "battaglia de li diversi pensieri," *Vita Nuova* XIV. 1.

55. See the *guida*'s later denunciation of carnal love: "Vedere adunque dovevi amore essere una passione accecatrice dell' animo, . . . vizio delle menti non sane e sommergitrice dell' umana libertà" (193). This love is consistently seen, in images suggested, perhaps, by Dante's phrase, "questo cieco carcere" (*Inf.* X.58–59—the phrase is quoted at 102), as a prison, precisely as entailing the loss of human freedom. And the *guida*'s final point, at the end of the *trattato,* will be that the only possible definition of *gentilezza* depends upon the proper use of the subject's free will.

56. Boethius' *pi* and *theta,* or practical and theological philosophy, are dressed out in a three-part outfit as a condescension to late medieval tastes—Aristotelian natural science had to be included as one of her "skirts."

57. In this "situational frame" the adverb *quasi* occurs several times. It is dramatically necessary, for had the narrator been completely cured by the

"thought" or by his friends, there would have been no catharsis left for the dream vision to accomplish.

58. See n. 7, above.

59. See esp. v.8; vii.10.

60. See A. Gaspary, *Storia della letteratura italiana,* tr. V. Rossi, 2nd., ii (Torino, 1900), 28, where the author refers to "codesto Virgilio boccaccesco."

61. The similarities to elements in the *Amorosa Visione* are fairly evident. Compared with that earlier lascivious dreamer, this one is quicker to understand the falseness of the pleasures that at first seem so seductive. That is, the dream itself presents them as being the opposite of what they at first seem. One may think of the *Corbaccio* as presenting a sort of gloss to the pleasanter versions of the pleasures of lust we find in the earlier works.

62. The formulaic *mi parea* + verb of sentience appears here again. See n. 7, above. And see such other uses here as "Allora mi parve che io dicessi" (90).

63. The color of the garment might well remind us of the vermilion cloth worn by the "reborn" animals in the triumph of Venus during the seventeenth canto of the *Caccia* (see n. 32, above). Playing here with Dante's sense of God's superior art (see esp. *Purg.* x), Boccaccio will later have the guide say that his robe "non è panno manualmente tessuto, anzi è un fuoco dalla divina arte composto" (104). In Purgatorio he is cooked in this garment as retribution for his two sins: his love of money and the way in which he accepted his wife's outrageous behavior. Thus, it might be argued, the vermilion is God's color scheme for him in that it corrects with heavenly charity his earlier misdirected appetites.

64. "me . . . per lo mio proprio nome chiamando" (73). This, and a few subsequent details (that the narrator is a *studioso,* one who hated the merchant life, loves philosophy, etc.) remind us of Boccaccio's closeness to his character.

65. *Aen.* vi.126, is redone as follows: "quantunque l'entrare in questo luogo sia apertissimo a chi vuole e entricisi con lascivia e con mattezza, egli non è così agevole il riuscirne . . ." (89).

66. Nor is "Venus's pigsty." The goddess's name makes this sole and unsavory appearance in the *Corbaccio.* But is she really any different in nature and function from the triumphant goddess at the close of the *Caccia?* Are not all those gamboling youths and maidens also in "il porcile di Venere"?

67. See the concluding line of the *Caccia:* "da cui ancora spero aver salute," in which the narrator hopes for the fulfillment of his sexual desires.

68. The narrator of the *Caccia* worries about these (XVIII.46–48), for whom he will pray as he will for true lovers.

69. It is worth anticipating my later discussion of Boccaccio's narrators to point out here what a poor intelligence our narrator possesses. Yet we are in his hands, in this as well as in the other vernacular fictions. In this one, more than in any other, he is raised from *stoltezza* to knowledge—that indeed is the main subject of the work.

70. "Assai bene conosco che ancora il raggio della vera luce non è pervenuto al tuo intelletto, e che tu quella cosa la quale è infima miseria, come molti stolti fanno, estimi somma felicità, credendo che nel vostro concupiscibile e carnale amore sia alcuna parte di bene; e per ciò apri gli orecchi a quello che io ora ti dirò. Questa misera valle è quella corte che tu chiami 'd'Amore' e quelle bestie che tu di' che udite hai e odi mugghiare sono i miseri, de' quali tu se' uno, dal fallace amore inretiti. Le boci de' quali, in quanto di cosí fatto amore favellino, niuno altro suono hanno negli orecchi de' discreti e ben disposti uomini che quello che mostra che pervenga alle tue; e però dianzi la chiamai laberinto, perché così in essa gli uomini, come in quello già faceano senze saperne mai riuscire, s'avviluppano" (123–25). The passage is clearly in the commentator's style, one in which Boccaccio was thoroughly at home. Since we have his own commentary on the *Teseida,* and either his own or a possible refraction of his own on the *Elegia di madonna Fiammetta* (both of these documents are discussed in chapter 2), we can sense here his desire to include a sort of *commento* in the body of the *Corbaccio* itself.

71. See Boccaccio's description in the *Genealogie deorum gentilium libri,* ed. V. Romano (Bari, 1951), IX, iv (94d), which derives, he says, from Servius: "Etate puerum, nudum, et alatum, et accinctum pharetra, arcum saggitasque gestantem." Three pages later (95b) he will add: "Oculos vero illi fascia tegunt, ut advertamus amantes ignorare quo tendant, nulla eorum esse iudicia, nulle rerum distinctiones, sed sola passione duci."

72. One of the medieval misogynist pieces that Boccaccio may have known is the *Proverbia que dicuntur super natura feminarum,* ed. A. Tobler, *Zeitschrift für romanische Philologie,* 9 (1885), 287–331. Among possible classical sources V. Cian, *La satira* (Milano, 1945), p. 218, draws a parallel between Juvenal's *Satires,* VI, and the *Corbaccio.* See also A. K. Cassell, "*Il Corbaccio* and the Secundus Tradition," *Comparative Literature,* 25 (1973), 352–63, for another misogynist source.

73. Lopriore's argument that the *Corbaccio* only attacks *femmine* and not *donne* (see n. 47, above) probably misses Boccaccio's point. The earlier *donne* (e.g., Criseida, Fiammetta) behave, after all, only like *femmine.* The good women in Boccaccio are those who spurn the religion of love—often having begun their amorous careers by honoring it (e.g., Biancifiore, Emilia).

74. It should be noted that no other fiction of Boccaccio so often praises the Virgin. See the anonymous "Risposta alle censure fatte sopra il Boccaccio dal maestro del sacro palazzo ed alcuni prelati di Roma," *Letture di Famiglia* (March 1859), Appendice, p. 12, where the *Corbaccio* is singled out among Boccaccio's works for its praise of the Virgin. The piece dates from 1571, according to its editor, Pietro Fanfani, and was almost certainly composed by Vincenzo Borghini on behalf of himself and three other members (Antonio Benivieni, Agnolo Guicciardini, Bastiano Antinori) of the Accademia della Crusca.

75. If there is a single word in the vocabulary of Boccaccio's *opere minori in volgare* that expresses what one loses by falling in love it is *libertà.* And see the second paragraph of the *proemio* of the *Decameron,* where the narrator, now free from love's toils, is "libero."

76. Here I anticipate the discussion of the "unwitting narrator" in my fourth chapter, where I shall return to this trope.

77. *Restauri boccacceschi* (Roma, 1945), pp. 161–62: The *Corbaccio* is "l'inevitabile, conclusivo *Adversus amorem.* Così—più che l'impegno del primo maestro di correggere l'*Ars amandi* coi *Remedia amoris*—Andrea Cappellano, dopo le esaltazioni e i precetti e la noia di sofisticare in una catena di coscienti paralogisimi religiose sanatorie che fornissero l'indipensabile dignità culturale alla disputa, lascia gemere nel *De amore* la frattura della sconcordanza finale : colle improvvise, secche negazioni dell'ultimo libro: *E quibus rationibus amor reprobetur, De vitiis mulierum, De amoris militia recusanda;* e Bon-

compagno come *explicit* della *Rota Veneris* offriva scuse e lamenti." To which, in a footnote, Billanovich collates Boccaccio's own "scuse senili" in *Episola* XXI (to Mainardo Cavalcanti).

78. "Mondo aristocratico e mondo comunale nell'ideologia e nell'arte di Giovanni Boccaccio," *Studi sul Boccaccio,* 2 (1964), 199: "Nella composizione del *Corbaccio* agì certo la suggestione del τόπος dei *Remedia Amoris* (Ovidio ed Andrea Capellano): e tuttavia non può sfuggire come essa rompa decisamente con tutta la tradizione accolta dal Boccaccio nelle opere precedenti: ché quella corte d'Amore, che egli tanto aveva sempre esaltato e della quale si sentiva a giusto titolo cortigiano, gli si rivela ora essere 'misera valle,' piena di dolori e di brutture; e mentre vanno infittendosi i richiami a Dio, alla Vergine, al credo religioso e al mondo dell'al di là, si proclama la fallacia dell'amore rispetto alla 'vera luce' della religione." A few pages farther on Padoan will refer to "questo nuovo atteggiamento moralistico" of Boccaccio (p. 203).

79. A. Tripet, "Boccace et son clerc amoureux," *Bibliothèque d'humanisme et renaissance,* 19 (1967), 18–21, sees the influence of Petrarch's "conversion" of Boccaccio in the *Corbaccio.* I shall return to the problem of Boccaccio's "crisis" in the Conclusion of this study.

80. Which indeed Boccaccio had become, at the latest in 1360. See G. Billanovich, "Il chierico Giovanni Boccaccio," *Atti dell'Istituto Veneto,* 103, parte 2ª (1944), 1–12, reprinted in *Restauri boccacceschi,* pp. 165–80. Padoan, among recent critics, has offered the most interesting discussion of Boccaccio's religious "crisi"—see "Mondo aristocratico e mondo comunale . . . ," pp. 187–203. He is especially convincing when he discusses (pp. 188–90) the darkening of the cultural world of northern Italy after the great plague of 1348 and the resultant increase in religious mysticism, which he does along the lines set down by Millard Meiss, *Painting in Florence and Siena after the Black Death* (Princeton, 1951). See also V. Branca, "Profilo biografico," pp. 119–20.

81. See Nurmela, in his edition, p. 9: ". . . il libro costuisce la prova d'un orientamento culturale, morale e religioso radicalmente diverso da quello che aveva ispirato tutte le opere volgari precedenti del poeta."

2. Christian Romance and Pagan Delusion

1. Without wishing to cloud the issue, I should say here that what I mean by irony was understood by such medieval authorities as Isidore of Seville as the basic definition of allegory: "Allegoria est alieniloquium, aliud enim sonat, aliud intelligitur" (*Etym.*, I, xxxvii, 22—Isidore goes on to define irony itself, one of the seven kinds of "otherspeech" subsumed under *allegoria,* as "sententia per pronuntiationem contrarium habens intellectum"). In a modern but similar vein, see the Funk and Wagnalls definition of irony (New York and London, 1946): "The use of words to signify the opposite of what they would usually express; ridicule under cover of praise or compliment; covert sarcasm or satire." That will do very nicely as a simple and inclusive statement of what I intend to discuss if we include some sense of the particular mechanism by which irony becomes most notable and effective in Boccaccio (as well as in many other writers): the separation of the author from his characters. For a study which draws attention to the relatedness of irony and allegory, see W. J. Kennedy, "Irony, Allegoresis, and Allegory in Virgil, Ovid, and Dante," *Arcadia,* 7 (1972), 115–34. And for the necessarily related topic of parody in medieval texts see J. H. Martin, *Love's Fools: Aucassin, Troilus, Calisto and the Parody of the Courtly Lover* (London, 1972), esp. pp. 13–16, which also offer bibliographical indications.

2. The modern discussion of the work probably begins with F. Novati, "Sulla composizione del *Filocolo,*" *Giornale di filologia romanza,* 3 (1880), 56–67, who points out contradictions in the treatment offered by B. Zumbini, *Il Filocopo del Boccaccio* (Firenze, 1879).

3. The task of Boccaccio's present and future students has been greatly softened by the *apparata* now available to them in the various volumes of the Mondadori edition, all of which contain carefully prepared indices. A. E. Quaglio's entry for "Venus" is the source of this number.

4. N. J. Perella, "The World of Boccaccio's *Filocolo,*" *PMLA,* 76 (1961), 330–39, presents a typical "modern" reading of the text—as he himself perhaps unwittingly admits. Speaking of the "irrelevant material" in the work, he indicates "the mythological figures that people the book. The role the gods are made to play is, *for the modern reader,* the most annoying feature of all, for too often these gods become the principal actors and ruling agents of a world which for all its fable-like elements is studded with a psychological realism that immediately distinguishes Boccaccio from his predeces-

sors" (pp. 330–31—italics added). A number of Perella's judgments are worth having here, for they are nearly polar to my own and help establish a context—if a negative one—for my interpretation of the work. E.g., although he notes in passing the Christian nature of the fifth book ("To be sure, there is in the end a general conversion to Christianity so as to put things right"—p. 331), his view of the work makes its Christian elements altogether superfluous: "A universe ruled by pagan deities offers Boccaccio a subterfuge which allows for the representation of a vision of life that is at bottom incompatible with Christianity, although it is not without its own high ethics. Boccaccio's way of circumventing a moral conflict of which he was himself free, but to which he could not be blind, was to exclude Christ from his world" (p. 331). That judgment would be incorrect even if Christ were not explicitly included in the work, but of course He is (e.g., I, 1, 15–17; V, 52, 2: "in una parte videro effigiata di colui la figura che fu dell'universo salute," etc.). In a similar vein Perella adds: "Boccaccio's 'paganism,' if we are to call it that, is more modern and complex; it is the paganism or 'heresy' that has come to be called courtly love" (p. 334). And there is the following observation, which is precisely as my own, or would be with the pivotal change of the mode of its third verb from conditional to indicative: "Biancofiore literally idolizes Florio, and, like him, falls into what would be blasphemy under a Christian sky" (p. 334). For this last, see the remark of J. C. L. Simonde de Sismondi, *De la littérature du midi de l'Europe* (Bruxelles, 1837), I, 276, regarding the mixture of two religions found in the *Filocolo* and the *Fiammetta:* "sa religion poétique est bien étrange, et paraît aujourd'hui une profanation." Even if Simonde de Sismondi felt in 1837 that the sky above *him* was a Christian one, he too failed to come to grips with the religious symbolism of the *Filocolo,* which has escaped almost all readers of the work.

5. Given the character of the *Filocolo* it is not surprising that the majority of its critics have wished to deal with the still vexed question of its sources. And a second consuming effort has been to sift through the work in order to find a residue of "biographical" information about its author. The major literary consideration has involved the relationship of the thirteen "questioni d'amore" to the later *Decameron.* For bibliography, see, as always, the "bibliografia essenziale" in the Mondadori edition (in this case, *Opere,* I, 710–12). And here we might pause to admire the enormous labor of A. E. Quaglio, who has edited and annotated the *Filocolo* brilliantly, echoing the judgment of P. V. Mengaldo (himself one of Italy's most brilliant philologists) of Quaglio's previous edition of the *Comedia ninfe:* "Alla fine, va ribadita la per-

suasione che questa edizione sia uno dei prodotti più maturi e rigorosi della nuova filologia italiana, da allinearsi ai modelli sicuri di metodologia in atto della critica testuale"—*GSLI,* 141 (1964), 418.

6. But for consideration of Amore in the frame of the *Filocolo,* see my Ch. iv, below, nn. 10 and 22.

7. Quaglio, *Opere,* I, 752, points to Boccaccio's gloss on *Inf.* XV.55, which takes up the importance of the ascendant according to the astrologers. For the scientific *esoterica* of the *Filocolo,* see Quaglio's *Scienza e mito nel Boccaccio* (Padova, 1967). For a study of the medieval valence of astral phenomena in another author, see Chauncey Wood, *Chaucer's Country of the Stars* (Princeton, 1970).

8. See I, 39, 1, and Quaglio's note. It is not clear whether Boccaccio continues the tradition of the OF text that the lovers were born on Palm Sunday ("Pasqua fiorita") or that of the Italian *Cantare di Fiorio e Biancifiore* which has them born on Pentecost ("Pasqua rosata"), although the former possibility is the more likely one.

9. See Boccaccio's discussion of Ovid's banishment by Augustus in *Esposizioni sopra la Comedia di Dante, Inf.* IV, *esp. litt.*, 124 (*Opere,* VI, 201), where one of his "duo crimina, carmen et error" (*Tristia,* II, 207) is described as follows: "La seconda cagione dice che fu l'avere composto il libro *De arte amandi,* il quale pareva molto dover adoperare contro a' buoni costumi de' giovani e delle donne di Roma. E di questo nel detto libro si duol molto e quanto può s'ingegna di mostrare peccato non aver meritata quella pena." See A. Monteverdi, "Un libro di Ovidio e un passo del 'Filocolo,' " in *Studia philologica et litteraria in honorem L. Spitzer,* ed. A. G. Hatcher and K. L. Selig (Bern, 1958), p. 336, where this passage and the intervention of the goddess and her son which follows are described: "*Santi* i versi, *divota* la lettura; e c'è la consapevolezza della virtù che i versi letti hanno esercitato sulle menti. Biancofiore smentisce il Boccaccio; o piuttosto, è il Boccaccio-poeta che smentisce il Boccaccio-letterato, e rende inutile con quel mirabile dialogo la pedentesca invenzione dell'intervento di Cupido." The reading is Romantic and hostile to Boccaccio. See discussion of Boccaccio's sense of Ovid at the conclusion of chapter 4, below.

10. I, 1, 3; and see Quaglio's thoroughly explicative note, *Opere,* I, 754.

11. The parody of Dante is uproarious. Observe merely the following: ". . . incontanente chiusi i libri, *abbracciandosi si porgeano semplici baci, ma più avanti non procedeano. . . .*" (II, 4, 7). Here Is Francesca: ". . . *la bocca mi basciò tutto tremante.*/ Galeotto fu 'l libro e chi lo scrisse:/ quel giorno *più non vi leggemmo avante*" (*Inf.* V.136–38, italics added). The effect is something like what one would experience watching a kindergarten version of *Inferno* V. Boccaccio's great love of Dante did not stand in the way of parody.

12. II, 76, 3. In the preceding narrative Florio and Ascalion, if only tacitly, do not make the same omission. Florio makes offerings to Mars and Venus (75, 1–2), and then leaves unvisited no other temple ("niuno altro in Montoro ne rimase che da lui visitato non fosse, e onorato con degni sacrifici"—75, 6).

13. Qauglio's note, *Opere,* I, 815, clearly sets forth Boccaccio's transmutation of *Metamorphoses* II.760ff., Minerva and Invidia there becoming Diana and Gelosia here. Gelosia appears in this scene only, but her effect on Florio works for some time, animating the conflict of the Fileno subplot.

14. Hymen, mentioned in I, 5, 3, recurs only now, in these two passages (III, 46, 5; 51, 7). His climactic appearance awaits us in Book IV.

15. That Biancifiore has learned her lesson is demonstrated by the invocations that occur in her prayer in III, 58, 2: "O Citerea, o Diana. . . ." Her earlier invocations tended to be addressed to Venus alone, and never explicitly included Diana. G. Di Pino, *La polemica del Boccaccio* (Firenze, 1953), is among the few to note the importance of Biancifiore's failure to offer sacrifice to Diana at the end of Book II. However, he insists that the conciliation of Diana and Venus does not "work" in the text: ". . . non è una reale conciliazione dei termini; è solo una pacificazione esterna delle linee del racconto, un adattamento escogitato con pregiudizio dello stesso simbolo di Diana" (pp. 75–76). His argument continues, "Diana rimane simbolo. Un simbolo inconciliabile: si chiamerà ancora Diana nel *Ninfale Fiesolano;* si chiamerà convenzione sociale nel *Decameron.* Voce che inquieta non più un altro simbolo, ma l'ansia stessa—e la poesia—dell'umano ardimento. Perché il prevalere dell'amore sulla castità non significa il trionfo del senso. È il trionfo di un principio attivo e drammatico contro la tiepidezza e la rinuncia. Diana e Venere hanno lungamente simboleggiato nell'arte del Boccaccio, fino alla risoluzione dell'*Ameto,* propriamente queste due disposizioni dello spirito umano" (p. 77). His remarks serve to illustrate again the way in which the

texts of the *opere minori in volgare* are forced to fit preconceptions of their meanings. Venus, and even Diana, is a far more complex and changing figure in Boccaccio's fictions than Di Pino realizes, and the significances he attributes to the two goddesses seem to derive from modern psychological instincts rather than from medieval or renaissance mythography.

16. He derives his name from the "Greek" *philos* and *colon* (="amore" and "fatica"), saying that it means "fatica d'amore," and thus yielding a further sense of his own identification with Hercules. See the article by Janet Smarr in *MLN,* 92 (1977), 146–52, concerning the importance of the choice of Hercules to Boccaccio.

17. E.g., Venus's advice, given in dream to Florio (II, 42, 7–23), which urges him to make sacrifice to Mars and to herself.

18. The transmogrifications of this lady await discussion in chapter 4, below.

19. "Reckoning with Boccaccio's *questioni d'amore,*" *MLN,* 89 (1974), 47–59.

20. See chapter 4, nn. 8 and 79.

21. For a typical description of the atmosphere of Boccaccio's scenes that involve discussions of love, see S. Battaglia, "Schemi lirici dell'arte del Boccaccio," *Archivum Romanicum,* 19 (1935), 67: ". . . è una condizione che oscilla fra il vago 'incantamento' dei poeti stilnovisti che amavano obliarsi a 'ragionar sempre d'amore,' e una certa insinuante amabilità da salotto." What is lacking in such treatments of the "questioni d'amore" is cognizance of the fact that Fiammetta *opposes* the values of the "court of love" with better moral principles. Even so astute a reader as Quaglio, in his note to the passage in which Pola brushes aside Fiammetta's objections (*Opere,* I, 876), characterizes Fiammetta's remarks as an "ostacolo" which is surmounted by Pola's rejoinder: "Però al presente lasciando con vostro piacere la vostra sentenza, terrò che licito sia l'innamorarsi, prendendo il mal fare per debito adoperare" (IV, 47, 2). It should be added that Quaglio's notes constitute one of the very few sources of intelligent criticism of the *Filocolo.* Fiammetta's "sermon" is, as Kirkham has shown, the center of the "questioni," both numerically (seventh of thirteen) and morally. Most of Boccaccio's readers, like the twelve other members of the "court of love," like lust (or

what they take to be Boccaccio's praise of it) so much that they tend to make it licit.

22. "Reckoning with Boccaccio's *questioni d'amore,*" p. 53. I have refrained from treating Fileno's long outburst against Venus and her son in III, 34–35, because Kirkham has—correctly, it seems to me—discussed that digression as a kind of anticipation of Fiammetta's "sermon" (pp. 57–58).

23. *Opere,* I, 872. He points out that the tripartite definition is similar to Dante's in *De vulgari eloquentia,* II, ii, 8, and is repeated by Boccaccio in the *Amorosa Visione* XXXVIII.40–88, and in the *Esposizioni* of *Inferno* V.100 (*Opere,* VI, 318). In the commentary to Francesca's "Amor, ch'al cor gentil . . . ," Boccaccio is not taken in—the love of which Francesca speaks is not *amore onesto* (or *amore utile*), but *amore dilettevole;* he continues, "Dico che questo Cupidine, o Amore che noi vogliam dire, è una passion di mente delle cose esteriori. . . ." In short, Boccaccio's treatment of lust in Dante's *Inferno* is roughly, indeed almost precisely, the same as Fiammetta's treatment of it here. The formulation is also found in the *Genealogie,* where Apuleius's *De dogmate Platonis* is given as a source (I, XV—18b): there are three kinds of love, "Quorum primum dixit esse divinum. . . . Alterum degeneris animi corrupteque voluntatis passionem. Tertium ex utroque permixtum." The following sentence gives Aristotle as source and combines Apuleius's three terms with the more usual "*honestum . . . dilectabile . . . utile.*" And see Mario Equicola d'Alveto, *Di natura d'Amore* (Venezia, 1587), p. 23[v], on Fiammetta's distinctions among different kinds of love in the *Filocolo:* ". . . la prima è d'Amore honesto, il quale debbiamo seguire; l'altra d'Amore vtile, che si può chiamare odio; & la terza d'Amor diletteuole, il quale maggiormente priua d'honore, adduce affanni, desta i vitij. . . ."

24. "Elli è guastatore di molti beni: e più tosto, ragionevolmente parlando, si dovria chiamare odio che amore" (IV, 44, 7). It is a little surprising that the close parallelism between this passage and the corresponding *locus* in the *Genealogie* has apparently gone unnoticed. Discussing these same three kinds of love, now with their Aristotelian provenance made patent, Boccaccio concludes with the following indictment of the lower form of *amore:* "Eum igitur rite pensatis omnibus non amorem, quin imo odium rectius vocaremus" (I, 15–18b). The later phrase is not much more than a Latin translation of Boccaccio's earlier sentiment.

25. "Ma però che alla proposta quistione né del primo né dell'ultimo è bisogno di parlare, del secondo diremo, cioè amore per diletto: al quale,

veramente, niuno, che virtuosa vita disideri di seguire, si dovria sommettere, però che egli è d'onore privatore, adducitore d'affanni, destatore di vizii, copioso donatore di vane sollecitudini, indegno occupatore dell'altrui libertà, più ch'altra cosa da tenere cara. Chi, dunque, per bene di sé, se sarà savio, non fuggirà tale signore? Viva chi può libero, seguendo quelle cose che in ogni atto aumentano libertà, e lascinsi i viziosi signori a' viziosi vassalli seguire." The vituperation of the last sentence sounds remarkably like that so frequently expressed in the *Corbaccio*. There carnal love is seen precisely as a loss of liberty and is even discussed in rather theological language as the loss of free will. In sum, it is practically impossible to find a difference in the message (or in the vehemence of the message) between these two texts. The difference exists in what surrounds them. In the *Corbaccio* carnal lovers are *posti in bando;* in the *Filocolo* they literally surround the speaker and recede to the limits of the work, which is itself narrated (unlike the *Corbaccio*) by a carnal lover.

26. Despite her moralizing and Christian view of love, Fiammetta is evidently one who lives in its toils. The difference between her and the other servants of Amore in the *Filocolo* is that she longs to be free and struggles against her subjection. If this is a correct characterization, it conceivably sheds some light on Boccaccio's own situation. We have reason to believe, for instance, that he was the sire of at least five illegitimate children (see Billanovich, *Restauri boccacceschi,* p. 183; Branca, "Profilo biografico," p. 78 and n.). It is clear that such were not the result of moralizing and Christian behavior. I am not arguing in this study that Boccaccio's life was not *improba,* but that, like those of his predecessors in Latin satire, his pages do not reflect his personal improprieties in any but corrective ways. The Fiammetta of the "questioni d'amore" may, in this respect, be taken as a moral self-portrait.

27. See the discussion of Boccaccio's view of Orpheus in chapter 4.

28. An expression of what can only be called the typical view of Boccaccio's own adherence to this "religion" is found in Luigi Malagoli, "Timbro della prosa e motivi dell'arte del Boccaccio nel *Filocolo,*" *Studi mediolatini e volgari,* 6–7 (1959), 109–11: "È un concetto che egli deriva della più ortodossa tradizione medievale: l'Amore è in alto, una forza superiore che regge la vita degli uomini, una divinità sempre presente." The judgment is repeated *verbatim* in Malagoli's *Decameron e primo Boccaccio,* 2nd ed. (Pisa, 1963), p. 76. The better reading is probably to see that the *signoria d'Amore* in Boccaccio represents the antithesis of heavenly love, not its complement.

29. See Quaglio's note to this passage, *Opere,* I, 875–76: " 'Quella luce' è ovviamente Venere, che simboleggia il Dio e l'amore cristiano, . . ." (p. 876). Both Boccaccio and Quaglio seem to be confused here. The passage which Boccaccio probably has in mind is *Aen.* II.590–92, where his goddess mother appears to Aeneas *in order to prevent his slaying of Helen.* Quaglio correctly points out that in *Comedia ninfe* XXI.14, Boccaccio refers to the heavenly omens sent down by Jove (the harmless flame around Iulus's head and ensuing confirmation of Anchises' prayer in the form of a meteor—*Aen.* II.680–94). But here again Boccaccio has garbled his Virgil, since it is *not* Venus who appears to Anchises. In the *Comedia ninfe* he would seem to have conflated the two Virgilian passages. In our passage in the *Filocolo,* on the other hand, he would seem to have only the first of them in mind, but to have misremembered its context. What is most striking, regardless of the incorrect nature of the Virgilian reminiscence, is the antagonistic relationship between Venus and Cupid that is necessary to the significance of the passage.

30. Fiammetta's response to Caleon culminates in an attack on Amore: "Questi ancora, chiamandosi e faccendosi chiamare iddio, le ragioni degli iddii occupa[="usurpa le prerogative divine"—Quaglio, p. 875]. Chi porria mai con parole le iniquità di costui narrare appieno? Egli, brievemente, ad ogni male mena chi 'l segue" (IV, 46, 15–16); she concludes: "convienci, poi[che] nelle sue reti siamo incappati, seguire la sua vita, infino a tanto che quella luce, la quale trasse Enea de' tenebrosi passi, fuggendo i pericolosi incendii, apparisca a noi, e tirici a' suoi piaceri" (IV, 46, 20).

31. For the blind Cupid see *Corbaccio,* 198. And see Erwin Panofsky, *Studies in Iconology* (New York, 1967), pp. 95–128, "Blind Cupid," a chapter which deals at length with this tradition.

32. E.g., Perella's *PMLA* article, p. 334n.: "Another unforgettable page on this theme [the delights of carnal love] is the scene of the consummation of the protagonists' love in Biancofiore's room at the top of the tower of Alexandria." That the page is more forgettable than it seems to Perella is clear enough, for their love is not there described as having been consummated. Perella, it should be pointed out, is far from being alone in misconstruing the letter of this text.

33. The situation is somewhat similar to Shakespeare's rustic treatment of the intended "marriage" of Florizel and Perdita in Act IV of *The Winter's Tale.* Their proposed sylvan wedding (which is not allowed to be completed) will later be given true status at court, as will that of Florio and Biancifiore.

34. E.g., at II, 48, 16, and III, 53, 3, she was nude, wrapped in a purple veil. See discussion of her colors, chapter 3, n. 71.

35. First in "Idalogos," *Zeitschrift für romanische Philologie,* 9 (1885), 437–79; 10 (1886), 1–21; then in *Contributo agli studi sul Boccaccio* (Torino, 1887), esp. pp. 70–85, and see also pp. 45–70.

36. The language repeats the feeling and some of the words of Cato in *Purgatorio* II: "Correte al monte a spogliarvi lo scoglio/ch'*esser non lascia a voi Dio manifesto*" (ll. 122–23); "Venga il vivo fonte che dalle preterite ordure, nelle quali come ciechi dietro a cieco duca siamo caduti, ci lavi, e *facciaci Iddio essere manifesto*" (V, 60, 3—italics added).

37. The last time that Jove, Juno, Hymen, Venus, Mars, or any of their co-divinities are mentioned favorably is in Filocolo's pre-conversion (and nearly Christian) prayer of thanksgiving in V, 34, 2–4. Amore, however, will reappear in the penultimate word of the text, about which phenomenon there will be something to say at the appropriate juncture. Otherwise the names of the pagan deities remain in the text only as the names of the planets—e.g., V, 95, 1.

38. At V, 96, 3, we learn that the whole romance was "in fact" written by the monk Ilario in Greek. The literary joke will be familiar to all admirers of Cide Hamete Benengeli, the putative author of *Don Quixote.* It also has the effect of reminding us that the *Filocolo* is precisely such a tale as a Christian monk might have written, had monks written tales. For a curious recognition of some of the Christian elements in the *Filocolo,* see O. H. Moore, "Boccaccio's *Filocolo* and the Annunciation," *MLN,* 33 (1918), 438–40, which identifies the dependence of certain formulations in Lelio's prayer to Jove for a son (I, 5, 9–11) on Luke 1:12–15. However, Moore draws back from recognizing that the *Filocolo* has anything to do with Christianity: "In every case, it should be remembered, the Scriptural allusion is dragged into the romance by Boccaccio without any artistic justification whatever" (p. 439). Here we have another telling example of the determination of readers of the *Filocolo* to avoid the intention of the text, even when the evidence points clearly in the direction of that intention.

39. One is reminded of Vittore Branca's view of the (far briefer) conclusion of the *Caccia di Diana,* which he characterizes as "una gratuita puntata finale, un espediente esterno per concludere" (*Opere,* I, "Profilo biografico," p. 59n.). Even for *this* conclusion, some 125 pages in length, the general at-

titude has been silent inattention. It is difficult to find a rational ground for such a reaction.

40. E.g., Idalogos's despite of women, Filocolo's stilling of the pains of love (for Fiammetta) in Caleon—to point to only two pieces of business in the fifth book.

41. Many readers have undoubtedly agreed with Gustav Koerting's estimate of the aesthetic "failings" of the work, *Boccaccio's Leben und Werke* (Leipzig, 1880), p. 500: "Ferner ist nicht in Abrede zu stellen, dass die wunderliche Mischung antiker and romantischer, heidnischer und christlicher Elemente, welche wir im 'Filocopo' finden, in dem Leser auch nicht entfernt das wohlthuende und befriedigende Gefühl von einer inneren Einheit des Dichtungswerkes aufkommen lässt, sondern dass im Gegentheile dadurch der unbehagliche Eindruck hervorgebracht wird, es mit einer bizarren und selbst grotesken, weil aus ganz disparaten Bestandtheilen sich zusammensetzenden, Geistesschöppfung zu thun zu haben."

42. See *Cervantes' Christian Romance: A Study of the Persiles* (Princeton, 1972).

43. Quaglio's notes to the *Filocolo,* which are the work of a master, are probably the best single source of critical insight into the work and are quick and reliable in their response to the Christian matter one finds therein. It is thus a bit disquieting to read his "Introduzione" to the text (*Opere,* I, 47–59) and find hardly a hint that the work might have any major Christian purpose.

44. The doubleness of Venus is not only a prominent feature of Boccaccio's mythography in the early works, but is clearly stated in the late works as well. See *Genealogie,* III, xxii: "De Venere magna VI[a] Celi filia" (where Venus is mainly treated as being planetary and marital), and III, xxiii: "De secunda Venere Celi VII[a] filia et matre Cupidinis" (where she is entirely licentious—"Et ex ea sola Cupidinem [natum volunt], nam pro Venere hac ego voluptuosam vitam intelligo . . ." (38c). For this second Venus, see also *Gen.,* XI, iv, "De Venere Iovis XI[a] filia, quae peperit Amorem," a passage that enlists the support of Augustine's *De civitate Dei* to heap blame upon carnal love. In the *Esposizioni* (*Inf.* V, *esp. all.,* 69–72), rehearsing the distinction already made in the *Genealogie* (III, xxii—37a), which refers to Homer's depiction of the marital Venus as wearing her *ceston,* Boccaccio again reflects the long tradition of the doubleness of Venus (incest, that is, all illicit love, derives from "incesto, cioè fatta senza questo '*ceston*' "—72):

when Venus appears without her *ceston* she encourages lascivious passion. And see *De mulieribus claris,* VII, "De Venere Cypriorum regina," for a savage attack on the carnal Venus and on those who worship her: "Et breviter omnes, tetra obfuscati caligine, quam sciebant a mortali femina editam, immortalem asserebant deam eamque infausti amoris, quem Cupidinem vocitabant, genitricem totis nisibus affirmabant; nec illi intercipiendi stultorum intuentium mentes variis gesticulationibus deerant artes" (VII, 4). Boccaccio will shortly add that it was Venus who "founded" prostitution (VII, 9—and see XLV, 6). For a discussion of later renaissance views of the two Venuses see ch. 5, "The Neoplatonic Movement in Florence and North Italy," of Erwin Panofsky's *Studies in Iconology* (New York, 1967), pp. 129–69. Such writers as Marsilio Ficino, returning to the original Platonic conceptions, make both Venuses beneficial, thus overturning the medieval tradition inherited by Boccaccio that sees the celestial and marital Venus as positive, the merely carnal Venus as negative. Without attempting in a footnote to construct a sorely needed history of the metamorphoses of Venus, I might suggest this much. There has generally existed an understandable tendency to associate three kinds of love with Venus: 1) a perfect intellectual love, having no physical component, 2) a positive sexual love, present in matrimony and resulting in the creation of offspring, 3) a negative sexual love, seeking mere sexual satisfaction, and having destructive and anti-social results. Since the basic literary (or painterly) tradition tends to polarize rather than to triangulate the aspects of Venus, a given writer (or painter) will formulate his particular double Venus from among these three basic possibilities. For Plato, later Platonists, and renaissance Neoplatonists, the tendency is to avoid the third aspect; their constructions will tend to make the celestial Venus represent perfect and intellectual love-knowledge, the earthly one a lower but necessary and praiseworthy form of procreation. Christianizing mythographers, on the other hand, tend to avoid the first aspect, seeing in the celestial Venus a metaphor of licit love, in the carnal one, despicable license. The matter is of great complexity and interest, and has never received the large and undeflected attention it so clearly calls for. But see R. H. Green, "Alan of Lille's *De planctu Naturae,*" *Speculum,* 31 (1956), 649–74, where there is a helpful discussion of the medieval tradition of the two Venuses as they are found in the work of Alain de Lille, Bernardus Silvester, Scotus Eriugena, and others. For a still more frontal approach to the topic, see G. D. Economou, "The Two Venuses and Courtly Love," in J. M. Ferrante and G. D. Economou, eds., *In Pursuit of Perfection: Courtly Love in Medieval Literature* (Port Washington, N.Y., and London, 1975), pp. 17–50, where there is discussion of the venereal formulations of Eriugena, Remigius of Auxerre, Albericus (the "Third Vatican Mythographer"), Bernardus, and Pierre Bersuire as these influenced such writers as Alain, Guillaume de Lorris and Jean de Meun, Chaucer, Chrétien, Wolfram, and Gottfried. In the same year, and still more to the point of this study, there appeared Earl G. Schreiber's brief but important attempt to offer systematic review of the changing medieval valences of Venus: "Venus in the Medieval Mythographic Tradition," *JEGP,* 74 (1975), 519–35. These two last items appeared after I had finished this book. Were this not the case, I would have made more detailed reference to them. For two brief recent discussions that also intersect with the concerns of this study, see D. W. Robertson, Jr., *A Preface to Chaucer* (Princeton, 1963), esp. pp. 124–27; Winthrop Wetherbee, *Platonism and Poetry in the Twelfth Century* (Princeton, 1972), esp. pp. 115–21. For one of the earliest literary references to the two Venuses, see Pausanias's speech in Plato's *Symposium.*

45. Among a plethora of classical allusions there is only a single biblical reference that is evident in the text—and it has to do with the questionable story of Susannah and the elders. See Daniel 13:50–60, referred to by Fiammetta at v, 28.

46. *Venus als Heilige und Furie in Boccaccios Fiammetta-Dichtung* (Krefeld, 1958). Pabst's work is extraordinarily rich and suggestive, and, while I disagree with a number of his particular findings (e.g., his tripartite goddess, Venus "als heilige Gottheit," "als Furie," and as the "santissima Venere" of the nurse [p. 19], probably adds a distinction to those of Boccaccio, whom I find taking Venus either as celestial [in the sense that she presides over matrimonial love] or as lascivious, while she is often praised as being celestial by the carnal-minded Fiammetta; that is, the carnal Venus is herself present in Fiammetta's consciousness *both* "als Heilige *und* Furie"), I am in strong agreement with his basic principle: "Nur wenn wir Venus und Tesiphone ernst nehmen, wenn wir sie als Illustration zu Boccaccios intensiver Auseinandersetzung mit der Schicksalsfrage auffassen, werden wir dem Sinn der Fiammetta-Dichtung näherkommen" (pp. 21–22). As we have seen in critical responses to, for instance, the *Filocolo,* most modern readers simply do not want to take Boccaccio's mythography seriously, mainly because it interferes with their belief that he is a "realist" or a "naturalist." What Pabst accomplished—though he has been paid little serious attention—was to put the *Elegia* back into its mythographic framework. Perhaps my main divergence from him is from the tendency in his argument which makes Fiammetta a victim rather than the agent of her own difficulties, e.g., "Venus ist in dieser Erzählung die eindeutige Verursacherin des Unheils" (pp. 14–15).

My view is that Boccaccio, like the Homer he did not yet know, tends to use the gods as "psychological manifestations" of the states of mind of his own characters. I hasten to add that this issue is a complex one. Pabst's study, in any case, which itself begins with an admirable review of previous critical responses to the *Elegia* (pp. 5–14), should have by now become the prolegomenon to any later study of the work. See also his *Venus und die missverstandene Dido* (Hamburg, 1955), esp. pp. 144–47.

47. Karl-Ludwig Selig, *Bibliothèque d'humanisme et renaissance,* XXI (1959), 253–54, is favorable to the study in a brief review. A. E. Quaglio reviewed it twice, in *GSLI,* 137 (1960), esp. pp. 435–36; and in *Lettere Italiane,* 12 (1960), 221–26. One is likely to agree with several of Quaglio's negative findings (to pass over some of the more niggling ones, his correct sense of Pabst's failure to relate the Venus of the *Elegia* to the Venus of the other works). However, if Pabst's conclusions may, to some, seem questionable, they are hardly to be dismissed as "eccentriche al problema dell'unità artistica dell'opera" (*GSLI,* p. 436). Nor is it easy to agree with the following: "In verità Venere, come gli altri dèi del Boccaccio, più entusiasta dilettante che ordinato sistematore della mitologia (e ciò suona, per un romanziere, come una dote) resta un elemento dotto e libresco dell'azione, non si fa mai personaggio" (ibid.). Here we enter the domain of such modern discussions of "character" in fiction as E. M. Forster's distinction between "round" and "flat" characters. It has very little to do with Boccaccio's likely sense of a "personaggio"—anyone, god or human, who performs actions in a fiction is likely to have been a "personaggio" to Boccaccio. His "dilettantism" in mythological matters (a questionable enough assertion: Boccaccio was good enough at the game to become, with the *Genealogie,* the *De casibus,* and the *De mulieribus claris,* the master mythographer of the renaissance), even if granted, does not remove the fact of Venus's crucial role in the work. One suspects that Quaglio chooses to disagree with Pabst because he does not wish to think of the *Elegia* as the kind of work Pabst's analysis tends to make it. At any rate, Pabst's study, with any and all its deficiencies, remains the most important attempt to break some new ground in interpretive studies of the work.

48. "La modernità della 'Fiammetta,' " *Convivium,* N. S. 1 (1947), 703–15. De Sanctis' influence here has been enormous. He is quoted (p. 705) as follows: "L'autore volge le spalle al Medioevo e inizia la letteratura moderna. Di un mondo mistico-teologico-scolastico non è piú alcun vestigio. Oramai tocchiamo terra: siamo in cospetto dell'uomo e della natura." The passage

has had wide currency and large effect. It was first printed in "Il Boccaccio e le sue opere minori," *Nuova Antologia,* 5 (1870), 243, and then in *Storia della letteratura italiana.* See the edition of N. Gallo (Torino, 1966), p. 345.

49. "Le 'fonti' autobiografiche nell' 'Elegia di Madonna Fiammetta,' " *Humanitas,* 3 (1948), 790–802. Here too Rastelli does not present his own position, but instead carefully demonstrates the bankruptcies of earlier ones, and cites Billanovich's *Restauri boccacceschi* (Roma, 1945) as the turning point in the history of "biographical" Boccaccio criticism. The sense in which he has wiped the slate clean and prepared the way for new and better understandings is graspable from the following: "Quindi il dire che egli attende all' *Elegia* per lasciare di sé un ricordo come poeta significa dire che egli la scrive per applicare in essa le regole medievali sul 'cursus,' sulle figure, sul tema amoroso come unico tema degno dell'arte, della canzone (aveva già ammonito Bernardo di Ventadorn), del poema, del romanzo, sull'amore che muove dal cuore e che si complica in tragedia (il suicidio) come lusso di gente raffinata e di raffinate società letterarie ecc. In questa direzione credo si debba venire a cercare che cosa il Boccaccio intendeva fare scrivendo la *Fiammetta*" (p. 801). For a recent treatment which opposes an autobiographical reading, see Robert Griffin, "Boccaccio's *Fiammetta:* Pictures at an Exhibition," *Italian Quarterly,* 18, No. 72 (1975), 75–94.

50. Two of Rastelli's other studies of the work take up the rhetorical element in Boccaccio's prose; see "Boccaccio rétore nel 'Prologo' della 'Fiammetta,' " *Saggi di umanesimo cristiano,* 2, No. 3 (1947), 10–18, and see "Spunti lirici e narrativi, motivi stilistici nella *Fiammetta* di G. Boccaccio," *Lettere Italiane,* 3 (1951), 83–98: "L'Elegia è una lunga lettera rettorica . . . di cui il nono capitolo è il congedo come il Prologo è l'esordio" (p. 98). Another casts an eye over some sources: "Le fonti letterarie del Boccaccio nell' 'Elegia di Madonna Fiammetta,' " *Saggi di umanesimo cristiano,* 4, No. 3 (1949), 68–79. Still another offers a traditional discussion of the usual scholarly problems: "Notizie storiche a bibliografiche sulla composizione e sulla fortuna dell' 'Elegia di Madonna Fiammetta' e del 'Ninfale Fiesolano' di G. Boccaccio," *Annali della biblioteca governativa e libreria civica di Cremona,* IV, fasc. 2 (1951), 22 pp. But it is only in "*L'Elegia di Fiammetta* (Il mito mondano e la caratterizzazione psicologica della protagonista)," *Studi Ghisleriani,* S. II, I (1950), 151–73, that we get an inkling of "che cosa il Boccaccio intendeva fare scrivendo la *Fiammetta.*" Rastelli, for all his hardheaded and welcome work, seems totally taken in by the lady in question. Fiammetta is indeed characterized as follows: "Incolpevole seduttrice fuori

d'ogni deliberato proposito o d'ogni benchè minima malizia, la medesima nobiltà e la bellezza la ponevano più in su che qualsiasi frivolo gioco" (p. 156). Or he sees Fiammetta exalted: "Su questo piedestallo sta Fiammetta tuttavia come donna, non come statua" (p. 163). In short, for all his intelligent argument against the Romantic view of the work, Rastelli sounds surprisingly like a Romantic reader himself.

51. "Per l'interpretazione della 'Fiammetta,' " *Miscellanea storica della Valdelsa,* 21 (1913), 68–71.

52. ". . . il Boccaccio fece per lei ciò che poi, dopo parecchi anni, fece ancora nel *Corbaccio* per la vedova schernitrice" (p. 71).

53. Some examples: C. Pellegrini, *Archivio storico italiano,* 72 (1914), 454: "Le poche pagine di Giuseppe Gigli . . . sono in realtà troppo povera cosa"; A. Della Torre, *Rassegna bibliografica della letteratura italiana,* 22 (1914), 118: the article "è non soltanto piccolo di mole, ma anche mancante di ogni qualsivoglia valore"; H. Hauvette, in his tremendously influential *Boccace* (Paris, 1914), *the* "event" of the sixth centennial: "Pareille interprétation est insoutenable, car il faut encore le répéter: pas un trait de caricature, pas une intention sarcastique ne se laisse deviner dans ces pages brûlantes de passion" (p. 155). Gigli had in fact been pursuing this line of interpretation of the *Fiammetta* for some time, first in his introduction to an anthology of the *opere minori* (Firenze: Sansoni, 1907) and then in his edition of the *Fiammetta* (Strasbourg: Bibliotheca romanica, Nos. 120–22). See O. Bacci, reviewing this second item, *Miscellanea storica della Valdelsa,* 19 (1911), 51.

54. Vittore Branca refers to it as the "primo romanzo psicologico e realistico moderno" ("Profilo biografico," p. 66). This is, after all, even if we are excruciatingly careful about not mixing medieval and modern terminologies (a "racket" that some medievalists tend to overwork in order to terrify timid moderns), what Boccaccio accomplished. That is not to say that its values are modern, but that it created what was to become a modern genre.

55. "Indicazioni per una lettura del 'Decameron,' " in the collection *Scritti sul Giovanni Boccaccio* (Firenze, 1964)—a reprinting of *Miscellanea storica della Valdelsa,* 69, Nos. 2 and 3 (1963)—pp. 7–19: "La *Fiammetta* è la storia di un doloroso processo irrazionale di cui ella è consapevole e contro cui non ha forza" (p. 13). This much is fine. Ramat goes on to see her irrationality in terms of "una deviazione nella natura innocente ove l'amore del senso è

l'iniziazione all' umanità razionalmente piena." That seems dubious, very much a twentieth-century view of sexual hygiene (vs. sexual depravity). Fiammetta is not in need of a psychoanalyst, but of a priest. Her conduct in church (see discussion, below) shows us that she has cut herself off from that kind of aid. For another similar statement, see Ramat's "Boccaccio 1340–1344," *Belfagor,* 19 (1964), 170: ". . . la novità consiste nella rappresentazione del pervertimento morale prodotto da amore, fonte di follia e non di sagezza, il cui tormento origina disarmonia interiore e non superiore pacificazione; per cui la *Fiammetta* si presenta, per volontà certa dello scrittore, come storia di una follia e di una disarmonia, come racconto di un doloroso processo irrazionale, contrario a quella naturale razionalità amorosa che talvolta abbiamo visto affiorare nelle pagine del Boccaccio e che sappiamo essere un motivo dominante del suo capolavoro."

56. For a similar understanding of melancholy resulting from love see Dino del Garbo's gloss to Guido Cavalcanti's *canzone Donna me prega* (in G. Cavalcanti, *Rime,* ed. Guido Favati [Milano-Napoli: Ricciardi, 1957], p. 370: "nam in amore, quando est ualde uehemens, aliquis remouetur a bona sua dispositione naturali et tendit versus melanconicam, sicut ponunt medicine auctores." And see *Rime* LXVII. 14: "questa mia trestizia." Perhaps the only critic who has thought that Dino's gloss (which will occupy us at greater length farther on in this chapter) is applicable to the *Fiammetta* is Carlo Muscetta. See his "Giovanni Boccaccio e i novellieri," *Storia della Letteratura Italiana,* II, *Il Trecento* (Milano, 1965), esp. 317–62: "L'amor-passione cantato da Cavalcanti e commentato da Dino del Garbo è qui analizzato nel suo tormento drammatico e nella nudezza della sua fisicità . . . con una sottigliezza psicologica non mai raggiunta, prima del Boccaccio . . ." (p. 354).

57. The importance of Seneca's drama to the *Elegia* was first noted by V. Crescini, *Contributo agli studi sul Boccaccio* (Torino, 1887), pp. 160n.–62n. Crescini showed clearly the dependence of the (crucial) scene between Fiammetta and the *balia* on the similar scene in *Phaedra* I. A. S. Cook, "Boccaccio, *Fiammetta,* Chap. I, and Seneca, *Hippolytus,* Act I," *American Journal of Philology,* 28 (1907), 200–04, pointed out the important correspondences between the Venus-Fiammetta encounter and passages in *Phaedra,* without taking note of Crescini's earlier treatment of Seneca in the *Elegia.* Crescini's ensuing rebuke of Cook is at least ungracious, for Cook had after all come up with different textual confrontations; if he had not done his homework he was at least right. See "Il primo atto dell' *Hippolytus* di Seneca

nel primo capitolo della *Fiammetta* del Boccaccio," *Atti del Reale Istituto Veneto di Scienze, Lettere ed Arti,* S. IX, V (1920–21), 14–15. And see M. Serafini, "Le tragedie di Seneca nella 'Fiammetta' di Giovanni Boccaccio," *GSLI,* 126 (1949), 95–105. Pp. 95–101 show the traces of six of Seneca's tragedies in chs. V, VI, and VIII of the *Elegia.* See also A. Roncaglia, "Sulle fonti del sonetto 'al Sonno' di Giovanni della Casa," *GSLI,* 125 (1948), 42–53, where the brief treatment of the sources of Fiammetta's prayer is probably to be preferred to that of Cornelia C. Coulter, "Statius, *Silvae,* V, 4 and Fiammetta's Prayer to Sleep," *American Journal of Philology,* 80 (1959), 390–95. P. Waley's view—that Boccaccio has widely amplified his sources—is undoubtedly correct: see "The Nurse in Boccaccio's Fiammetta: Source and Invention," *Neophilologus,* 56 (1972), 164–74. Her reading ends in a "biographical" key: "Although the character and function of the nurse are prominent features of the sources [Seneca and Ovid] upon which Boccaccio drew for his tragedy of love, he expresses through her not only the conventional exhortations to Stoic virtue but also a disillusion with love which may well be his own" (p. 173). Her article is marred by small errors of fact, e.g., that the nurse is "too old and slow-moving to prevent [Fiammetta's] dash up the stairway" (VI, 20—p. 166); "the expected Panfilo was a different man by the same name" (VII, 8—p. 166); perhaps more alarming is the fact that her study refers to no critical work later than Serafini's (1949), which means that the labors of such as Pabst and Rastelli are not even referred to. There is also the dubious notion that Boccaccio—since the nurse does not refer to them—was unaware "of the counsels contained" in the *Remedia amoris* (pp. 173n.–74n.).

58. Some months after writing this passage its author came upon the following: J. C. L. Simonde de Sismondi, *De la littérature du midi de l'Europe* (Bruxelles, 1837), I, 274–75: "On sent que Fiammetta est dévorée par l'ardeur qu'elle exprime, et quoiqu'elle n'ait pas le moindre rapport avec Phèdre, celle-ci se présente au souvenir, car dans l'une et dans l'autre, 'C'est Vénus tout entière à sa proie attachée.' "

59. See "Ciascheduno il beneficio della sua libertà, come gli pare, può usare. Se tu fortemente ami lui, tanto che di ciò pena intollerabile sostieni, egli di ciò non t'ha colpa, né giustamente di lui ti puoi dolere: tu stessa di ciò ti se' principalissima cagione. Amore, ancora che potentissimo signore sia, e incomparabili le sue forze, non però, te invita, ti poteva il giovine pignere nella mente: il tuo senno e gli oziosi pensieri di questo amore ti furono principio; al quale se tu vigorosamente ti fossi opposta, tutto questo non avvenia,

ma, libera, lui e ogni altro averesti potuto schernire, come tu di' che egli di te non curantesi ti schernisce" (VI, 15). It is the nurse who speaks, and her "reading" of Fiammetta's dilemma is important—even essential—for its insistence that love is a form of captivity which is not enforced but willingly chosen. Either she is wrong or almost all previous criticism of the *Fiammetta* is wrong.

60. See *Georgics* IV.457–59. And see *Teseida* III.33, for the comparison of Amore's effect on Palemone and Arcita to the poisonous bite of the serpent.

61. "Once bitten, twice shy" is not a proverb that fits Boccaccio's loving ladies. See Mensola's acquiescence to Africo's *second* sexual assault, *Ninfale fiesolano* 305.

62. The occasion—a "giorno solennissimo"—is traditionally understood to be Easter Saturday. See *Filocolo* I, 1, 17; *Comedia ninfe* XXXV.105.

63. See Boccaccio's commentary on this classical scene, *Comm. Teseida, Opere,* II, 472.

64. The omission of Juno, if intentional on Boccaccio's part, may be programmatic, since Juno is generally associated by Boccaccio with marriage.

65. ". . . e li sacri oficii, appena da me uditi non che intesi . . ."

66. I, 6. Hauvette, *Boccace,* p. 145n., has observed the quotation of *Vita Nuova* II.5. And several other elements of that work are also obviously borrowed here. What Hauvette and many others have failed to see is the irony that underlies the borrowings; nothing could be less like Dante's love of Beatrice than Panfilo's love of Fiammetta which, if it resembles anything in Dante, is more like Paolo's love of Francesca. It is so often the case that criticism of the *opere minori in volgare,* even when it takes notice of a literary borrowing in a text, is bent on having its "biography" of Boccaccio at any price, that one comes upon the following in Hauvette's *Boccace* with a smile and a sigh: "On est cependant autorisé à se demander si cette première recontre à l'église, qui rappelle si étrangement l' 'innamoramento' de Pétrarque à Sainte-Claire d'Avignon, et quelques scènes de la *Vita nuova,* n'est pas un écho d'une tradition poétique alors vivace. Je me borne à poser ce point d'interrogation" (p. 51n.). If Hauvette never followed his better instincts in this regard, his view of the *opere minori* is shared by many intelligent read-

ers. The desire to seek out the "biographical" truth behind the fictions is a common phenomenon. Let two examples suffice. J. H. Whitfield, "Boccaccio and Fiammetta in the 'Teseide,'" *Modern Language Review,* 33 (1918), 29–30, crowns his argument that Boccaccio "is" Palemone (and not, as Crescini had argued, Arcita) by adducing Filippo Villani's description of Boccaccio's stature and appearance to that of Palemone. R. M. Lumiansky, "Aspects of the Relationship of Boccaccio's 'Il Filostrato' with Benoit's 'Roman de Troie' and Chaucer's 'Wife of Bath's Tale,'" *Italica,* 31 (1954), 1, suggests that some of Boccaccio's reason for including Pandaro in the plot of the *Filostrato* may have resulted from his own actual use of a go-between in his wooing of Maria d'Aquino. Only after completing this study did I come upon the excellent monograph of Bernhard König, *Die Begegnung im Tempel: Abwandlungen eines literarischen Motivs in den Werken Boccaccios* (Hamburg [Hamburger Romantische Studien, Band 45], 1960). Starting with the meeting of Fiammetta and Panfilo, König demonstrates, with patience and skill, that the "autobiographical" elements of Boccaccio's fictions are, on the contrary, essentially literary in their provenance. Had I read König's work when I should have, I would have frequently made use of his findings in my own discussions.

67. The nurse cites classical text with precision. See *Phaedra* I.249: "Pars sanitatis velle sanari fuit." Here and elsewhere in this discussion of the *Elegia* the excellent classicizing notes by Maria Segre Consigli, in Giovanni Boccaccio, *Opere,* ed. Cesare Segre (Milano: Mursia, 1966), have been of great assistance.

68. See the close similarity in tone and subject to Boccaccio's allegorical exposition of *Inf.* V: "Ma i moderni giovani fanno tutto il contrario . . ." (*Esposizioni, Inf.* V, *esp. all.,* 31).

69. Even on the social scale. The idleness of rich ladies (and gentlemen) is an often present spectacle in Boccaccio's work. While one is impressed by his own courtly ambitions in Naples, one can also often sense his middle-class disgust with the empty lives of the wealthy, lives which they attempt to fill with the dangerous game of lust. One thinks of Ovid's line—as Boccaccio was likely to have done also: "Divitiis alitur luxuriosus amor" (*Remedia,* 746).

70. The "Fiammetta" of the *Caccia di Diana,* "la bella donna, il cui nome si tace," it will be remembered, rebels against Diana (XVI.48–54); "Come Diana questo udì, nel loco/non stette guari più, ma sen salio,/partendosi turbata. . . ." (XVI.55–57).

71. "E lui di Venere chiamate figliuolo, dicendo che egli dal terzo cielo piglia le forze sue, quasi vogliate alla vostra follia porre necessità per iscusa" (I, 15).

72. See again the view of the nurse, n. 59, above.

73. It is in fact generally avoided, and even played down by so astute a reader as Quaglio (see n. 47, above). Hauvette's response is typical of many: ". . . l'apparition de Vénus et son discours à Fiammetta rappellent désagréablement les premiers livres du *Filocolo*" (*Boccace,* p. 152). The remark only serves to illustrate Hauvette's distaste for much that is medieval in medieval literature.

74. See chapter 3, n. 71.

75. Here, as in the *Caccia di Diana* and *Filocolo,* Diana would seem to be associated not only with virginity, but also and particularly with chastity in marriage.

76. This overt statement helps to make Pabst's essential view of Venus as fury in the *Fiammetta* extremely difficult to refute.

77. See St. Augustine, *Enarratio in Psalmos* (*PL,* XXXVI, 1231–32): "Omnes dii gentium daemonia"—cited by Jean Seznec, *The Survival of the Pagan Gods* (New York, 1961), p. 17n. This is not to suggest that Boccaccio's attitude toward pagan divinities was the same as that expressed by St. Augustine—nothing would be further from the truth—but that he had a tradition in which to see the daemonic quality of carnal love in terms of false gods and goddesses.

78. In her room Panfilo is more reverent than in a temple. The "religious" language of love is frequent in her speech.

79. In this and much else she closely resembles the Troiolo of the *Filostrato.*

80. See again Hauvette's remark, quoted above, n. 53: ". . . pas un trait de caricature, pas une intention sarcastique ne se laisse deviner dans ces pages brûlantes de passion."

81. Again see the nurse's remarks at VI, 15, when she puts forth her clear understanding that Panfilo never had any intention of returning to Fiam-

metta—his false promise is merely seen as one of the "costumi che s'usano nella corte del tuo iddio." Boccaccio has obviously reversed the pattern of male and female roles from that found in false Criseida and deserted Troiolo in the earlier *Filostrato.*

82. See the more than slightly ridiculous encounter of the *balia* and a foreigner whom she takes to be a friend of Panfilo. The young man leaps off his boat, crashing into the old woman and sending her reeling. The touch would be completely wrong in a "serious" romance. It is a piece of low comedy. As is the whole "non-recognition" scene—his friend will turn out to be someone other than Panfilo, of course (VII, 8).

83. Giuseppe Billanovich, *Restauri boccacceschi* (Roma, 1945), p. 11, describes Fiammetta as "suggestionata e malata, nella tristezza di conoscere il suo morbo e di specularne il continuo progresso." His description, despite its accuracy, does not take into account the medieval medical background. There is a long tradition in which passionate love was indeed considered a disease. This malady was rediscovered by J. L. Lowes, "The Loveres Maladye of Hereos," *Modern Philology,* 11 (1914), 491–546. The phrase that gives this brilliant piece of detective work its title is found in Chaucer's *Knight's Tale,* A 1372–73. (When one considers Chaucer's dependence in that work on the *Filostrato* one wonders why it was only in 1970 that a scholar would point out the relevance of the concept to Boccaccio—see the ensuing discussion in this note.) As Lowes demonstrates, *amor hereos* (variously *amor heroycus,* etc.), in one medieval medical authority after another (Arnaldus of Villanova, Bernardus Gordonius, *et aliis*) "is always associated with the discussion of *melancolia*" (p. 503). For a typical definition, see Arnaldus: "Alienatio, quam concomitatur immensa concupiscentia, irrationalis, & graecè dicitur herois, id est domina rationis: nam herois est corrupta scientiatio, qua iudicatur apprehensum delectabilius aut excellentius esse, quam sit, quapropter excitat vehemens desiderium ad quaerendum rem illam, & suam cogitationem in ea frequentius: Cum haec species manifestatur in concupiscentia indiuidui humani, qua indiuiduum unius sexus complexionari desiderat indiuiduo sexus alteri, vulgariter dicitur amor, & a Medicis amor heroicus. id est immensus & irrationabilis"—*Opera omnia* (Basel, 1585), pp. 270–71. M. Ciavolella, "La tradizione dell' 'aegritudo amoris' nel 'Decameron,' " *GSLI,* 147 (1970), 496–517, traces the disease from Hippocrates' fusion of *malinconia* and *follia* (p. 503), through various medieval authorities, including Dino del Garbo ("Et uocatur talis passio 'ereos' ab auctoribus medicine"—in Favati's edition, p. 372), to the *Decameron.* Since he accepts Quaglio's inclination to believe that Boccaccio had direct knowledge of

Dino's commentary on *Donna me prega* only after 1366 (a judgment which I find most difficult to accept—see n. 155, below, and the following discussion), he does much less with his discovery than he might have, and applies it, among Boccaccio's fictions, only to the *Decameron.*

The "medical research" of Lowes and Ciavolella opens up a world of possibility that many proponents of "amour courtois" as the prime Boccaccian mode will not find pleasing. The following passage from Lowes, considering the likelihood that the conventional "sigma" of "falling in love" should be taken more critically than they generally have been, is worth quoting. These "sigma" indeed "constitute precisely the sort of medical lore that always filters through into lay thought and speech, and, with due recognition of the fact that *hereos* is not the only influence involved, the medieval literature of love must none the less be re-read in its light" (p. 543). In a footnote, Lowes draws our attention to the definition of love found at the beginning of the *De amore* of Andreas Capellanus: "That is substantially (in part even verbally) the definition of the medical writers, and Andreas' work is full of other reminiscences" (p. 543n.). The net draws tighter. May I ask the reader to consider my first allusion to Fiammetta's illness (n. 56, above)? There I adduced Dino del Garbo's discussion of *melanconia;* and see the more lengthy discussion of Dino's presence in Boccaccio's thought in my consideration of the gloss to the *Teseida,* below, which will link Dino's and Andreas's definitions of love. For all his excellent work, Lowes too falls victim to the common belief that Boccaccio was a proponent of carnal love. Discussing *Teseida* IV.26–29, where he finds the *sigma* in Arcita/Penteo, he draws back at the brink of comprehension: Chaucer, when he made use of this passage, "proceeded to rearrange and combine [the *sigma*] in the light of his knowledge of the malady" (p. 525n.)—which denies to Boccaccio exactly such knowledge as he surely had, mainly because Lowes too is convinced that Boccaccio was a champion of such love, rather than an opposer, despite the fact that the "symptomology" of carnal love in Boccaccio—if it did not influence Chaucer, which it may have done—at least preceded him.

84. The language probably reflects Dante's "ingiusto fece me contra me giusto" (*Inf.* XIII.72). That the speaker there is Pier delle Vigne, a suicide, may have been significant to Boccaccio.

85. Had Boccaccio read his pages aloud to his friends, as Franz Kafka apparently did, would they not have, like Kafka's friends, frequently joined him in laughter?

86. Though not quite so biting in its tone, the *Elegia* has similarities to Shakespeare's *Troilus and Cressida,* another great work that pricks the bubble of pretense which lovers rear over their carnal affections. What is not present in Boccaccio's work is the upstage presence of a Pandarus who speaks "no more than truth" (I.i.64) or a Thersites ("All the argument is a cuckold and a whore"—II.iii.78) who might display the bitter truth more openly. Still, the nurse does a fair job of doing just that, at least on occasion, and few have chosen to listen to her.

87. VI, 20. Her earlier equation of Venus and Tisiphone (I, 21) is here given further validity—hers is a love which leads to madness and death. See also Tisiphone's "poisoning" of Palemone in *Teseida* V.13 and Boccaccio's gloss to the passage.

88. It is possible, even likely, that Boccaccio had a model in mind: *Aeneid* IV.659, where the distracted Dido kisses the couch on which she had lain with Aeneas. L. 650 may even have suggested to Boccaccio that she spoke to her bed: "incubuitque toro dixitque novissima verba." Dido's suicidal intent is surely to be seen mirrored in Fiammetta's.

89. ". . . che più al mio simigliante il [dolore] conosco quasi che altro alcuno."

90. Boccaccio's own view of Dido is complicated. In the *Esposizioni* (*Inf.* V, *esp. litt.*, 65–83) he sets out his fullest defense of her (but see *De mulieribus claris,* XLII, for a similar gesture), concluding: "Fu adunque Dido onesta donna e, per non romper fede al cener di Siccheo, s'uccise. Ma l'autore seguita qui, come in assai cose fa, l'oppinion di Virgilio, e per questo si convien sostenere." (The whole question is of some curiosity—see the notes of Padoan, *Opere,* VI, 859–60, Quaglio, *Opere,* I, 767, and Branca, *Opere,* III, 682–84, for essential background and bibliography.) However, Boccaccio is frequently the child of Virgil and Dante in his view of Dido, especially in the earlier works. A brief survey will help to clarify the point. Apart from a fleeting reference in the *Teseida* (VI.45, 3), where Dido is merely mentioned as the wife of Sichaeus, she is referred to in four of these, *Filocolo, Comedia ninfe, Amorosa Visione,* and *Fiammetta.* Her appearances in these texts fall into three main topographical categories:

1) Boccaccio twice refers to the Virgilian scene in which the false Ascanius—Cupid—fans the flames of love in Dido as he sits in her lap: *Filocolo,* II, 1, 5; *Fiammetta,* I, 19.

2) He more frequently refers generically to the Virgilian Dido, betrayed by Aeneas, who is portrayed as a suicide, still sadly burning with love for Aeneas (and once—in the *Comedia ninfe*—specifically as forgetful of her "promise" to Sichaeus, following *Aen.* IV.552, and *Inf.* V.62): *Filocolo,* II, 18, 12; IV, 20, 4; *Comedia ninfe* XXIII.29–30; *Amorosa Visione* XXVIII.4–XXIX.30 (this last represents Boccaccio's major effort to "re-do" Virgil).

3) But his far more frequent practice is to make of Dido, in the spirit of Ovid, an *exemplum* of subjection to Amore, twice alone, but usually in a small company of similar *exempla:*

Filocolo, III, 67, 4: Helen, Dido, Leander.
IV, 54, 2: Dido and Ariadne.
IV, 83, 3: Medea, Dido, Deianira, Phyllis, Leander.
V, 8, 42: Dido and Biblis.
Comedia ninfe I.4: Helen, Dido, Hypsipyle, Medea.
XV.12: Semiramis and Dido.
XXXV.83: Dido, Iphis, Biblis.
XXXVI.35: Dido and Biblis.
Fiammetta I.17: Paris, Clytemnestra, Achilles, Scylla, Ariadne, Leander, Dido.
V.22: alone.
V.27: Semiramis, Cleopatra, Helen, Dido.
VIII.5: alone.

From this summary it seems clear that, whatever the attitudes toward Dido of his characters or narrators, Boccaccio himself, in the *opere minori in volgare,* thinks of her as moving and beautiful, but also as a guilty figure, sharing Dante's view of her as she is found in the pages of Virgil, and like Dante seeing her against a Christian moral matrix which makes her guilty of the sin of *lussuria.* The company she keeps is certainly illustrative on that score and joins Boccaccio's sense of Ovid's presentation of her to that he found in Virgil. How then do we account for the *two* Dido stories in the *Esposizioni?* For there Boccaccio devotes some four pages to the guiltless Dido (who lived and died *before* Aeneas came to Carthage, and who committed suicide rather than submit to the marital desires of the king of the neighboring Musitani) and a single page to the incorrect version narrated by Virgil, which concludes with the words with which this note began. What seems possible, even likely, is that during his stay with Petrarch at Padova (mid-July to early October 1368—see Branca, "Profilo biografico," pp. 163, 166) Boccaccio either read Petrarch's letter to Federico Aretino (*Sen.,* IV, v) or heard Petrarch speak about its contents. This epistle was composed between 1364 and 1367 (see E. H. Wilkins, *The Prose Letters of Petrarch* [New York, n. d.]), and is likely to be the source of Boccaccio's new sense of Dido. For this lengthy exercise in the allegorical interpretation of the *Aeneid* features a discussion of the true history of Dido, citing patristic and historiographic sources (see the Italian edition of the *Seniles* by G. Fracassetti [Firenze: Le Monnier, 1869], pp. 252–53); it begins by asserting that Dido was utterly chaste, tells the basic story that we will later find in Boccaccio, and concludes by declaring that she indeed kept faith with her husband. In the *Trionfi* Petrarch undoubtedly shocked many a reader when he placed Dido among the chaste rather than among the great lovers of the past. His treatment of her there clearly reflects the knowledge he is so pleased to put forth in the letter to Aretino, and he puts forth his position in the two passages that treat of Dido (*Tr. pud.* 10–12, 154–59) with typically Petrarchan scorn for the ignorance of others. Both passages use the phrase "'l publico grido" to describe the opinion of those who acceded to Virgil's version of the story. The attack is undoubtedly aimed squarely at Dante, and surely strikes Boccaccio too—especially for his treatment of Dido in *Amorosa Visione* XXVIII–XXIX. Whether or not Petrarch ever showed the *Trionfi* to Boccaccio is not known. But whether or not Boccaccio ever read them, one may be nearly certain that Petrarch would not have chosen to be silent about his discovery. One imagines his great satisfaction in being able to inform Boccaccio that his beloved Dante (about whom Petrarch had probably heard far too much from Boccaccio) was wrong—and that he was too. (As is not surprising, a rereading of Giuseppe Billanovich's *Restauri boccacceschi* has chastened this writer's enthusiasm for his "discovery": Billanovich refers to Petrarch, "che gli [Boccaccio] è indubbiamente maestro anche in questa contradizione a Virgilio e a Dante . . ." [p. 138n.]).

In short, Boccaccio's view of Dido seems to have been fairly consistent throughout the early works, only changing when he became aware of Petrarch's discovery. (A probable further result of this discovery is Boccaccio's defense of Virgil's lie—*Genealogiae,* XIV, 3—*Seniles,* IV, V, also defends Virgil's reasons for "lying.") For other references to Dido see *Filocolo,* I, 1, 1; *Amorosa Visone* V.14, VIII.68, XLII.41. For a discussion of the uses of *exempla,* see S. Battaglia, "L'esempio medievale," *Filologia Romanza,* 6 (1959), 45–82.

91. See most recently Vittore Branca's perception, "Profilo biografico," p. 67: her passion is "una passione che mena a 'martiri,' a 'dolorosi passi,' come quella di Fedra o di Francesca (anch'essa lettrice di 'franceschi romanzi' " [see *Elegia,* VIII, 7, concerning her pleasure in Tristan and Isolde finding happi-

ness in death]). If the *Elegia* is the "primo romanzo psicologico e realistico moderno" (Branca, p. 66), it may well remind its reader of another lady who chose death in love, who is sometimes compared to Francesca, but who is really more closely related to Fiammetta—Emma Bovary, heroine of the greatest "romanzo psicologico e realistico moderno."

92. "Profilo biografico," p. 66n.: "Dantesca è il titolo stesso: *'per elegiam stilum intelligimus miserorum,' De vulg. eloq.*, II, 4, 6: cf. 'a' casi infelici, . . . con lagrimevole stilo seguirò' " [Fiammetta's own words in the prologue]. But there are a number of other likely sources. See P. V. Mengaldo, "L'elegia *'umile'* (*De vulgari eloquentia,* II, iv, 5–6)," *GSLI,* 143 (1966), 177–98, for a thorough examination of the wide medieval context of the word as it comes into Dante. See also the *Accessus* to Ovid's *Amores* in R. B. C. Huygens, *Accessus ad Auctores,* 2nd ed. (Leiden, 1970), pp. 36–37: "Et sciendum est quod Tragedia dea est facti carminis de gestis nobilium et regum, Elegia autem dicitur dea miseriae (contingunt etiam in amore miseriae et adversitates) et scribitur impari metro et exametro" (see Horace, *Ars poetica,* 75: "versibus impariter junctis querimonia primum"). C. Segre, "Strutture e registri nella 'Fiammetta,' " *Strumenti critici,* VI, No. 18 (1972), 135, points to Giovanni da Genova for an early equation of *elegia* and *miseria,* and to John of Garland for the following definition of *carmen elegiacum:* "id est miserabile carmen quod continet et ricitat dolores amantium."

93. See Giuseppe Di Stefano, "Jacques Legrand (†1415) Lecteur de Boccace," *Yearbook of Italian Studies,* 1 (1971), 248–64. Di Stefano publishes (pp. 259–64) the medieval French translation of Legrand's little text *De poetria* (*Archeologesofia* II. 4—MS.B.N. Par., franç. 143, f. 399^{r}.–401^{v}.), from which the following generic criticism is drawn (400^{r}.): "Oultre plus doiz sçavoir que, se les ditz des poetes parlent des pasteurs, lors ilz sont appellez bucolicques, et, se ilz parlent des hommes notables, ilz sont appellez eroyques, et, *se ilz parlent des meschans, ilz sont appellez elegiacques,* et, se ilz contiennent aucune lamentacion, ilz sont appellez threnes, et se ilz parlent de la mort, ilz sont appellez epitaphes" [italics added]. The word *meschans* is clearly to be taken in the sense of "unfortunate," not of "bad."

94. For Boccaccio's self-consciousness about the epic tradition, see remarks about the opening of the *Teseida,* below. For his sources, see V. Pernicone, "Il 'Filostrato' di Giovanni Boccaccio," *Studi di filologia italiana,* 2 (1929), 93–106; and now M. Gozzi, "Sulle fonti del 'Filostrato,' " *Studi sul Boccaccio,* 5 (1968), 123–209, by far the best treatment of the problem to date.

95. "FILOSTRATO È IL TITOLO DI QUESTO LIBRO, E LA CAGIONE È QUESTA: PER CIÒ CHE OTTIMAMENTE SI CONFÀ CON L'EFFETTO DEL LIBRO. FILOSTRATO TANTO VIENE A DIRE QUANTO UOMO VINTO E ABBATTUTO D'AMORE: COME VEDER SI PUÒ CHE FU TROIOLO DALL'AMOR VINTO SÌ FERVENTEMENTE AMANDO CRISEIDA E SÌ ANCORA NELLA SUA PARTITA." If the title has explicit reference to Troiolo here, it will refer explicitly to the narrator in the next line, where he identifies himself as "Filostrato" in the rubric of the *proemio.* Each is "vinto e abbattuto d'amore." For the possible influence of Petrarch's lost comedy on the title of the work see A. S. Bernardo, *Petrarch, Laura, and the Triumphs* (Albany, N.Y., 1974), p. 172.

96. The *martiri* and *sospiri,* commonplaces in the amorous tradition, are nonetheless likely to derive from Francesca's: see *Inf.* v.116, 118.

97. He is the nearly precise obverse of the narrator of the *Corbaccio,* moving from freedom to bondage as swiftly as the latter moves from bondage to or at least toward freedom.

98. Branca's note (*Opere,* II, 852) catches the obvious quotation of a famous simile in Dante, but it stops short of pointing out the clear antithetical relationship of Boccaccio's text to Dante's.

Inferno II.127–142

Quali fioretti dal notturno gelo
chinati e chiusi, poi che 'l sol li 'mbianca,
si drizzan tutti aperti in loro stelo,
tal mi fec' io di mia virtude stanca,
e tanto buono ardire al cor mi corse,
ch'i' cominciai come persona franca:
"Oh pietosa colei che mi soccorse!
e te cortese ch'ubidisti tosto

a le vere parole che ti porse!
Tu m'hai con disiderio il cor disposto
sì al venir con le parole tue,
ch'i' son tornato nel primo proposto.
Or va, ch'un sol volere è d'ambedue:
tu duca, tu segnore e tu maestro."
Così li dissi; e poi che mosso fue,
intrai per lo cammin alto e silvestro.

Filostrato II.80–81

Quali i fioretti, dal notturno gelo
chinati e chiusi, poi che 'l sol gl'imbianca,
tutti s'apron diritti in loro stelo,
cotal si fé di sua virtute stanca
Troiolo allora, e riguardando il cielo,
incominciò come persona franca:
"Lodato sia il tuo sommo valore,
Venere bella, e del tuo figlio Amore."

* * * *

Poi Pandaro abbracciò mille fiate
e basciollo altrettante, sì contento
che più non saria stato se donate
gli fosser mille Troie; e lento lento
con Pandar solo, a veder la biltate
di Criseida andò, guardando attento
se alcun atto nuovo in lei vedeva,
per quel che Pandar ragionato aveva.

It would seem at least probable that Boccaccio was aware of what followed the simile in *Inferno* II, that he intended Troiolo's prayer of thanksgiving to Venus and Cupid to be a parody of Dante's words of gratitude to Beatrice and Virgil. Further, Troiolo follows Pandaro as Dante follows Virgil. We should not forget that Virgil is leading Dante into Hell. The next line in the *Commedia* is the first of the nine lines inscribed over the portal of Hell. The next line of the *Filostrato* describes Criseida standing in her window. In at least some sense each of the two protagonists is about to begin a voyage into Hell. At the outset Troiolo will think his *inferno* a *paradiso* (e.g., III.56.7: "tu m'hai d'inferno messo in paradiso," and see the beginning of the narrator's dream in the *Corbaccio,* where that former lover also commences by considering a hellish place delightful), but will soon enough discover that the religion of love he has so enthusiastically embraced will create for him a hell on earth.

99. E.g., of Criseida's "debate" within herself as to whether she should give herself to Troiolo or no (II.67–78), Hauvette (*Boccace,* p. 85) has this to say: "[The monologue] nous découvre toute l'inconsistance de cette tête de linotte; d'un poète moderne, on n'hésiterait pas à dire que c'est un chef-d'œuvre de rosserie" It is exactly that, but Hauvette's procrustean view of Criseida as a character who very much resembles a Romantic heroine stands in his way. I might here point out that this is not the first time in these notes that Hauvette's instincts have moved in precisely the right direction, only to be deflected by his sense of what Boccaccio must be up to. And if I have used Hauvette as a convenient representative of the "biographical school," we should also note that he is often a more sensitive reader than most adherents to that tradition of reading Boccaccio. For instance, we might consider the early essay of C. S. Lewis, "What Chaucer really did to 'Il Filostrato,' " in his *Selected Literary Essays,* ed. W. Hooper (Cambridge, 1969—the essay was written in 1932), p. 33, where Lewis adverts to the *doctryne* and *sentence* found in Chaucer: "To Boccaccio, I suspect, this would have seemed as much an excresence as it does to the modern reader." Lewis is not recommended as a guide either to Boccaccio or to Chaucer. Nor is R. P. apRoberts, "Love in the *Filostrato,*" *Chaucer Review,* 7 (1972), 23: "Finally we must observe that Boccaccio draws Criseida as perfect in all her actions except one. Criseida's only fault is that she was not faithful, and the only adverse criticism of her by Troilo, Pandaro, and the narrator arises from this fault and is limited to it. Her beauty, her exquisite manners, her superior bearing, her good reputation, and her superior virtue are insisted upon over and over again in tributes by the narrator, Pandaro, Troilo, and Diomede."

That is a bit like claiming that Eve was perfect except that she was prideful—in all other respects she was the epitome of womanly virtue, and no one, not God, nor the serpent, nor Adam, blames her for any other fault. To treat a work that makes of its central female character a highly developed and articulated *exemplum* of female inconstancy as though it were written to praise this creature is not a hopeful sign. What makes the matter worthy of note is that this reading is far indeed from being atypical.

100. For a discussion of a possible source of the first six *ottave* of the passage, see Morton W. Bloomfield, "The Source of Boccaccio's *Filostrato* III, 74–79 and Its Bearing on the MS Tradition of Lucretius' *De rerum natura*," *Classical Philology*, 47 (1952), 162–65; this is an attempt to assert that there must have been an earlier MS of *De rerum natura* circulating in Italy than the one discovered by Poggio in the early fifteenth century. Bloomfield's argument is not ultimately convincing. As he himself admits, there are no precise verbal echoes (and for such an important claim that would seem something like a necessity) of Lucretius (I, 1–25) in the Boccaccio passage. And the evidence he cites, the all-pervasive power of Venus over various parts of the cosmos; the recitation of the specific effects of Venus on plants, birds, fish, and animals; the image of Venus softening the might of Mars—all these are common enough tropes to make his hypothesis seem at least questionable.

101. This would clearly seem to be Branca's perception (*Opere*, II, 856): "Il canto di Troiolo è continuamente punteggiato da calchi della poesia religiosa e anche liturgica, e soprattutto da reminiscenze stilnovistiche e dantesche, filtrate attraverso esperienze canterine e popolaresche." Branca also points to the presence of the words of address used here for Venus—"O luce eterna"—in Boccaccio's praise of the Virgin in *Rime* CXVIII, without apparently thinking that there might be an antithetic relation between the two texts. Yet the antithesis seems obvious. See the sestet of that sonnet:

> Volgi gli occhi pietosi allo mio stato,
> Donna del cielo, e non m'aver a sdegno,
> perch'io sia di peccati grave e brutto.
> Io spero in te, e 'n te sempr' ho sperato:
> prega per me, ed esser mi fa degno
> di veder teco il tuo beato frutto.

Troiolo's praise is directed to Venus as granter of sexual pleasure in a religion of love in which *dolce frutto* (see *inter alia*, III.94.7) is the sexual act, not the Son of God. Nor has he in mind the procreation of offspring—the only other hope which might "redeem" his carnal desires. If we may grant that Troiolo prays to a good goddess at the beginning of this prayer (but see remarks that will follow shortly), the praise which he offers her is hardly to be commended. For an interpretation of these six *ottave* which is diametrically opposed to my own, see Peter Dronke, "L'amor che move il sole e l'altre stelle," *Studi medievali,* 6 (1965), 389–422, who argues (pp. 417–22) for a positive view of Troiolo's song in what may be understood to be a statement of the "naturalist" position with regard to sexual love in medieval love poetry. This is not an attempt to deny that such a tradition existed in some writings of the period, but to argue that it is inapplicable here except as parody. Troiolo is not asking to share any of the celestial gifts of *Venus caelestis,* nor is he asking for the offspring which are seen as her main beneficence on this earth. A major reinforcement of my disagreement with Dronke here arises from the fact that he considers only the first six *ottave* of Troiolo's song, stopping short at *ottava* 79. The song in fact continues for *ten more ottave* (a fact that one would not be able to deduce from Dronke's treatment), and they, while continuing the religious language of the earlier stanzas (as Branca has pointed out), make it plain that Troiolo's interests are exclusively carnal. If, as Dronke argues, Troiolo here honors the celestial Venus, what is Cupid doing in his prayer (III.79.3; 80.4; 83.5)? The point of Boccaccio's blending of the attributes of the celestial and the carnal Venus in Troiolo's prayer is probably to indicate that Troiolo has got his two Venuses confused. At any rate, that is what I would argue that Dronke has done. For a view of the *Filostrato* which is much as my own, see Chauncey Wood's forthcoming book, *The Mood of Chaucer's Troilus,* the first chapter of which is a suggestive study of Boccaccio's epic. Michael Blechner was kind enough to send me a copy of the unpublished paper which he delivered at the Tenth Conference on Medieval Studies, Western Michigan University, 6 May 1975, "Foolish Love in Boccaccio's *Il Filostrato.*" His views are also quite similar to mine.

102. See Guido Vitaletti, "Benedizioni e maledizioni in amore," *Archivum Romanicum,* 3 (1919), 212, for a brief discussion of the first of these *topoi* in *Filostrato* III.83–85.

103. *Caccia di Diana* XVIII.26–27, "ché l'etterno Signor credo che gioia/abbia dicendo in sé: 'Io la formai.' "

104. E.g., st. 88, in which Athena and Mars (a suitable god in time of the Trojan War), and even Jove, are seen as inferior to love:

Segua chi vuole i regni e le ricchezze,
l'arme, i cavai, le selve, i can, gli uccelli,
di Pallade gli studi, e le prodezze
di Marte, ch'io in mirar gli occhi belli
della mia donna e le vere bellezze,
il tempo vo' por tutto, ché son quelli
che sopra Giove mi pongon, qualora
gli miro, tanto il cor se ne innamora.

105. In I.27, Criseida is described as being *grande,* her face being of *bellezza celestiale,* as having *una donnesca altezza*—the words may be drawn from Boethius's initial description of Lady Philosophy in the *De consolatione.* (For an unblinkingly serious discussion of the "actual" anatomical aspects of Boccaccio's heroines, see M. R. Ruggieri, "Aspetti dell' 'Eterno femminino' nel Medioevo e nel Rinascimento," in *Studi in onore di Pietro Silva* [Firenze, 1956], p. 257: ". . . l'ideale fisico muliebre vede spesso caratterizzato da un'ampia, spedita, candida fronte, da sottilissime, tenuissime ciglia non d'altro colore che le tenebre, da un collo che si alza come dritta colonna sotto il quale ondeggia il candido e spazioso petto.") For a suggestion that the *Fiammetta* is written with the *De consolatione* very much in mind, see Pabst, *Venus als Heilige und Furie,* p. 29. There is probably a good deal more Boethius in Boccaccio's *opere minori in volgare* than has generally been supposed.

106. But see Branca's opinion (*Opere,* II, 858–59) that in his early works Boccaccio himself was hostile to Fortuna, only accepting her, "scolasticamente e dantescamente, come 'general ministra e duce' della Provvidenza," in the *Decameron* and the late works, citing as evidence his letters of the early period, as when he refers to himself as *inimicus fortunae.* However, in the *Teseida,* the *proemio* of Book VI.1–5, which is addressed to Fortuna, is put in exactly such terms ("L'alta ministra del mondo Fortuna"—VI.1.1). See Alberto Limentani's note (*Opere,* II, 894) for some of the obvious verbal resonances of *Inf.* VII.69ff. For Branca to argue, however, that Boccaccio's characters' complaints against Fortuna are transferable to himself is not a convincing argument. The context of their complaints is likely to make *them* seem vain and wrong.

107. See *inter alia* V.1.7; 29.5; 31.6.

108. The fullest expression is found at V.62–65, a passage modeled on Cino's *canzone* "La dolce vista e 'l bel guardo soave." See Branca's note, *Opere,* II,

685. The observation was first made by G. Volpi, "Una canzone di Cino da Pistoia nel 'Filostrato' del Boccacio," *Bullettino Storico Pistoiese,* 1 (1899), 116–18. See S. Debenedetti, "Troiolo cantore," *GSLI,* 66 (1915), 414–25, who reads the quotation of Cino in a soft-hued "biographical" light (p. 425: "quella magnifica pagina di Cino che lo racconsolava nell'abbandono"). And see D. De Robertis, "Per la storia del testo della canzone 'La dolce vista e 'l bel guardo soave,' " *Studi di filologia italiana,* 10 (1952), 7 and n.

109. *Troilus and Criseyde* v 1828–41, *The Works of Geoffrey Chaucer,* ed. F. N. Robinson, 2nd ed. (Boston: Houghton Mifflin, 1961).

110. See D. W. Robertson, Jr., *A Preface to Chaucer* (Princeton, 1963), p. 240: "Many have been misled by Boccaccio's deliberate assumption of a personal point of view to see autobiographical elements in his early poetry and to think of the emotions expressed there as being actually those of the author"; see also p. 475: "Boccaccio . . . liked to identify himself with his heroes, or at least pretend to do so."

111. She is referred to thrice by name (II.80.8; VII.59.8; VIII.16.4) and is the unnamed object of veneration in III.74–89. Her son, Amor, is far more frequently named: Branca's index gives 64 *loci,* to which must be added at least that at I.38.1, which apparently got lost in the shuffle.

112. While Troiolo's prayer of thanksgiving is addressed to the celestial Venus, his gratitude is for carnal favors. As I have previously suggested, he has confused the two goddesses. See Quaglio's remark, in his review of Pabst's study of the *Fiammetta,* that the two Venuses of the *Comedia ninfe,* the *Fiammetta,* and the *Filocolo* share the same iconography, *Lettere Italiane,* 12 (1960), 225n.–26n. This is indeed often the case (though not always) in other works as well. Which Venus Boccaccio or one of his characters has in mind can only be ascertained from the purposes she expresses or is asked to carry out.

113. See "sarà da me di Cupido contato/e delle sue battaglie . . ." (III.1.6–7). For discussion of the "epic" dimension of the *Teseida,* with particular reference to Boccaccio's desire to fill a gap in vernacular letters left by Dante, see Alberto Limentani's "Introduzione," *Opere,* II, esp. pp. 231–33. And for Boccaccio's use of Statius, see his "Boccaccio 'traduttore' di Stazio," *La Rassegna,* 8 (1960), 231–42.

114. For Boccaccio as glossator see nn. 127 and 128, below.

115. If there are two Venuses, there are also two aspects of Cupid in Boccaccio. See discussion at n. 31, above, of the marital Cupid of the *Filocolo,* and see Boccaccio's brief later discussion, *Genealogie,* III, xxii (36c), which depends from Ovid's phrase *geminorum mater Amorum* (*Fasti* IV. 1).

116. See the opening and closing lines of the summarizing second *ottava* of Book III, an invocation addressed to Cupid: "Ponga ne' versi miei la sua potenza . . . e a l'un fu di morte caso amaro." In eight lines we move from love to death.

117. It seems a nice "realistic" touch that Arcita is so ravaged by his passion that he in fact looks quite a different person (IV.27–28). However, since the world of romance accepts the most incredible disguises without blinking (e.g., Shakespeare's ladies fobbing themselves off as men), Boccaccio is not here so much insisting on a "realistic" detail for its own sake as using it to figure the destructive force of passion, precisely by rehearsing the symptomology of the disease called "love." See n. 83, above.

118. It would seem probable that this choice of name is likely to reflect something of its most famous bearer—the Pentheus who died at the hands of the followers of Bacchus, and in this sense was killed by the power of sexual passion. See V.58.5, where the story is briefly but clearly referred to; in his gloss to the passage Boccaccio retells the sad story of the dismemberment of Pentheus. The tale is also referred to in *Comedia ninfe* XVIII. 18.

119. IV.43–48; 67–71; 75–77. The first of these prayers is addressed to Apollo as self-disguiser in the service of his love for King Ameto's daughter; the third to Apollo and Venus jointly. Thus all three prayers are amatory.

120. See discussion of VII.80, below. As there is a celestial and an earthly Venus, there are three Dianas—celestial, earthly (in which form she signifies chastity), and infernal. This last Diana is Proserpina, and it is to her that Palemone's prayer is addressed (IV.31–32). See *Aeneid* IV.511: "tria virginis ora Dianae."

121. There is a fourth "temple scene" (VII.96–102) which follows these three, and in which the court and the champions (along with their retinues)

offer sacrifices to Mars, as only befits the prelude to a combat. In this scene, however, there is no reference to prayer. Boccaccio has already accomplished all that he wanted to in the three competing prayers of the first three temple scenes.

122. It is put in a more complicated way—by the pity that Neptune felt when he besought Vulcan to free Mars and Venus from the golden net.

123. Emilia does not "bargain" with the gods as do Palemone and Arcita.

124. The one-line description of the Temple of Diana, rather than diminishing its importance, makes it seem a less vain place when its austerity is compared to the pomp found in the preceding temples.

125. It is as old as any number of classical myths and as recent as Graham Greene's *The Heart of the Matter.*

126. For reflections of the term in the *Vita Nuova* (with bibliography), see F. Beggiato's article "razos," *Enciclopedia Dantesca,* IV (Roma, 1973), 869.

127. There is, however, the possibility that he also wrote a gloss to the *Elegia di madonna Fiammetta.* This was first proposed by V. Pernicone, who published the text of a gloss to the *Elegia* he had collated from two MSS (Laurenziano XLII, 7, and Riccardiano 1126), pp. 171–212 of his edition of the *Elegia* (Bari: Laterza, 1939). His finding was accepted by A. Roncaglia, "Appunti lessicali dal Boccaccio minore," *Lingua Nostra,* 2 (1940), 53–55, but strongly attacked by U. Bosco, *Nuova Antologia,* 157, fasc. 1628 (16 Jan. 1940); V. Branca, *La Rassegna,* S. IV, 48 (1940), 13–16; and M. Serafini, "Le tragedie di Seneca nella 'Fiammetta' di Giovanni Boccaccio," *GSLI,* 126 (1949), 103–04. (Serafini's later argument is interesting, and might detain us first. His point is that since only one of the *chiose* points to Seneca their author must not be Boccaccio. His reasoning is that Boccaccio either would have noticed many of his Senecan borrowings—in order to display his erudition—or none of them—in order to keep his source hidden. But see A. Limentani's just observation that Boccaccio's glosses to the *Teseida* only exceptionally point to a literary, rather than a generic mythographic, source—e.g., the gloss to VI.53.1, Virgil's Camilla as model for Boccaccio's "Ida piseo"—*Opere,* II, 895; since Boccaccio borrows fairly often from Virgil in the *Teseida* but only once points in his direction, we have a precisely similar situation, and one which has not detracted from the genuineness of these

glosses, which are universally accepted as being by Boccaccio.) Pernicone attempted to answer the earlier and more challenging opposition of Branca and Bosco in "Sulle chiose all' elegia di Madonna Fiammetta del Boccaccio," *Leonardo,* 12 (1941), 49–60. One of his *ripostes* obviously delighted him. Branca had argued that elsewhere Boccaccio had (correctly) referred to the animal in the Pyramus and Thisbe story as a "leonessa," while the author of the *chiose* has it a "leone." Pernicone suggests that Branca study his own edition of the *Amorosa Visione* (Bari: Laterza, 1939) where, at XX.48, the animal in question is a "leone." See Branca's return in his next edition of that text (Firenze: Accademia della Crusca, 1944), p. CXLIX, n. 2, and the *A* and *B* texts of the Mondadori edition (*Opere,* III, 74, 198), which now show "leona" and "leena." The question was resolved, for all practical purposes, by A. E. Quaglio, *Le Chiose all' elegia di Madonna Fiammetta* (Padova, 1957), which met with general acceptance (see, *inter alia,* Limentani's review, *Convivium,* N.S. 26 [1958], 479–81). This book-length study opens with a complete and fair review of the problem (pp. 1–14), goes on to consider the tradition of the four MSS which contain the *chiose* (Branca had discovered Vaticano Rossiano 946 and Quaglio still another MS to add to Pernicone's two), and argues that the author is far more likely to have been someone like de' Bassi (see Giulio Bertoni, "Pietro Andrea Basso," *GSLI,* 78 [1921], 142–46, for a brief description of his fifteenth-century gloss of the *Teseida;* see also Ezio Levi, "Adriano de' Rossi," *GSLI,* 55 [1910], 201–65, esp. pp. 237–49, for a similar description of a late fourteenth-century gloss to the first book of the *Teseida*). Quaglio then turns to the internal evidence, and under nine rubrics gives good (if not always compelling) reasons for thinking that the *chiose* are not by Boccaccio (pp. 33–76). The first MS tradition is then offered (the text of the MSS discovered by Pernicone and Quaglio—pp. 115–66), and is followed by the MS found by Branca, the Rossiano (pp. 167–95). As always, Quaglio's scholarship and argumentation are sound, even brilliant, and his conclusions seem well founded.

One striking aspect of the four MSS that has escaped serious notice is that each of them breaks off with a gloss of Deianira in ch. VIII. Since she is hardly the last glossable of the *Elegia* (Jocasta, Hecuba, etc., follow hard upon) one is forced to wonder at the "coincidence." Why should all four MSS break off at exactly the same point? It seems at least probable that a fourteenth- or fifteenth-century glossator having a go at explicating the text of the *Fiammetta* would have wanted to complete his work, and also likely that a later copyist, coming upon an incomplete gloss and believing it to have been composed by someone other than Boccacio, would have finished the job he had found in an incomplete state. While it is true that several explanations might account for the identical point of rupture in all four MSS (coincidence is not one of them), the most likely hypothesis is that some or all of the copyists thought that they were copying the words of Boccaccio himself, and thus left the gloss incomplete. Under this hypothesis the glosses that are preserved may indeed be considered the remains of a lost Boccaccian original. The hypothesis has the merit of accounting for at least some of the orthographic and other variations from Boccaccio's usual practices so carefully put forward by Quaglio and would also support Pernicone's entirely reasonable observation that they are in no major respect at variance with Boccaccio's basic procedure as glossator in the *Teseida*'s *marginalia*—a good deal of "philology" and mythography, only momentary flights into allegory (for this last, see the striking similarity to the gloss on Venus in the *Teseida* found in the gloss here, n. 144, below).

128. The modern history of the *chiose* begins with G. Vandelli's discovery of a Boccaccio autograph containing them, "Un autografo della 'Teseide' (Laurenziana, Doni e Acquisti, 305)," *Studi di filologia italiana,* 2 (1929), 5–76, which concludes by pointing out that Boccaccio took as his model the gloss attributed to Lactantius Placidus on the *Thebaid.* A quarter century earlier P. Savj-Lopez, "Sulle fonti della 'Teseide,' " *GSLI,* 36 (1900), 57–78, had seen other codices containing the *chiose* and concluded that "vi fu chi volle faticosamente illustrare qualche episodio del poema cercandovi allegorie." Vandelli's discovery of the autograph proved conclusively that the laborious allegorizer was none other than Boccaccio himself. But he himself finds the two lengthy allegorical notes (on the temples of Mars and Venus) "singolarissime" (p. 65), evidently in the sense that they seem strange things for Boccaccio to have said: "Né meno straordinario della estensione ci riesce il significato allegorico che queste chiose dichiarano contenuto nelle parti del poema a cui riferiscono . . . e lo scrittore lo viene dimostrando con minuziose e sottili considerazioni, non senza lambiccature e stiracchiature in buon numero" (p. 64). Vandelli's puzzlement with his own discovery has, if anything, been only increased in other hands. A. Limentani, the editor of the Mondadori *Teseida,* some years ago, in his article "Tendenze della prosa del Boccaccio ai margini del 'Teseida,' " *GSLI,* 135 (1958), 524–51, characterized the Boccaccio of those lengthy *chiose* as "ingolfatosi in una confusa ed assurda analisi allegorica . . ." (542). Since Limentani's purpose was to study the *style* of Boccaccio's prose in the *chiose,* it is perhaps not fair to attack him for this judgment. But the author of this study cannot but wonder: If his best readers will not believe Boccaccio, why should they believe him? For information regarding another MS containing the gloss see E. Follieri, "I com-

menti al 'Teseida' del Boccaccio ed un codice corsiniano (Rossi CLXXVI, 44.B.12)," *Atti della Accademia Nazionale dei Lincei,* 11 (1956), 351–57. For Boccaccio as glossator, beginning with the *Teseida,* see Giorgio Padoan, *L'ultima opera di Giovanni Boccaccio* (Padova, 1959), pp. 47–49. For two forthcoming studies of the glosses to the *Teseida,* see the first chapter of Piero Boitani's monograph (which the author has kindly sent me in typescript) concerning the *Teseida* and the *Knight's Tale* (Oxford: Blackwell's *Medium Aevum* series) and my own article, "The Validity of Boccaccio's Self-Exegesis in His *Teseida,*" *Medievalia et Humanistica* (1977?).

129. "Sì come tra due signori li quali sieno l'uno da l'altro lontano, sono molte volte gli ambasciadori mezani a fare sapere a l'uno la intenzione dell'altro, così è tra noi e Iddio la orazione; e perciò qui l'autore la finge avere forma di persona acciò che possa dire quello che intende, perciò che dal farla persona prende conseguentemente cagione al disegnare la casa di Marte, sì come cosa da questa orazione veduta" (VII.29,1—p. 453). It is interesting to compare Panfilo's discussion of prayer in his concluding commentary on Cepparello (*Decameron* I.1.90), where the *mezzano* may be either good or bad himself, but mediates between us and God if we are pure of faith.

130. For Boccaccio's *nodosi e aspri* see *Inf.* XIII.5 and 7.

131. "Ad intelligenzia della qual cosa è da sapere che in ciascuno uomo sono due principali appetiti, de' quali l'uno si chiama appetito concupiscibile, per lo quale l'uomo disidera e si rallegra d'avere le cose che, secondo il suo giudicio, o ragionevole o corrotto ch'egli sia, sono dilettevoli e piacevoli; l'altro si chiama appetito irascibile, per lo quale l'uomo si turba o che gli sieno tolte o impedite le cose dilettevoli, o perché quelle avere non si possano" (VII.30, 1—p. 454). The description of these two appetites probably reflects, at some distance, Aquinas's formulations a century earlier (see *Summa Theologica* I, q. 81. a. 2; I–II, q. 23, a. 1).

132. Boccaccio uses the plural *Ire,* he says, because there is not only vicious, irrational wrath, but another kind which may be rational—righteous indignation is what he seems to have in mind. This leaves a door open to a necessary positive sense of Mars, such as one finds in Teseo's patron in Book I.

133. "E non solamente a questa ostinazione il tetto d'acciaio fa fuggire *la divina grazia* che di sopra viene, cioè il salutevole consiglio della ragione . . ." (VII.30,1—p. 455, italics added).

134. Since Boccaccio's (and Petrarch's) cultivation of Homer is not a subject of this study, I seize this opportunity to point to an extraordinary work concerning this subject, Agostino Pertusi, *Leonzio Pilato fra Petrarca e Boccaccio* (Venezia, 1964).

135. This study, unsurprisingly enough, finds itself in basic accord with J. V. Fleming, *The Roman de la Rose: A Study in Allegory and Iconography* (Princeton, 1969). For a recent attempt to mediate between the "hard line" of Robertson and Fleming and the "naturalist" interpretation of that work, see T. D. Hill, "Narcissus, Pygmalion, and the Castration of Saturn: Two Mythographical Themes in the *Roman de la Rose*," *Studies in Philology,* 71 (1974), 404–26. If anything, Boccaccio's treatment of carnal love is less ambiguous than that of Jean de Meun.

136. That doves are Venus's birds is a medieval commonplace. And see Boccaccio's gloss to VI.20,2: ". . . i colombi sono uccelli de Venere. . . ."

137. See *Inf.* V.116–20, Dante's question to Francesca, which also makes use of these three words, so popular in the tradition of love poetry, in the rime position.

138. Even the Tisiphone-like Venus of the *Elegia* (I, 17) warns Fiammetta against the excesses of "abominevole fuoco" like that of Myrrha, Semiramis, Biblis, Caunus, and Cleopatra. Janet Smarr has suggested to me that the fact that Boccaccio shows us nine victims of Venus significantly reflects his sense of the importance of the number nine to Dante. I would add that there are nine exempla of lust found in *Inferno* V, a fact first pointed out, I believe, by Ernst Robert Curtius, *European Literature and the Latin Middle Ages* (New York, 1963), p. 369.

139. One of Boccaccio's recurring mordant criticisms of carnal love and its concomitant "religion" is that only the rich have time for such activity. His readers have far too often taken him as a would-be member of the "court of love," as an amatory as well as a social *arriviste.* See his gloss here: "voluttuosa vita senza riccheza non potersi avere né lungamente seguire" (p. 471). And see, again, Ovid's "Divitiis alitur luxuriosus amor" (*Remedia,* 746).

140. In Boccaccio Venus's usual iconography involves her being partly nude and partly flimsily attired in purple. Here her *veste tanto sottil* have no color-

ation, but in the gloss she is "in parte nuda e in parte d'una porpora sì sottile coperta . . ." (p. 471). For consideration of the iconography of the sleeping Venus, see Millard Meiss, "Sleep in Venice: Ancient Myths and Renaissance Proclivities," *Proceedings of the American Philosophical Society,* 110 (1966), 348–82.

141. One of the few scholars to have paid significant attention to the gloss, if not for the direct study of Boccaccio's poem, is D. W. Robertson, Jr. See *A Preface to Chaucer* (Princeton, 1962), pp. 106n., 110, 260n., 370, 371.

142. The gloss to *ottave* 50–66 occupies pp. 462–72 of the Mondadori text. All the following citations of the gloss are from these pages.

143. As a medieval writer he inherited a long-standing Christian tradition of the same thing being capable of antithetic conception, either *in bono* or *in malo.*

144. See the gloss on *Venere Santissima* from the *chiose* to the *Elegia,* ed. Quaglio, *Le Chiose all'elegia di Madonna Fiammetta* (Padova: Cedam, 1957), p. 169: "dui sonno gli ussi [Quaglio: the Rossiano MS reads *vissi*] di Venere, cioè Venere licita e Venere illicita. Venere licita è de star lu marito con la sua moglie e però dice santissima; illicita si è de appetere lu marito altra donna che la sua e la donna oltro omo che 'l marito." If the orthography and expression are not Boccaccian, the thought is nearly identical to that expressed here.

145. The sentence stands as a gloss to a *locus* in the *Filocolo* as well. Biancifiore's bedchamber is flooded with light: "Luceva la camera, sì come chiaro giorno fosse" (IV, 118, 3); the light issues from the jewels that are the eyes of the "good" Cupid who will serve, in Filocolo's judgment, as their Hymen, Juno, and Venus, that is, as their god of marriage.

146. *Restauri boccacceschi* (Roma, 1945), p. 161.

147. See Guido Cavalcanti, *Rime,* ed. Guido Favati (Milano-Napoli: Ricciardi, 1957), pp. 359–78, for the Latin text. And see p. 348 for bibliographical notices. See also O. Bird, "The Canzone d'Amore of Cavalcanti According to the Commentary of Dino del Garbo," *Mediaeval Studies,* 2 (1940), 150–203; 3 (1941), 117–60. Bird offers a partial translation with commen-

tary. Bird seems unaware that the only MS which we possess of the Latin text of this commentary is a Boccaccio autograph (Vaticano Chigiano L. V. 176).

148. See again A. E. Quaglio, "Prima fortuna della glossa garbiana a 'Donna me prega' del Cavalcanti," *GSLI,* 141 (1964), 336–68. The Florentine doctor's Latin was *volgarizzato* by Jacopo Mangiatroia in the late fourteenth century. For the attribution of the MS to Boccaccio see A. Palescher, *GSLI,* 8 (1886), 364–73; but see the firm arguments of M. Barbi, who, in his critical edition of the *Vita Nuova* (Milano: Hoepli, 1907), pp. clxxiv–clxxviii, made the sure identification.

149. I quote from Favati's text, here from p. 359.

150. E.g., on Cavalcanti's "Risplende in sé perpetuale effecto": "Et propterea quod intellectus non est uirtus corporea particularis sicut sunt uirtutes sensitiue, cum amor de quo loquimur hic sit quedam passio corporalis et particularis, talis passio non habet esse in intellectu, cum in eo etiam non sint alie passiones corporales, ut sunt ira, tristitia, timor et similia" (p. 366); on "Fuor di salute": "idest: hec passio ponit iudicium [Boccaccio's *giudicio* comes back to mind] hominis extra salutem . . ." (p. 368); on "Et non si giri per trovarvi gioco": "nec etiam aliquis adhereat ei quia credat in ipso inuenire sapientiam multam uel paucam, quia in ipso nulla est sapientia neque discretio: imo potius quasi ultimo ille qui amat, cum bene est in feruore ipsius, devenit in fatuitatem et insipientiam" (p. 375).

151. Quaglio, "Prima fortuna . . . ," pp. 354–55.

152. "Prima fortuna . . . ," p. 348.

153. "Profilo biografico," p. 32n., disagreeing with Quaglio's opinion as to Boccaccio's interest in Guido.

154. "Prima fortuna . . . ," p. 348.

155. "Prima fortuna . . . ," p. 348. In a footnote Quaglio admits that part of the nurse's outburst against Amore in the *Fiammetta* (I, 15) is similar to Dino's paragraph (p. 373 of Favati's edition), "Deinde cum dicit . . . hanc passionem versantur," but continues by saying that such concepts,

common to the "casistica del tempo," may also be found elsewhere in Boccaccio. It becomes clear from such passages as these that Quaglio's argument rests on a major assumption, namely that Boccaccio's early works are written in praise of carnal love. This is, of course, a wisdespread assumption. See for example, G. A. Levi, "Boccaccio," in his *Da Dante a Machiavelli* (Firenze, 1935), p. 173, on the particular subject of Boccaccio's addiction to adulterous passion: "Di quelle gioie era sempre avido, ma del matrimonio era nemico."

156. "Prima fortuna . . . ," p. 365: "Ora soltanto possiamo render conto esatto del fatto che la glossa garbiana, anche se citata, non è stata usufruita nelle *Chiose* al *Teseida.* In clima stilnovistico, nel quale il Boccaccio del *Teseida* operava immerso nella tradizione lirica di Dante e Cino, non poteva trovar posto e accoglienza un' euristica amorosa che, ignorandola, coartava la misura tonale di *Donna me prega,* testo celebratissimo di una maniera poetica, esemplare scolasticamente: la novità della lettura fruttò, e altrimenti non poteva essere, una cursoria citazione."

157. Favati, p. 364, italics added in both passages. The *loci* are of some importance. It is at least likely—one should probably be less hesitant—that Dino's passage reflects the most important single definition of carnal love known to the late middle ages, that found in the opening words of the first chapter of the *De amore* of Andreas Capellanus: "Amor est passio quaedam innata procedens ex visione et immoderata cogitatione formae alterius sexus. . . ." Dino's text continues: "et uult dicere quod passio que est amor causatur ex apprehensione alicuius forme uisibilis, que quidem comprehenditur, ut postea dicet, sub ratione complacentie: que complacentia causatur aut quia uidetur sibi forma illius rei pulcra, uel ex gestibus illius forme, qui sibi placent, quicumque gestus sint illi." Dino's definition is reasonably close to that of Andreas. See n. 83, above.

158. To show how closely Boccaccio's definition follows Dino's, I beg the reader's patience for a final demonstration, in tabular form:

Boccaccio	Dino del Garbo
1. amore	amor
2. è una passione	passio est
3. nell'anima	quaedam anime
4. piaciuta	ex apprehensione
5. per alcuna cosa	alicuius rei

That Boccaccio intends to be understood as quoting Dino is made apparent by the phrase which precedes the definition: "Dice adunque sommariamente che . . . ," in which the subject of the verb *dice* is clearly Dino.

159. One further citation shall suffice: ". . . et licet, ut dixi prius, in amore de quo loquimur hic concurrat aliqua apprensio intellectus: tamen passio amoris non habet esse in intellectu; et ideo appetitus in quo habet esse amor non est intellectiuus, sed sensitiuus. Similiter autem, quia hic appetitus sensitiuus non est regulatus a ratione, imo est efferens et diuertens a ratione, ideo amor procedit a uirtute que non est rationalis sed sensibilis" (Favati, ed., p. 368).

160. A curiosity about which this writer appeals to his colleagues for enlightenment occurs in the sixteenth-century Platonizing treatise by Mario Equicola d'Alveto, *Di Natura d'Amore* (Venezia, 1587), p. 8ʳ. Equicola, discussing *Donna me prega,* "dove tratta d'amore, non secondo i Poeti, ma secondo i Filosofi," refers to "Dino Del Bel Corbo fiorentino." Is there an earlier tradition, of which Boccaccio might have been aware, that gives Dino's name in this fashion? If there is one, we might have another clue as to the meaning of the title of the *Corbaccio,* which might then be thought of as an assault on carnal love in the manner of Dino.

161. Favati, ed., p. 372.

162. M. Landau, *Giovanni Boccaccio, sua vita e sue opere,* tr. C. Antona-Traversi (Napoli, 1881), p. 235.

163. See n. 120, above. Diana is the moon in the sky, goddess of chastity on earth, Proserpina in hell. In the gloss, it must be conceded, her tripleness seems more the result of Boccaccio's mythographic tradition than a covert Christian intention.

164. Boccaccio's gloss reminds the reader that "Giunone è dea de' matrimonii." See the identical notation in glosses to X.40.2; XII.68.4.

165. Emilia's explanation of Arcita's death is curious (X.68–70): Venus has killed her fiancé, Acate (IV.35), and now Arcita because she hates the Amazons. This does not seem to square with the facts (Venus is perfectly willing to let Palemone have her). A few *ottave* later she refers to her prayer to Diana in Book VII, but does not here seem to think of Venus's antipathy toward

Diana—as she has previously done (VII,81,7), and as she will do to explain these same deaths at XII, 40–42. Theseus's reply will eventually enlighten her (XII.43).

166. The verse is "spoken" by the urn that contains his ashes (XI.91). Arcita's words in the sixth line reflect Dante's Capaneus (*Inf.* XIV.51): "Qual io fui vivo, tal son morto," as is also noted by Limentani (*Opere,* II, 899). The eternal blasphemer, whose original lies in Statius's *Thebaid,* gives a fitting final dimension to Arcita. For parallels between the death of Tristan and that of Arcita, see Daniela Branca, "La morte di Tristano e la morte di Arcita," *Studi sul Boccaccio,* 4 (1967), 255–64. For a brilliant study of the classical and medieval sources of *Teseida* XI.1–3, see Giuseppe Velli, "L'apoteosi di Arcita: ideologia e coscienza storica nel 'Teseida,' " *Studi e problemi di critica testuale,* 5 (1972), 33–66. What is missing in Velli's view of Arcita is a strong enough sense of his damnation; see XI.3.7–8: "e quindi se ne gio/nel loco che Mercurio li sortio." That *loco* is Inferno. As X.99–101, makes plain, Arcita knows that this is his destiny, but hopes (as does Fiammetta in *Elegia,* VI, 19) that he will be granted a pleasant rather than a horrible eternal situation in the afterlife, i.e., in Christian terms (or at least Dantesque ones) they both hope for a place in Limbo ("Eliso" to Arcita) rather than in Inferno itself. But his own awareness, as his death approaches, of the nearness of Acheron and of the "nere ombre, misere, tapine" (101.6) would seem to indicate that Mercury is leading him where he belongs, to Hell proper. In the *Esposizioni* Boccaccio refers to the Emperor Claudius as being described by Seneca as "cacciato di paradiso e menatone da Mercurio in inferno" (*Inf.* IV, *esp. litt.,* 338). For Mercury as psychopomp, in addition to the passage in the *Elegia* referred to above, see also *Genealogie,* II, 7; III, 20.

167. This is the first time in the text that the two goddesses are joined (see *Filocolo,* esp. III, 52, where Diana and Venus agree to intervene on behalf of the lovers together), although a small detail some 270 pages earlier has perhaps helped prepare us for this moment: Boccaccio's gloss to IV.73.8, says that the star Citerea "volgarmente è chiamata la stella Diana." Whatever the importance of this astronomical information, the union of the two is evidently necessary to the marital conclusion of the work. (While Diana is absent from the marriage of Ipolita and Teseo [I.134], her spirit of chastity is present in Ipolita herself and her Amazons.)

168. See his words: "la forma tua non è atta a Diana/servir ne' templi né 'n selva montana" (43.7–8).

169. I.134.2: "di Citerea il tempio fero aprire"; XII.48.7–8: "per che Teseo fece il tempio aprire/di Venere. . . ." Hymen is the only other god mentioned: I.134.7;XII.49.3.

170. Juno has three main roles in the *Teseida:* the opposer of the Thebans (e.g., III.1.1; IV.16.6; 17.6; X.95.7), the jealous wife of Jove (glosses to V.58.4; VI.38.4; XI.30.4), the goddess of matrimony (VII.83.2; X.40.2; XII.68.4; 75.7). The three roles have little, really nothing, to do with one another. It is perhaps a weakness of Boccaccio's mythography that it is frequently inconsistent, since it reflects the highly varied valences of the gods in Boccaccio's various sources. Or perhaps that is one of its pleasures.

3. Pagan Integument and Christian Design

1. P. G. Ricci, "Dubbi gravi intorno al 'Ninfale fiesolano,' " *Studi sul Boccaccio,* 6 (1971), 109–24, argues that the *Ninfale* is unlike, in various particulars, Boccaccio's other works of the 1340's, and is thus either not by him (a possibility that Ricci does not really defend) or is a very early work, contemporary with the *Caccia* and the *Filostrato* (and thus forming an early triad of works which do not celebrate Fiammetta). Only F. Maggini's advice—that the *Ninfale* is too accomplished a work to have been written so early in Boccaccio's career—keeps him in doubt about his hypothesis. One of his reasons for thinking the work of very early date or not by Boccaccio is dealt with intelligently by R. H. Terpening, "Il mito di Calisto e l'attribuzione del *Ninfale fiesolano,*" *Studi e problemi di critica testuale,* 7 (1973), 17–23, who shows that Boccaccio's treatment of this myth is various, and not unilateral, as Ricci would have us believe. Still, the question of the date of the *Ninfale* is very much an open one. And for another way in which the work is like the *Caccia* and the *Filostrato,* evidence which perhaps lends support to Ricci's argument, see n. 71, below.

2. "Era in quel tempo la falsa credenza/degl' iddii rei, bugiardi e viziosi" (6.1–2); see *Inf.* I.72, "al tempo degli dei falsi e bugiardi."

3. See E. Carrara's belief that the *Ninfale* is a literary reflection of Boccaccio's own seduction of a nun, "Un peccato del Boccaccio," *GSLI,* 36 (1900), 123–30. Such an event may or may not have actually occurred. It is the close positivism of Carrara's argument which it is impossible to accept.

4. The scene is clearly reminiscent of the *Caccia,* in which work the hidden narrator (IX.2–3) also gazes on a beloved *bella donna* (XVIII. 55–58). See also *Comedia ninfe* XLIX. 1–3.

5. He tells Girafone that he is tracking *una cerbietta,* one so beautiful that God Himself must have made her with his own hands (76). The singling out of one's love as being especially (and carnally) pleasing to God is a familiar motif, one that begins in the *Caccia* (XVIII.26–27) and runs through many of the *opere minori.*

6. See the previous discussion of *tristitia* and *melanconia* in chapter 2.

7. See M. Landau, *Giovanni Boccaccio* (Napoli, 1881), p. 332: "Il miracolo, che il poeta fa succedere presso l'altare di Venere, somiglia più una parodia che un vero miracolo. . . ." Landau, believing that Boccaccio approves of Venus, thinks his powers have failed him here. He hinges a perfectly correct perception to a widely accepted but highly dubious thesis.

8. See the "miracolo" in the *Caccia* (XVII.39–40) when Venus turns the burnt animals into men. Their "vite nuove" are probably meant to be understood as being equally short-lived.

9. The boar that Africo kills comes roaring through the woods with several arrows already in his back (214.7). In this respect he resembles Africo himself, who has similarly been wounded earlier (by Cupid's arrow) and who now rushes through the woods into the presence of nymphs. Both will die of a chest wound inflicted by Africo's weapon. Possibly to underline the identification, Boccaccio has the name Africo appear three times in this ottava.

10. His loose long blond hair makes him a natural transvestite—if one had not known who he was, one would have never thought he was a man, as Boccaccio makes plain (211–12). One is reminded that his "femininity" is related to a Christian *topos* of some standing: our appetitive soul is composed of an "Adam" and an "Eve," of masculine reason and feminine desire. It is clear which element is predominant in Africo.

11. The nymphs, about to bathe in the heat of the day, are verbally reminiscent of Francesca and Paolo (236.4): "sanz'alcun sospetto." Balduino (*Opere,* III, 811) notes Boccaccio's frequent use of *Inf.* V.129, but does not have any-

thing to say about its context, which may well be present here, since Africo and Mensola are about to be joined in a love which leads to death.

12. E 'nnanzi che spogliato tutto fosse,
le ninfe eran nell'acqua tutte quante;
e poi spogliato verso lor si mosse,
mostrando tutto ciò ch'avea davante.
Ciascuna delle ninfe si riscosse,
e, con boce paurosa e tremante,
cominciarono urlando: "Omè, omè,
or non vedete voi chi costui è?"

13. For a different view, see F. Maggini, "Le similitudini del 'Ninfale fiesolano,' " *Miscellanea storica della Valdelsa,* 27 (1919), 2: in the *Ninfale* "abbiamo la vita serena della campagna e gli affetti più gentili e soavi, espressi in una forma spontanea, elegante, efficace." His view of the thirty similes in the work—despite their at times violent humor—is roughly as this quotation would indicate. And see the remark of D. J. Donno, in the introduction to his translation of the work (New York, 1960), p. x: "Implicit in the story is the idea that violence to nature is evil."

14. The style of Boccaccio's comedic instinct is absolutely "modern" in at least one respect: He is a genius at showing what occurs aesthetically when words are taken literally, i.e., the comic effect is overwhelming. Diana has warned the nymphs that if a man should ever approach them they must run for their lives (21). All of them except Mensola take this as the letter of the law. The two times that the *brigata* encounters Africo, its members scatter like sheep running from a wolf (Boccaccio uses "classical" similes on both occasions—63 & 240). Of course there is a "moral" component here. But the predominant effect is comical in very much the same way that Bergson thought mechanistic behavior was funny. Africo is their "panic button." Show them a man, they run like sheep. See Ovid's double simile describing the rape of the Sabines, *Ars amatoria* I.117–20.

15. It is amusing to note that Africo will later kill himself with a *dardo* in the breast as Mensola attempts to do here. The mollifications of Venus are short-lived.

16. Sworn, of course, by the authority of Venus—see 292.5.

17. The words of Boccaccio's rubric above *ottava* 304 offer the briefest means of establishing the point:

> Le dolci parole e lusinghe avièno
> il cor di Mensola infin convertito
> al disio d'Africo e a l'appetito:
> con gran piacer insiem si congiugnièno.

18. Our "facitore" will later interrupt in order to separate her *peccato* from the rape (374.5–6).

19. For an early recognition of Boccaccio's large indebtedness to Ovid in the *Ninfale* see B. Zumbini, "Una storia d'amore e morte (il 'Ninfale Fiesolano' del Boccaccio)," *Nuova Antologia,* XIX, fasc. 5 (1 marzo 1884), pp. 12–13.

20. Dario Rastelli, "Pagine sul 'Ninfale Fiesolano,' " *Saggi di umanesimo cristiano,* 7, Nos. 2–3 (1952), 71, thinks otherwise. Unlike the death that takes off Paolo and Francesca, "La morte, poi, che coglie i due protagonisti non è un castigo, un'espiazione, non rappresenta la catarsi tragica di una colpa. . . . Essa non ha il compito di riscattare un amore che abbia perso o che si avviasse a perdere qualcosa della sua purezza, ma suggella invece quella medesima intatta purezza restia a scendere sul piano di una qualsiasi comune cronaca terrena. Anzichè sfiorire, resta in un' aura di suggestivo, incantevole vagheggiamento ideale."

21. Balduino speaks of the conclusion, "che troppo spesso i lettori moderni hanno avuto il torto di considerare estranea all'economia dell'opera," as revealing Boccaccio's plan to construct "una più complessa e compiuta parabola storica" (*Opere,* III, 283). But his view of what the parable means is sharply divergent from my own. He continues (p. 284) by describing Africo's passion for Mensola and its effect on the *anima ingenua* of the nymph as leading to "la scoperta della vita nella sua pienezza, nei suoi valori più autentici e puri (la bellezza, l'amore, il miracolo di una creatura che nasce, il sentimento della maternità); ma non meno contano [sic], dopo la morte dei giovani amanti . . . quel senso di continuità della vita che si coglie nella meravigliosa giovinezza di Pruneo amorosamente allevato dai nonni e poi nella sua ascesa politico-sociale." He concludes by pointing to the importance of the Florentine matter of these *ottave,* derived from the chronicles. This characterization, which offers a linear sense of development, is counter to my own, which rather sees a relationship of antithesis: Mugnone/Cialla: Girafone/Ali-

mena:: Africo/Mensola: Pruneo/Tironea. In this view of the work natural relationships do not necessarily produce civilized results. Pruneo's "parents"—insofar as his moral values are instilled by "parental" teaching—are not Africo and Mensola nearly so much as they are Girafone and Alimena.

22. This is the title found in the MSS. From the fifteenth century and into our own, printed texts have been under the title *Ameto.*

23. Marco Landau, *Giovanni Boccaccio,* p. 146.

24. "Profilo biografico," p. 57.

25. See the *postille* of Francesco Sansovino (Venezia, 1558). These notes are dedicated to his "lady," Gaspara Stampa, in a gesture that evidently reflects Sansovino's sense of Boccaccio's own practice as lover-poet. His reading, which has Lia-*bellezza terrena* and Fiammetta-*bellezza divina* sometimes has little to do with the text, but is at least "allegorical" in character.

26. See "L'allegoria dell' 'Ameto' del Boccaccio," *Atti e memorie della R. Accademia di scienze, lettere ed arti di Padova,* 2 (1866), 5-32: "Infatti in questa composizione sotto la veste letterale classica si nasconde un contenuto allegorico affatto cristiano: s'inneggia a Venere, e questa Venere è Dio. Così si ascende dalle lascivie dell'amore volgare alla contemplazione dell'amore divino" (p. 18). These findings are repeated in Crescini's *Contributo agli studi sul Boccaccio* (Torino, 1887), pp. 92–112, e.g., "L'opera del Boccaccio, che ha un fine morale come la *Commedia* dantesca, esalta dunque la pietà celeste e l'influsso benefico delle sette virtù, e mira a dimostrare con l'esempio di Ameto come gli uomini debbano redimersi seguendo la ispirazione divina e le virtù stesse . . ." (p. 97). For a later similar appreciation, see N. Sapegno, *Il Trecento,* 3rd. ed. (Milano, 1966), p. 307: "Questi [Ameto] è dunque il simbolo dell'umanità incolta e selvaggia, ingentilita dall'amore: amore dei sensi dapprima, ma che poi si purifica e, sorretto dalle virtù cardinali e teologiche, s'innalza alla contemplazione della Verità suprema."

27. *Opere,* II, 667.

28. Landau, for instance, while recognizing that this is an allegory, laments that Boccaccio fails to tell what happens *afterwards* to Ameto and the nymphs (*Giovanni Boccaccio,* p. 147). And see S. Battaglia, "Schemi lirici dell'arte del Boccaccio," *Archivum Romanicum,* 19 (1935), 69: "In definitiva egli è

rimasto schiacciato dalla sua stessa concezione macchinosa che nell' *Ameto* si proponeva di dimostrare il sorgere e l'evolversi della civiltà umana attraverso la luce intellettuale di Eros; e se lo scrittore fosse vissuto nel pieno Quattrocento a contatto del pensiero ficiniano, avrebbe potuto simulare una veste filosofica a questo suo timido teorizzare sull'amore; ma per il momento egli possiede solamente quel tanto dell'atteggiamento neoplatonico implicito nella teorica dello Stil novo, e anch'esso del resto sopraffatto dal gusto per il bucolico e dagli schemi ovidiani." But Battaglia's sense of what the *Comedia ninfe* tends to be about helps to explain his troubled and even confused sense of Boccaccio's problem with the work (p. 70): "In questa galleria di quadri troppo luminosi e allucinanti e di figure muliebri troppo nude e vistose, il Boccaccio ha chiarificato la sua posizione estetica, come contemplativa valutazione di pura bellezza terrena, goduta per se stessa, senza veli metaforici e senza preoccupazioni etiche. In questa ambizione esclusivamente d'arte, per cui l'estetica ritrova in se stessa la sua morale e i suoi fini, il Boccaccio ha individuato forse per primo la sensibilità umanistica." More recently, and in a similar vein, see G. Giacalone, *Boccaccio minore e maggiore* (Roma, 1959): "Il vero Boccaccio però rimane quello della prima parte del romanzo e quello delle narrazioni delle ninfe . . ." (p. 65).

29. See A. Schiaffini, *Tradizione e poesia nella prosa d'arte italiana dalla latinità medievale a G. Boccaccio* (Genova, 1934), p. 261: "Quasi tutta la prosa dell' *Ameto* è così manierata, esteriore e decorativa. . . ."

30. *Opere,* II, esp. pp. 668–73. And in a similar vein see Branca, "Profilo biografico," p. 59: "Il trionfo delle virtù—e della Virtù—rimane nelle due opere [*Comedia ninfe* and *Amorosa Visione*] una pura aspirazione, un astratto coronamento."

31. In Claricio's defense of Boccaccio against his detractors (Venezia, 1531—a reprinting of the 1521 Milano edition) it is interesting to find that the anonymous *detrattori* seemed to have linked the two works as being similarly displeasing, apparently on a stylistic basis (p. N, ii[r]).

32. Of the celestial presence at the conclusion A. Gaspary wrote: "È la Venere celeste, la vera deità che si manifesta"—*Storia della letteratura italiana,* tr. V. Rossi, 2nd ed. (Torino, 1900), II, 17.

33. Further to establish the implicit metaphor, one should note that the first of the nymphs, Mopsa, describes the striptease she performed to bring

Affron round to her (allegorically, to his senses)—XVIII.34–35. That life continues to imitate art is suggested by a news item in the Rome *Messaggero* of 30 April 1975 which describes the striptease performed by one Diana King as part of a religious service in a Unitarian church in Dallas, Texas. In his role as commentator, the pastor of the church, Bill Nichols, is quoted as saying "L'aspetto erotico di questa danza non è un peccato; dopo tutto noi veniamo concepiti eroticamente."

34. The *Comedia ninfe,* like the *Amorosa Visione,* is divided into fifty parts; there are nineteen *canzoni* in *terza rima* (and thus not, strictly speaking, *canzoni* but *ternarii*) and thirty-one sections of prose.

35. The allegorical sense of this *canzone*—as of those that follow—is only finally clarified, in general terms at least, in ch. XLVI, but its overtones are already fairly clear. Quaglio's notes, in the critical tradition begun in modern times by Crescini, are crisply to the point. Here is his terse recapitulation of the allegorical significance of Lia's song: "Il ternario è la presentazione degli attributi allegorici di Lia, la protagonista dell'opera, cioè la Fede cristiana, che nasce da un fiume (*Cefiso*), simbolo del battesimo; la quale diversamente dal fratello Narciso sa amare e condurre gli amanti, fra i quali, come vedremo, il rozzo Ameto, attraverso la purificazione della contemplazione, al gaudio eterno" (*Opere,* II, 910).

36. "Ella ancora, nata di dio, vorrà di dio avere figliuoli, e non d'un semplice cacciatore"—V, 19. That he thinks of carnal love as creating children is another sign that he is not the usual Boccaccian lover.

37. "A me non costa nulla il provare: se io piacerò, *consolazione etterna* riceverò nell'animo" (V 23—italics added). Even the phrase he uses to describe his imagined sexual success shows the direction in which Boccaccio is leading the work.

38. One thinks of the similar sacrifice, first intended for Diana but given in rebellion to Venus in the *Caccia di Diana* XVII.

39. It is probably just to maintain that the language of the religion of love is turned back on itself in the *Comedia ninfe* to reassume a Christian significance. For a study of the relationship of two Florentine birth salvers of the early Quattrocento to the text of the *Comedia ninfe* that displays a similar understanding see Paul F. Watson and Victoria Kirkham, "Amore e Virtù:

Two Salvers Depicting Boccaccio's 'Comedia delle Ninfe Fiorentine' in the Metropolitan Museum," *Metropolitan Museum Journal,* 10 (1975), 35–50.

40. The nymph in question seems to be Acrimonia.

41. The parallel construction of the seven tales and the identities of the lovers may be presented quickly as follows:

CHAPTER	NYMPH (VIRTUE)	COLOR OF GARMENT	DEDICATED TO	LOVER (FLAW)
XVIII	Mopsa (*saggezza*)	*rosato*	Pallas	Affron (*il dissennato*)
XXI, XXIII	Emilia (*giustizia*)	*sanguigno*	Minerva	Ibrida (*il superbo*)
XXVI	Adiona (*temperanza*)	*purpureo*	Pomona	Dioneo (*il dissoluto*)
XXIX	Acrimonia (*fortezza*)	*bianco*	Bellona	Apaten (*l'apatico*)
XXXII	Agapes (*carità*)	*vermiglio*	none, then Venus	Apiros (*il gelido*)
XXXV	Fiammetta (*speranza*)	*verde*	Vesta	Caleone (*il desperato*)
XXXVIII	Lia (*fede*)	*d'oro simile*	Cybele	Ameto ("umanità incolta e selvaggia")

A tabular description of the nymphs as virtues and the lovers with their qualities may be found in Sapegno, *Il Trecento,* p. 307. Quaglio's similar list (*Opere,* II, 673) is marred by what one assumes to be a printer's error which transfers Apaten's epithet to Dioneo and omits Acrimonia's and Apaten's names.

42. See Hauvette, *Boccace* (Paris, 1914), p. 114: ". . . tout est superficiel et frivole dans cette laborieuse allégorie: l'identification de Dieu avec Vénus pourrait n'être qu'inattendue; en réalité elle frise l'inconvenance, quand on lit les exploits licencieux dont se vantent ces prétendues vertus, cardinales ou théologales. . . . La disparité absolue, paradoxale entre le signe employé et la chose signifiée atteint ici les confins du grotesque; il faudrait peu de chose pour que le récit versât dans une indécente bouffonnerie." To take the *Comedia ninfe* not as a botch, as Hauvette essentially takes it, but as an intentional send-up of allegorical poetry is at least logically sound. It is amusing to listen to Hauvette fume at Boccaccio's "serious" work for being buffoonery, while he swoons at Boccaccio's buffoonery, e.g., "Pour Boccace, l'amour a un caractère sacré" (p. 86)—his response to the carnality at the end of *Filocolo,* III.

43. See the fifty-eight Neapolitan ladies of the *Caccia.* As Quaglio observes, these allusions furnished positivistic criticism of the *Comedia ninfe* with a

good deal of its prime interest in the work. His brief and cogent notes (pp. 926, 929, 934, 942, 947, 951, 959) offer his own sense of the state of the problem, which may be summarized as follows: Two of the ladies (Mopsa, Adiona) are securely identified; two others (Agapes and Lia) are associated with particular Florentine families, but further identification seems dubious; one (Emilia) is identified by some, considered a fictional creation like Fiammetta by others (see Branca, "Profilo biografico," p. 59n., for a resumé of the main pertinent bibliography); another (Acrimonia) is identifiable as "la bella lombarda" of *Amorosa Visione* XL.66, and the "monna Vanna" of the *ternario* "Contento quasi" (*Rime* LXIX)—but who she may be we do not know; and the last (Fiammetta) is portrayed as the illegitimate daughter of Roberto d'Angiò, inheriting this part of Boccaccio's familiar pseudo-biography. In short, and although the entire issue is confused and confusing, we can say that there seems to be a mixture of the historical and the fanciful at work in the literary beings of these nymphs. This is certainly true for their husbands. The first three ("Nero," "Giovanni," and Pacifico) are clearly identifiable Florentines. The last three have no clues whatsoever attached to them and seem clearly fictional. (Lia has no husband, only her beloved—and fictional—Ameto.) There is the further complication of Boccaccio's supposed autobiographical "self-portraits" in Ibrida and Caleone, beloved of Emilia and Fiammetta, respectively. They have been the focus of considerable attention in the "biographical" studies of the *opere minori.* C. Antona-Traversi, in one of his numerous notes to Landau's *Giovanni Boccaccio* (Napoli, 1881), claims that Boccaccio's first audience knew who all these ladies were (p. 147). That seems a hopeful notion.

44. See Rosemond Tuve, *Allegorical Imagery* (Princeton, 1966), for a discussion of the difference between at least some medieval expectations of allegory and our own.

45. "Botticelli's Mythologies: A Study in the Neoplatonic Symbolism of His Circle," *JWCI,* 8 (1945), 38.

46. That something by way of a heightening in Ameto's moral consciousness should occur as the four cardinal virtues yield to the three theological virtues seems fitting.

47. See Quaglio, *Opere,* II, 959, accepting Crescini's reading for the second possibility. Teogapen's hymn (XI) was the last previous fully Christian exposition in the text.

48.
Io conosco che li ben sovrani
e gl'infimi qua giù furon creati
interi, e ben, dalle divine mani,
e 'nnanzi a' nuovi secoli formati
essere in tre persone e una essenza
etterno il sommo ben da cui sian dati.
(XXXIX, 19–24)

The passage goes on to describe the birth, death, and resurrection of Jesus, turns an approving eye on marriage ("e legittimi e giusti ancor gli amori/del matrimonio tengo"—XXXIX.61–62), and concludes with hopes for Paradise.

49. Aldo Scaglione, *Nature and Love in the Late Middle Ages* (Berkeley and Los Angeles, 1963), finds it difficult to take these words at face value (p. 120). However, see the *chiose* to *Teseida* VII.50 & 65 (*Opere,* II, 463 & 472): "la quale Venere è doppia . . ."; "Per il pomo, il quale dice Venere avere in mano, vuole dimostrare la stolta elezione di quegli che così fatta vita ad ogni altra prepongono." The Venus of whom "non si parla" in the *Teseida* is seen to be the only Venus of the *Comedia ninfe.* Within the symbolic structure of the work the other Venus is an accommodative form of her true celestial self.

50. Several aspects of the scene are modelled on Dante's. See the verbal echo in "del divino viso l'effigie" (XLII, 5) of "la nostra effige" (*Par.* XXXIII.131, for the likeness of Christ).

51. XLVI, 5: "e brievemente, d'animale bruto, uomo divenuto essere li pare"; *Caccia* XVIII.11–12: "di cervio mutato in creatura/umana e razionale esser per certo."

52. Here Boccaccio adverts to the ancient *topos dolce/utile* which will be prominent in the *cornice* of the *Decameron* (*Proemio* 14).

53. "Similemente vede che sieno le ninfe, le quali più all'occhio che allo 'ntelletto erano piaciute, e ora allo 'ntelletto piacciono più che all'occhio; discerne quali sieno i templi e quali le dee di cui cantano e chenti sieno i loro amori, e non poco in sé si vergogna de' concupiscevoli pensieri avuti, udendo quelli narrare; e similemente vede chi sieno i giovani amati da quelle e quali per quelle sieno divenuti" (XLVI, 3).

54. See A. Schiaffini, *Tradizione e poesia* (Genova, 1934), p. 257, who says that the work, "rinnovando l'egloga, si prova a dar forma classica latina a un

mondo allegorico cristiano, a conciliar Dante con Virgilio." His sense of priorities seems absolutely right, in that Boccaccio fits the classical to the Christian rather than the obverse, such as we find the arrangement in later Neoplatonists (e.g., Marsilio Ficino), who fit Christianity into the preferred pagan structure. The distinction, one which is not easily made, is one that is of the utmost importance to any deliberation that concerns the nature of European intellectual history.

55. See V. Branca, " 'L'Amorosa visione,' (Origini, significati, fortuna)," *Annali della R. Scuola Normale Superiore di Pisa,* S. II, 11 (1942), 283–90: The *Amorosa Visione* is "l'opera boccaccesca più presente a quel rinnovamento di schemi letterari e di atteggiamenti sentimentali che caratterizza la cultura poetica dell'Umanesimo e del Rinascimento" (p. 290). And see *Opere,* III, 21, for a brief record of the work's Italian and European *fortuna.*

56. It is at least possible that the little poem (twenty *ottave* in length) known as "La visione di Venus" which seems to be of fourteenth-century origin is one of the progeny of the *Amorosa Visione.* The text is published by A. D'Ancona, *Giornale di filologia romanza,* 1, (1878), 111–18. Where G. B. Baldelli had thought the work to be certainly by Boccaccio, D'Ancona prefers to remain dubious, if willing to consider the possibility (pp. 111–12). The poem resembles a shorthand version of the *Amorosa Visione.* Its narrator, alone in his bed, is approached by Venus, who takes him to a field where he sees happy lovers, and then, on a cloud, takes him to heaven. There he sees a *nobil giovinetto* on a throne (it is clearly Amore). Two spirits—one is *onestà,* the other *cortesia* (are they related to the two anti-guides of the *Amorosa Visione?*)—hold a crown over Amore's head. The dreamer sees the seven virtues and the seven liberal arts, and then a *triumphus Cupidinis.* The dreamer longs to enter Amore's service, but the pageant disappears, and he is left alone and sad, but eager to tell what he has seen to "ciaschedun ch' ha gentil core" (XX.2). While the poem is no longer discussed as possibly being by Boccaccio (it certainly seems not to be), it is perhaps interesting to consider it as the possible result of a reading of the *Amorosa Visione* and perhaps the *Comedia ninfe* as well by an unknown coeval of Boccaccio.

57. *Giovanni Boccaccio* (Napoli, 1881), p. 151. See V. Branca's even less kind judgment, *Opere,* III, 20: "questo mediocrissimo poemetto." That is surely unfair to Boccaccio. N. Sapegno, in his article "Giovanni Boccaccio," in the *Dizionario biografico degli Italiani* (Roma, 1968), p. 845b, calls the work "la scrittura più povera, scolorita e prosaica del Boccaccio. . . ."

58. Where the narrator is clearly not "Boccaccio," but the lady in question. Boccaccio's tactic here should have long ago alerted his readers—especially those of the "biographical" school—that one must take care not to make easy assumptions about the identity of Boccaccio's narrators.

59. These were first printed in Claricio's 1521 edition (the *editio princeps*—see V. Branca in *La Bibliofilia,* XL [1938], 460–68), where they are printed near the end of his "Apologia" (p. O, vii,[r] in the Venetian reprint of 1531), and where Claricio refers to the last of them as a "madriale." A. Gaspary, *Storia della letteratura italiana* (Torino, 1900), II, 18, identifies them as "due sonetti caudati" and "un sonetto doppio caudato." H. Hauvette, *Boccace* (Paris, 1914), p. 131n., refines the description of the third sonnet to " 'rinterzato' et 'caudato.' " Branca, attacking the inexact descriptions of Claricio and others, up to Landau, says exectly what Hauvette had said, it is "un sonetto rinterzato e caudato," *Opere,* III, 557. Branca describes Boccaccio's acrostic exercise as follows: "Nella loro bizzarra stranezza, nella loro artificiosità arida, gli acrostici dell' *Amorosa Visione* rappresentano un vero capolavoro che non teme confronti" (*Opere,* III, 554).

60. I.e., they spell the Italian word for "mine," *Opere,* III, 554.

61. Boccaccio's rubric to the sonnets, which announces their acrostic nature (one can imagine his anxiety lest his *coup de foudre* go unnoticed) concludes: "E però che in quelli il nome dell'autore si contiene, altrimenti non si cura di porlo." The statement is true for all the vernacular works, not merely for the rest of the *Amorosa Visione,* and may reflect Dante's *apologia* for naming himself at *Purg.* XXX.55 ("quando mi volsi al suon del nome mio,/che di necessità qui si registra"—XXX.62–63).

62. In this connection one is likely to think of the gloss to *Teseida* III.35.5–8 ("E così sa Amore adoperare/a cui più per servigio è obligato:/colui il sa che tal volta fu preso/da lui e da cota' dolori offeso"): in the margin of the text, next to the word *preso* is Boccaccio's notation "che sono io." This authorial intervention is treated by Vandelli (see "Un autografo della 'Teseida,' " *Studi di filologia italiana,* 2 [1929], 47), as further proof that the *Teseida* is to be considered autobiographical. Limentani's gloss to the gloss (*Opere,* II, 891) takes another tack: "Il referimento in chiosa a sue pene d'amore è la punta di maggior civetteria nel fantasioso edificio dell'autobiografia del Boccaccio." Perhaps no smaller point clarifies so directly the conflicting responses that may be drawn from the evident spectacle of Boc-

caccio's profession of the religion of love. I shall return to these concerns in the following chapter. But here I should underline the fact that the love by which both narrator and glossator own themselves caught is not seen as pleasant. That is, as was the case with Fiammetta in *Filocolo,* IV, the speaker admits to being caught in the toils of Love without enjoying or approving of his situation. He is, after all, "preso da [Amore] e *de cota' dolori offeso*" (italics added), as Fiammetta (*Filocolo,* IV, 46, 20) admits to being caught in his nets in a tone of lamentation rather than one of joy. In a sense both Vandelli and Limentani would seem to be right, the latter in that his remark points to the coquettishness of Boccaccio's stance as love-struck glossator, one who stands in the margin next to a love-struck narrator, who himself narrates the *dolori* of Arcita and Palemone. Yet Vandelli's view has the virtue of reconciling what we do know about Boccaccio's life, which includes the fact that he was frequently embroiled in carnal affections, with the ironic view of carnal love that we find in the fictions. As the expression has it, it takes one to know one.

63. For some of the precedents of this equation in Dante and in Cavalcanti, see Branca, *Opere,* III, 645.

64. The textual history of the *Amorosa Visione* is one of the more interesting problems in Boccaccio studies. It would be futile to attempt to reproduce briefly Branca's masterful contribution in this area—another territory which he may fairly claim as being his own—and which is currently in dense resumé in *Opere,* III, 541–49. What Branca has been able to demonstrate is that the second redaction of the poem, which he believes was effected between 1355 and 1360, is entirely Boccaccio's own revision. It is most interesting to have such a document. One only regrets that Branca and/or his publisher did not choose to print the two versions alongside one another (rather than one after the other, as has been done) in the Mondadori edition. For a close analysis of textual problems raised by Branca's 1944 edition, see Gianfranco Contini, *GSLI,* 123 (1946), 69–99.

65. Quotations and citations are from the later *B* text, with notice of variant readings in *A* when such occur (mere orthographical changes will not be recorded).

66. In *A* both ladies are called *donna gentile.* It is as though Boccaccio wanted to remove a possible source of confusion, for in *B* his mortal lady is *donna leggiadra,* this apparition *donna lucente.*

67. Boccaccio's fifty chapters in the *Comedia ninfe* and even more probably the fifty *canti* of the *Amorosa Visione* reflect a sense of inferiority to the great(er) Dante—that is, to attempt half a *Commedia* seemed daring enough to Boccaccio. And perhaps no other of his works, all of which are studded with bits and pieces of Dante, offers him as warm and moving a tribute. See V.70–88, where Boccaccio includes Dante, in his version of the *bella scola* of *Inferno* IV, as the only modern in the exalted presence of the great writers of the past (the list begins with Virgil at V.7; see also *Filocolo,* V, 97, 4–6, for a similar treatment). It is pointed and poignant that Boccaccio shows Dante as being crowned with the laurel, an honor that escaped him during his lifetime (and thus considerably downgrading all subsequent prizes for literary excellence; it is worth considering that Boccaccio most likely composed these lines within months of Petrarch's coronation on the Capitoline in April 1341—an event which surely struck him). The wave of praise sweeps into the next canto, where Dante is "il maestro dal qual io/tengo ogni ben" (VI.2–3), and where Boccaccio longs that Dante had lived longer. The obvious reason for this hope is that the two poets might then have known one another, that Boccaccio might have proffered his gift of praise in person. So emotional is his response to the sight of Dante that the work comes to a standstill. Neither the "pilgrim" nor his author seems to wish to continue. The guide's stern admonition is touching: "Why do you stare so? Do you perhaps believe that you can bring the dead back to life with gazing?" (VI.23–24).

68. *Opere,* III, 560; and see p. 16, as well as Branca's earlier discussion, "'L'Amorosa visione,' (Origini, significati, fortuna)," *Annali della R. Scuola Normale Superiore di Pisa,* S. II, 11, (1942), 279n. He discards the "ipotesi incerte e contraddittorie" that have previously been advanced ("la Virtù, la Fede, Venere celeste, la Ragione, la Fortezza, la Madonna"). One of these, however, seems a likely candidate, as I shall shortly argue. At any rate, the notion of a medieval writer constructing an allegorical lady who has no specific allegorical significance is at least a strange one, and seems rather to be based on our own ignorance than on any justification which may be found in Boccaccio's text.

69. Branca, *Opere,* III, 560, shows that the crown, apple, and sceptre that she wears and carries are the three *signa* of royalty in *Decameron* X.1.17 and *Teseida* XI.36 (and also that the apple and sceptre are royally conjoined in *Filocolo,* IV, 74, 7).

70. Gaspary, in a review of Koerting's *Boccaccio's Leben und Werke* (Leipzig, 1880), remarks, in polemic with Koerting but almost in passing, "Diese Führerin ist die himmlische Liebe, die Venere celeste"—*Literaturblatt für germanische und romanische Philologie,* 2, No. 1 (1881), 25.

71. The color—perhaps for the sake of the rhyme—is *viole.* Boccaccio's "color symbolism" is not consistent, but we do have a large amount of evidence which suggests a likely connection here between the color and Venus. In the earliest works, we find exceptions. The *Caccia* has Venus totally nude (XVII.31); her followers put on vermilion robes (XVII.44), while the nymphs, when they worshipped Diana, wore purple ones (II.29). In the *Filostrato* Venus does not appear in the action and is thus not described. However, beginning with the *Filocolo,* in all the rest of the early works, with the exception of the *Ninfale fiesolano* (the only later work in which she appears and is not described in terms of her vestments or lack of them, and where Diana's color is purple—12.8), she is partly nude, partly clothed in purple (*Filocolo,* II, 48, 16; III, 53, 3; *Teseida* VII.65—where the color of her *veste tanto sottil* is only given as purple in the gloss; *Comedia ninfe,* XXXII, 37; *Elegia di madonna Fiammetta,* I, 16).

72. For Boccaccio's frequent, even compulsive, references to the Judgment of Paris, see Branca's note, *Opere,* III, 679 (but for *Comedia ninfe,* XXX, 3, read XXXI, 3).

73. *Amorosa Visione* I.49–51: " 'Lascia,' diss'ella, 'adunque i van diletti/e seguitami verso quell'altura/che posta vedi inanti a' nostri aspetti (ch'opposta vedi qui a' nostri petti"—*A*); *Comedia ninfe* IV.52–57: "Né per me sentirà mai nullo amaro/tempo chi con saver la mia bellezza/seguiterà, come già seguitaro/color li qua', dopo lunga lassezza,/lieti posai appresso i loro effetti/nel ben felice della somma altezza"; *Comedia ninfe* XLI.10–12: "Chi di me parla, alle cose superne/la mente avendo con intero core,/spregiando il mondo e le cose moderne."

74. As Branca would have it, *Opere,* III, 561: "il paragone della Guida celeste con Giunone indica uno spontaneo ricorrere della fantasia dello scrittore alla cultura mitologica. . . ."

75. See the discussions in Ch. ii of the marriage scenes in the *Filocolo* and *Teseida.*

76. For the influence of the French work in Italy, see L. F. Benedetto, *Il 'Roman de la Rose' e la letteratura italiana* (Halle, 1910).

77. One of the many features of correspondence between the *Amorosa Visione* and Petrarch's *Trionfi* is the presence of an enigmatic and "allegorical" *guida* in both works. Giuseppe Billanovich, "Dalla 'Commedia' e dall' 'Amorosa Visione' ai 'Trionfi,' " *GSLI,* 123 (1946), 25–26, suggests that the guide in the *Trionfo d'Amore* is none other than Boccaccio. His solution fulfills all the six conditions laid out by Carlo Calcaterra for a successful candidacy, *Nella selva del Petrarca* (Bologna, 1942), pp. 145–49. (Calcaterra's lengthy list of candidates, which does not include Boccaccio, culminates in the election of Giovanni d'Arezzo.) However, R. di Sabatino, in reviewing Billanovich's *Petrarca letterato* (Roma, 1947) in *Studi petrarcheschi,* 2 (1949), 232, objects that on two grounds Billanovich's solution is unacceptable: Boccaccio, as the younger of the two, would not refer to Petrarch as "figliuol mio" (*Trionfo d'Amore* I.60—but see Billanovich, art. cit., pp. 26n.–27n.); Petrarch did not know Boccaccio in his youth (*Trionfo d'Amore* I.52–54—but the lines do not claim acquaintanceship on the *guida*'s part with more than the reputation of the young Petrarch as being inclined to love). Billanovich's hypothesis, advanced tentatively, indeed in the form of a question ("L'amico . . . non sarà dunque Giovanni Boccaccio, il caro autore dell'entusiasmante *Amorosa Visione?*"), remains entirely attractive.

Perhaps more interesting than this small, if important, detail is the at times amusing history of the critical resistance to the plain notion (it is plain to anyone who has read the two works with any care and the simulacrum of an open mind) that the *Trionfi,* whether or not they were "inspired" by the *Amorosa Visione* (which they most probably were, at least in the sense that Petrarch took the basic concept of his work from Boccaccio), reflect large amounts of the earlier work. The modern debate probably began with E. Proto, "Sulla composizione dei 'Trionfi,' " *Studi di letteratura italiana,* 3 (1901), 1–96, who was the first to oppose the nineteenth-century notion that, if there were any influence to be found, it was that of Petrarch on Boccaccio (see M. Landau, *Giovanni Boccaccio,* p. 155). H. Hauvette, *Boccace,* p. 135, sides with Proto when he says, ". . . lorsque Pétrarque composa ses *Triomphes,* il tira certainement plus d'inspirations de l'*Amorosa Visione* que de la *Divine Comédie.*" The approximate reverse of this position is found in Calcaterra's *Nella selva del Petrarca.* The major contribution in this large, problematical, and important area of Boccaccio and Petrarch studies is—once again—by Vittore Branca. Dealing gently with such totally incorrect views as that of R. Serra, "Dei 'Trionfi' di Francesco Petrarca," *La Romagna,* 16 (1927), 8–35, 109–63—e.g., "E così sempre. Non lo spunto di un verso mai o di un'immagine, non uno scorcio mai, un atteggiamento, un fantasma, una forma che richiami, pur una volta, nel Petrarca, il Boccaccio" (p. 122—Branca kindly explains that this piece, published posthumously, was Serra's *dissertazione di laurea,* written in fourteen days and not retouched for publication), Branca lays out many precise reverberations of Boccaccio's text in Petrarch's (including the presence of an enigmatic *guida*), pp. 700–06 of his "Per la genesi dei 'Trionfi,' " *La Rinascita,* 4 (1941), 681–708. Billanovich, arguing from other materials and from another slant, comes up with a highly similar result, art. cit., pp. 1–52, and see *Petrarca letterato,* pp. 145–76. E. Raimondi, first in *Convivium,* N. S. 1 (1948), 438n., and then in *Studi petrarcheschi,* 3 (1950), 223–226, disagrees with both Branca and Billanovich. Here is an example of the quality of his defense of Petrarch's "originality": "La sua vicenda di uomo distesa nel tempo tra l'amore, la morte, la fama e l'eterno, è l'origine vera dei *Trionfi*" (p. 226 of the review in *Studi petrarcheschi*), hardly a convincing position to argue from, since one's experiences as a man of letters is generally conceded to include, in shall we say major ways?, the letters of others. Doubts—or a moderate "qualche riserva"—had already been expressed in the same journal, 2 (1949), 53–56, concerning the Branca/Billanovich position by G. Martellotti. But it is probably fair to say that even the most Romantically inclined Petrarchan must now assent that his author owes, in the *Trionfi,* a great deal to the Boccaccio of the *Amorosa Visione.*

78. II. 1–18 (variants from the *A* text are italicized, and the original readings are offered in the right-hand margin):

"O somma e graziosa intelligenzia	
che muovi il terzo cielo *e ogni sua idea,*	o santa dea
metti nel petto mio la tua potenzia:	
non sofferir che fugga, o *santa dea,*	Citerea
a me l'ingegno all'opera presente,	
ma più sottile e *via* più in me ne crea.	*omitted*
Venga il tuo *buon* valor nella mia mente,	*omitted*
tal che 'l mio dir d'Orfeo risembri il suono,	
che *placò il duca della morta gente.*	mosse a racquistar
Infiamma me più tanto ch'i' non sono,	la sua parente
che l'ardor tuo, di ch'io tutto m'invoglio,	
faccia *esser grato* quel di ch'io ragiono.	piacere

Poi che condotto m'ha a quest'*alto* soglio	*omitted*
costei, che *sol seguir lei* mi si face,	cara seguir
menami tu colà *dove io gir* voglio,	ov'io ir
acciò che' passi miei, che van per pace	
seguendo 'l *chiaro* raggio *di* tua stella	*omitted;* della
venghino a quell'effetto che ti piace."	vengano

79. See Branca, *Opere,* III, 562: "All'inizio di una visione 'amorosa,' che ha per fine l'esaltazione della donna e dell'amore come via alla virtù, è naturale l'invocazione alla potenza che il poeta ritiene principio di questa forza." He characterizes the invocation as existing in "un' atmosfera quasi filosofica," noting in *B* "tendenze più riflessive e religiose della maturità" (to account for the substitution of the phrase "o santa dea" for the "Citerea" of *A* in line 4), and suggesting that the Dantesque reminiscences of the passage also help to account for the "tono esteriormente più religioso del poema" (p. 563). The "religious tone" is here—but is it not the tone of the religion of love, in which Venus is as often called "santa dea" as she is called by name? Branca's reading, it can and will be argued, is based on a hypothesis that requires closer attention, namely that the narrator of the *Amorosa Visione* celebrates a higher, more philosophical kind of love. The poem is probably Boccaccio's most complicated (if not his most complex) work, but it does offer enough by way of negative indication to make Branca's reading suspect.

80. Contesting Gaspary's identification of the *guida* and *Venere celeste,* A. Della Torre, *La giovinezza di Giovanni Boccaccio* (Città di Castello, 1905), p. 114, points out that the *guida* of Canto I and the *dea* of Canto II are not the same. His argument assumes that there is only one Venus—or that the *dea* invoked is the celestial one. Neither of these positions is intrinsically valid. F. De Sanctis, "Il Boccaccio e le sue opere minori," *Nuova Antologia,* 5 (1870), 238, sees Boccaccio as invoking Venere in Canto II—by which he evidently intends the carnal goddess.

81. It is true that the narrator will temporarily escape from his guide in his pursuit of carnal love (XL–XLVII), and that she will, once she has made her alliance with the *donna bella,* leave the two of them alone for some moments (XLVIII–XLIX). But her clear purpose is to continue in her office until the dreamer/narrator has achieved true happiness—which is not the kind he himself seeks.

82. As Branca has noticed (*Opere,* III, 563): "Con una preghiera molto simile aveva iniziato anche la *Comedia ninfe* (terzine del proemio), che nasce e si sviluppa da posizioni sentimentali e intellettuali affini a quelle dell' *Amorosa Visione*" (see his longer discussion in his article on the *Amorosa Visione, Annali della R. Scuola Normale Superiore di Pisa,* S. II, 12 [1942]). Yet if the allegorical aspects of the works are similar, it is not necessarily true that the narrators of either work will share the beatitude of Ameto, who *is* drawn up into a higher love. My discussion here anticipates what will be said of Boccaccio's narrators in the following chapter, to which the reader may wish to refer at the present time.

83. The following exercise will make the point clear. If we were to find a fragment of a fourteenth-century manuscript on which are written only the following words, have we found a *laude* to the Virgin or carnal praise of a lover's beloved? "Graziosa donna della mia salute,/il tuo servitor ti chiede aiuto;/le misericordie tue dammi tutte/acciò che posseder possa 'l frutto. . . ." All we could safely say on the basis of that much is that there were some rather inept fourteenth-century poets.

84. ". . . tal che 'l mio dir d'Orfeo risembri il suono,/che placò il duca della morta gente"—II.8–9; in *A* the second line reads "che mosse a racquistar la sua parente."

85. For brief treatments of Orpheus's role in three medieval works (Boethius's *De consolatione,* pp. 78–79; the glosses on Boethius by Guillaume de Conches, pp. 96–98; the lyric "Parce continuis," pp. 98–103), see Winthrop Wetherbee, *Platonism and Poetry in the Twelfth Century* (Princeton, 1972). What emerges in Wetherbee's view of the Orpheus found in these three texts is a perhaps too modern view of an ambiguous note in the various authors. E.g., according to Wetherbee the poem that concludes the third book of the *De consolatione* (*metr.* 12) and two of the poems in the following book (*metr.* 3—concerning Ulysses and Circe—and *metr.* 7) have in common "an undertone of suppressed feeling which is at odds with their ostensibly exemplary purpose" (p. 79). This may or may not be so, but a medieval reader was certainly likely to take Lady Philosophy's Orpheus as monitory. (For the suggestion that the "vasta concezione morale-cristiana" of the *Amorosa Visione* possibly derives from Boethius, see V. Branca, "Per la genesi dei 'Trionfi,' " *La Rinascita,* 4 [1941], 697n.–98n., and see *Opere,* III, 584. For a brief but important consideration of the scholarly neglect of Boccaccio's dependence upon Boethius, see G. Velli, "L'apoteosi di Arcita," *Studi e*

problemi di critica testuale, 5 [1972], 40–43.) Guillaume de Conches sees Orpheus's failure to bring Eurydice back from the lower world (which he glosses as "earthly delight") as his great failure, one that demonstrates that he had not mastered the earthly impulse in himself. His turning back, for Guillaume, leaves him "ut canis reuersus ad uomitum." Wetherbee gives the reference to Proverbs 26:11 (without reminding the reader of the rest of the text): "As a dog returneth to his vomit, so a fool returneth to his folly." Boccaccio certainly knew Boethius and seems to have known either Guillaume's commentary or some form of it. While in the *Genealogie* (V, xii, "De Orpheo Apollinis filio VIIII°," pp. 244–47 of Romano's edition) Boccaccio derives his Orphic material from a variety of sources, as was his continual practice, there seems to be a clear dependence on the formulations of Guillaume. Fulgentius is cited as the source for the significance of Orpheus's name ("quod interpretatur vox optima"—p. 246). But this would seem to be all of Fulgentius's brief treatment of Orpheus, which allegorizes the myth as a recounting of the origin of the arts (*Mythologicon,* III, x, "Fabula Orphei et Euridicis," ed. R. Helm [Leipzig, 1898]), that Boccaccio has in mind. Guillaume's text also admittedly borrows from Fulgentius (citing Fulgentius in medieval "classical studies" being the rough equivalent of citing Curtius in contemporary medieval studies), and gives the same phrase for Orpheus's name ("id est optima vox"). Much of the rest of Boccaccio's gloss seems inspired by Guillaume—as even the citation of Fulgentius may be. See E. Jeauneau, "L'Usage de la notion d'*integumentum* à travers les gloses de Guillaume de Conches," *Archives d'Histoire Doctrinale et Littéraire du Moyen Age,* 24 (1957), 45–47, where Guillaume's gloss on Boethius's treatment of Orpheus (MS Troyes 1331, fol. 69^{r-v}) is printed in full. Some correspondences:

	GUILLAUME	BOCCACCIO
Orpheus	vox optima (citing Fulgentius)	optima vox (citing Fulgentius)
Eurydice	naturalis concupiscentia	naturalis concupiscentia
pratum	terrena	temporalia disideria
Aristeus	virtus	virtus
inferi	terrena delectatio	terrena

Both writers, despite the differences in their accounts, make the descent of Orpheus a morally inferior act. For a wider view of the situation of Orpheus in our period see John Block Friedman, *Orpheus in the Middle Ages* (Cambridge, Mass., 1970). Friedman devotes pp. 136–42 to Boccaccio's view of Orpheus; however, in his treatment he only considers the *Genealogie.* One may note that his discussion of Boethius's Orpheus (pp. 93–95) is a good deal more to the purpose of this study than that of Wetherbee, which is referred to above. See also August Buck's study, which, although it is primarily interested in later figures (Ficino, Poliziano, etc.), does touch on (pp. 18–19) Orpheus as *poeta-theologus* in Petrarch (*Invective* III) and Boccaccio (*Genealogie,* XIV, 8): *Der Orpheus-Mythos in der italienischen Renaissance* (Krefeld, 1961).

86. See E. R. Curtius, "Poetry and Theology," Ch. xii of *European Literature and the Latin Middle Ages,* tr. W. R. Trask (New York, 1953), pp. 214–27. And see R. Hollander, "Dante *Theologus-Poeta,*" *Dante Studies,* 94 (1976), 91–136.

87. *Esposizioni,* IV, *esp. litt.,* 317–23. Boccaccio gives more of the Orphic matter, apparently according to the view of the poets, in the following three paragraphs, but the basic opposition occurs in these first two treatments. See also *Esposizioni, Inf.* I, *esp. litt.,* 75, for the "theological" Orpheus.

88. Eurydice's snakebite (see *Georgics* IV.457–59) enters importantly in the *Elegia di madonna Fiammetta* (I, 3)—not with happy connotations, one need hardly add.

89. See R. Hollander, *Allegory in Dante's Commedia* (Princeton, 1969), p. 47n. The hypothesis advanced there is in need of adjustment along the lines suggested in the discussion of Orfeo's relationship to Linus, below. In addition, Dante's view of the "carnal" Orfeo may have been very close to the one proposed here for Boccaccio.

90. It is interesting to note that F. Torraca, quoted by Quaglio, *Opere,* I, 873, had suggested that Caleon's description of Orfeo derived from Boethius (III, *metr.* 12). Quaglio prefers to think it is the result of a *luogo comune.* If Torraca is correct—and Fiammetta's response could lend support to his case—the argument presented here is given further weight.

91. See, however, the case of the missing guitar. The maidservant Glorizia laments that she has not a musical instrument such as *la cetera d'Orfeo* to sound her joy at the private "wedding" of Filocolo and Biancifiore (IV, 121, 7). But just as Filocolo had turned Cupid into Hymen and Juno (121, 3), she now turns Orphic melody into something better when, with a *bastonetto,* she bangs beautiful melodies out of the four golden trees in the corners of the room (see IV, 85, 9).

92. See *De civitate Dei* XVIII. 14, for the conjunction of Orpheus, Musaeus, and Linus as the first poets to sing of the gods. The tradition is a long one. Again see Curtius, n. 86, above.

93. Two other allusions, at IX. 10 and XXVI. 38, both to the "cetera d'Orfeo," may be little more than that, though they too may have similar intention.

94.

Quella virtù che già l'ardito Orfeo
mosse a cercar le case di Plutone,
allor che forse lieta gli rendeo
la cercata Erudice a condizione
e dal suon vinto dell'arguto legno
e dalla nota della sua canzone,
per forza tira il mio debole ingegno
a cantar le tue lode, o Citerea,
insieme con le forze del tuo regno.
(II. 1–9)

See *Rime* VIII, the sonnet "Quel dolce canto col qual già Orfeo" for the obverse of this trope. There not even such sweetness would suffice to praise the *bellezza* of the poet's lady.

95. Branca holds that Boccaccio's description of Orfeo here is full of sympathy—more so than in other *loci* because here the *rievocazione* of Orfeo, "tutto assorto nell'amore, risuoni più avvivata di simpatia, quasi il Boccaccio lo senta così più vicino e veda in certo modo in lui uniti e identificati amore e poesia . . ." (*Opere,* III, 669).

96. *Opere,* III, 669.

97. Orfeo's speech, with its apostrophes of Amore (in *B* there are three, as there are in Francesca's speech) has much in common with *Inferno* V, its opening and conclusion especially so: see "Amore, a questa gioia mi conduce" (XXIII. 14) and "Amor condusse noi ad una morte" (*Inf.* V. 106); the concluding rimes ("felice," "radice") probably reflect those rimes at *Inf.* V. 122 & 124; and more than the specific echoes there is the entire atmosphere of the episode—the loving couple, only one of whom speaks, and the sense of lovers joined eternally, as well as the close identification of the observing poet with the loving souls. Boccaccio's own words on this last sub-

ject are worth having here. Of Dante's "pietà mi giunse, e fui quasi smarrito" (*Inf.* V.72) Boccaccio says: "In queste parole intende l'autore d'ammaestrarne che noi non dobbiamo con la meditazione semplicemente visitar le pene de' dannati; ma, visitandole e conoscendole, e conoscendo noi di quelle medesime per le nostre colpe esser degni, non di loro, che dalla divina giustizia son puniti, ma di noi medsimi dobbiamo aver pietà e temere di non dovere in quella dannazione pervenire e compugnerci ed affliggerci, acciò che tal meditazione ci sospinga a quelle cose adoperare, le quali di tal pericolo ne traghino e dirizinci in via di salute" (*Esposizioni, Inf.* V, *esp. litt.*, 138–49). I do not offer this passage as evidence of Boccaccio's sentiments in the *Amorosa Visione,* but allow myself to suggest that his view of *Inferno* V, a text so present behind the surface of this canto, changed a good deal less than most of his critics would like to believe.

98. In the *A* and *B* texts the lists are:

A:	*B:*
Orfeo	Orfeo
Ambepece	Arion
Temistio	Essiodo
Essiodo	Lino
Timoteo	Timoteo

With or without the Augustinian/Dantesque Linus of the *B* text, Orfeo is here presented as a *poeta/theologus.* Hesiod's presence is enough to make that clear. Branca's long note to the passage (*Opere,* III, 578–80) probably draws too heavy a line between the young and the mature Boccaccio and fails to distinguish between the two aspects of Orfeo that are so clearly present, from the *Teseida* onwards, in Boccaccio's works.

99. Branca points to both of these origins, *Opere,* III, 564–65.

100. See Philip Damon's discussion of this motif in Dante and its medieval background, "Geryon, Cacciaguida, and the Y of Pythagoras," *Dante Studies,* 85 (1967), 15–32. And for the motif in Petrarch see T. E. Mommsen, "Petrarch and the Story of the Choice of Hercules," *JWCI,* 16 (1953), 183–89. See also the article by Janet Smarr regarding the choice of Hercules in Boccaccio, referred to in ch. ii, n. 16.

101. E.g., "Tu guardi là, ché forse ti diletta/il cantar che tu odi, il qual piuttosto/pianto si dovria dire 'n lingua retta" (II.52–54).

102. "Dove cercando vai gravoso affanno?
Vien dietro a noi, se vuoli il tuo disire.
Solazzo e festa, come molti fanno,
qua non ti falla, e poscia salir suso
ancor potrai nell'ultimo tuo anno.
Il luogo è chiaro e di tenebre schiuso:
vien, vedi almeno, e salira' ten poi
se ti parrà noioso esser quaggiuso."
(III.53–60)

103. The allegorical significance of these two creatures is one of the more difficult problems of the *Amorosa Visione.* Branca, who confesses his bafflement (*Opere,* III, 567), does come up with one formulation which is provocative: "Il 'bianco' e il 'rosso' alluderebbero quindi ai due aspetti di chi si lascia dominare dalle passioni." One may add to that the documentation of the medieval love lyrics in which lovers turn either or both of these colors (for the white, which gives Branca the most difficulty, see, *inter alia, Vita Nuova* XXXVI.1, where pallor is the "color d'amore"). But this does not help to explain why there should be two youths, rather than one. Perhaps Boccaccio wanted to figure in them the duplicity of earthly things. If this was in fact his intention, the two youths do behave in appropriate ways. In this connection it may be remembered that Amore, when he appears in the poem (XV.14–17), is seated on two eagles, while standing on two lions. (This remarkable acrobatic feat was similarly performed by him in *Filocolo,* III, 19, 2.) The iconography points to his imperious power—but also to his duplicity. In *A* his face is described as a mixture of white and red (XV.22–24); in *B* it is like "neve ad ora messa/in porpora, cotal mista rossezza/nell'angelico viso aveva impressa"—another indication of the likelihood that Boccaccio thought of the two youths as associated with Amore. In the *Rime* (IX.6–7) Boccaccio describes his lovely lady's coloration in terms of "vermiglie rose i bianchi gigli/misti. . . ." This tradition, whether by agency of Boccaccio or by that of another (and perhaps earlier and even common) source, may be found preserved in Rubens' "Triumph of Divine Love" (canvas No. 1700 in the great Prado Museum in Madrid) where Venus's train includes two boys who stand to the left side of her chariot (which is drawn by two lions). The shorter one is dressed in white, the taller in red (see Boccaccio's description in the *A* text: "l'uno era corto e bianco in suo colore/e l'altro rosso"—III.51–52; the *B* text removes the detail: "l'un rosso e l'altro bianco in suo colore"). Their "icons" would seem to have carnal rather than divine associations, as

the one robed in white holds a flaming brand, the one in red, a bow in his left hand and a flaming round object in his right (an apple?). They would seem to be morally set off from the celestial Venus whom they accompany, much as in Boccaccio's text they are at odds with the *guida*—whom I take to be a representation of the higher kind of love.

104. It is not surprising to find that in a work by Boccaccio the space given over to love is well more than double that allowed to the three other subjects combined.

105. . . . "Parti vedere
quel ben che tu cercavi qui dipinto,
ché son cose fallaci e fuor di vere?
E' mi par pur che tal vista sospinto
in falsa oppenion t'abbia la mente,
ed ogni altro dovuto ne sia istinto.
Adunque torna in te debitamente:
ricorditi che morte col dubbioso
colpo già vinse tutta questa gente. . . ."
(XXX. 13–21)

Her speech continues at some length. This much of it shows clearly the emphasis that is put on the fact that carnal love leads to death. In all the rout the only lovers whose endings are not unhappy are Florio and Biancifiore, seen briefly (XXIX. 31–36) as "contenti" *after* "lor agro dolore" ("lor trapassato dolore" in *A*). They contrast sharply with Dido, the "star" of the triumph of Love, who has two *canti* to herself, and ends in "perpetuo duolo" (XXVIII. 87—"etterno duolo" in *A*). Unless the *guida* is either foolish or wrong, it is impossible to read the triumph of Love in a positive light. Florio and Biancifiore are the sole example of a loving married couple in the entire lengthy list, and it is their *unhappy* "courtship" which is remembered in the triumph, that is, the part of their relationship which was governed by their worship of Amore, before they turned to better gods. Those that conclude the rout, Lancelotto and Tristano (XXIX. 38 & 41), adulterous protagonists of "romanzi francesi" and thus *exempla* of lustful passion, return to the peccant note which Boccaccio wants for the entirety of the triumph, stretching from Jove himself to Tristano in a sad *translatio amoris.* (See *Esposizioni, Inf.* V, *esp. litt.* 135, of Tristano: "d'amore men che onesto amò la reina Isotta, moglie del re Marco . . ."; for a more general discussion, see R. M. Ruggieri,

"Dante, Petrarca, Boccaccio e il romanzo epico-cavalleresco," *Lettere Italiane,* 8 [1956], 385–402.)

106. "Tu t'abbagli te stesso in tanta erranza
con falso immaginar, per le presenti
cose che son di famosa mostranza."
(xxx.40–42)

See *Purg.* xxxi.34–36.

107. See Branca's long note to the allegory, *Opere,* iii.710–12.

108. E.g., *Inf.* viii.109f., xvii.43f. See R. Hollander, *Allegory in Dante's Commedia* (Princeton, 1969), pp. 301–07.

109. Precisely who this lady might be has been the subject of lengthy disquisition. See Branca's note, *Opere,* iii, 717–18, for a presentation of the problem with bibliography.

110. Indeed Lia is identified as she who "trasse Ameto/dal volgar uso dell'umana gente" (xli.35–36), thus allowing a dating of the *Amorosa Visione* as being almost certainly posterior to the *Comedia ninfe.*

111. See Branca's note (*Opere,* iii, 728–29). This is Boccaccio's most precise identification of his beloved. As Branca points out, the very precision of the identification works—in various ways—to cast uttermost doubt on its historical authenticity. E.g., no historical lady of that name has ever been traced; if she had existed Boccaccio never could have named her, for fear of reprisal to her and to himself.

112. In fact she is portrayed, though one must admit that the trope is conventional enough, as being loved by Love. At any rate she is the only presence in the triumph who is not shown in servitude to Love, with the possible exception of Florio and Biancifiore, who were once under his dominion.

113. "Io son discesa dalla somma altezza" (xvi.2); "al ciel ritornarò po' che m'aspetta" ("poi tornerò al cielo a chi m'aspetta" in *A*—xvi.27).

114. "Iddio mi v'ha mandata/per darvi parte del ben che possede" (xvi.8–9).

115. "Sariesi detto che di paradiso/fosse discesa da chi intentamente/l'avesse alquanto rimirata fiso" (XLIII.43–45).

116. See *Opere,* III, 747: "l'appagamento carnale ha il preciso significato allegorico di compimento dell'amore virtuoso, di ultimo coronamento dello sforzo al bene determinato dell'Amore."

117. See the first epilogue of Flaubert's *Education sentimentale* for a similar effect in the most anti-climactic work ever written. In the realm of retrospective comparison, there is the climax of the *Roman de la Rose,* which Boccaccio would certainly seem to have in mind here.

118. This would also seem to be the view of Gaspary, *Storia della letteratura italiana* (Torino, 1900), II, 21: "Quando dovrebbe cominciare la parte morale, il poema finisce; è rappresentata la terra, che sarebbe il peccato, l'Inferno, e mancano il Purgatorio ed il Paradiso."

119. She is referred to as "la bella donna" (L,5) but the context makes her identity certain.

120. This is surely the central problem of the *Amorosa Visione.* Landau, *Giovanni Boccaccio* (Napoli, 1881), p. 154, is understandably upset by the work's conclusion. How can the *guida,* he asks, "consente poi alla fine che tutto si consacri all'amore di una bella donna, la quale nulla ha in sè di celeste?" His translator, Antona-Traversi, gives him credit for being the first to note the contradictions of the work's conclusion (p. 223) and tries to resolve them by bypassing them (as opposed to Dante, Boccaccio eventually comes "alla glorificazione della carne, nella quale è il riposo e la pace"—p. 224). That is just what Landau, with what one can only consider just cause, is concerned about. But see Louise George Clubb, "Boccaccio and the Boundaries of Love," *Italica,* 37 (1960), 191, for an understanding similar to that of Antona-Traversi: "The reward promised to the poet at the end of his spiritual journey in the *Amorosa Visione* is ultimate pleasure with the enticing lady of his dream." What can the *guida celeste* have to do with such carnal love? Hauvette, *Boccace* (Paris, 1914), p. 138, is also disturbed, but is content to settle for a Boccaccio who did not do his job very well: "Assurément, entre le signe employé et la chose signifiée, il y a une incompatibilité qui va jusqu' à l'incongruité."

121. See L.58–60: "Io non curo se poi da alcun spregiate/fien forse le sue rime o sua sentenza,/sol ch'a voi sieno dilettose e grate." His not caring

about his *sentenza* is certainly a clue to the ironic intent of the work that should have been noticed long ago.

122. See L.79–81: "Rimirate alla fiamma poi, che ascosa/dimora nel mio petto, ed ispegnete/quella con l'esser verso me pietosa."

123. See the judgment of Aldo Scaglione, *Nature and Love in the Late Middle Ages* (Berkeley and Los Angeles, 1963), p. 121, who refers to "the obvious and miserable failure, logical and aesthetic, of this poem. . . ."

124. It is difficult to discern the reasons for Giorgio Padoan's judgment that the *Amorosa Visione* is inspired by altogether different principles from those that inspire the *Comedia ninfe* and the *Ninfale fiesolano*—"Mondo aristocratico e mondo comunale . . . ," *Studi sul Boccaccio,* 2 (1964), 144–45.

4. The Book as *Galeotto*

1. However, it has a certain similarity to the voice we hear in the frames of the *Elegia* and the *Decameron,* as I shall point out below.

2. This dominant view of the matter will be considered at greater length in the Conclusion.

3. We should remember that the narrator of the *Remedia* (see ll. 7–12) is himself a lover. See the discussion with which this chapter concludes.

4. See V. Branca, "Schemi letterari e schemi autobiografici nell'opera del Boccaccio," *La Bibliofilia,* 49 (1947), 24–29, for a review of the presenc of "questa enciclopedia di discettazioni erotiche" in Boccaccio. G. Billanovich, esp. in *Restauri boccacceschi* (Roma, 1945), and G. Padoan, esp. in "Mondo aristocratico e mondo comunale . . .," *Studi sul Boccaccio,* 2 (1964), are similarly sensitive to Boccaccio's wide use of Andreas's *regulae amoris.* See also the many *postille* of Branca and Quaglio in the various Mondadori volumes. However, even if we include Billanovich's discussion of the retractions found in Ovid's *Remedia amoris,* in the conclusions of Andreas and of Boncampagno da Signa, and in Boccaccio's *Corbaccio,* no one seems to have considered the possibility that Boccaccio read *all* of Andreas (or Ovid, for that matter) in the tradition of such retractions. This is perhaps a result of the tendency, of recent vintage, to consider that a retraction is only a *pro forma* literary device,

a way of coyly preserving one's former opinions, not of denouncing them. However, it is at least possible that such writers as Andreas were heading toward their retractions as they began, that is, were writing in an ironic mode, and only praising what they knew they would ultimately condemn.

The single article devoted entirely to the influence of Andreas on Boccaccio is by C. Grabher, "Particolari influssi di Andrea Cappellano sul Boccaccio," *Annali delle Facoltà di lettere filosofia e magistero dell' Università di Cagliari,* 21 (1953), 67–88, from which I extract the following indicative judgment: "Connessa con tutta la trattazione intorno all'amore è, nel Cappellano, l'idea della sua onnipotenza poiché l'amore è una passione naturale che governa l'universo mondo e, se arreca tormento, è anche principio di elevazione. . . ." (p. 70). Grabher's positive view both of Andreas's doctrines of love and Boccaccio's view of those doctrines is considerably weakened by his peremptory abridgment of Andreas's opening definition of love, from which he quotes the first five words, "Amor est passio quaedam innata," in the footnote which depends from the word *naturale* in the quotation above. If one wanted to believe that the *passio* of which Andreas speaks is *naturalis,* he is indeed almost forced to cut him off at this point, for he continues as follows (let us begin at his beginning): "Amor est passio quaedam innata procedens ex visione et *immoderata cogitatione* formae alterius sexus, ob quam aliquis super omnia cupit alterius potiri amplexibus et omnia de utriusque voluntate in ipsius amplexu *amoris praecepta* compleri" (text in S. Battaglia's edition [Roma, 1947], italics added for some particularly "unnatural" aspects of this *passio*). For a sharply divergent view of Andreas, see D. W. Robertson, Jr., "The Subject of the *De Amore* of Andreas Cappellanus," *Modern Philology,* 50 (1953), 145–61. And see his expanded treatment in *A Preface to Chaucer* (Princeton, 1963), esp. pp. 84–85, 393–448. While different medieval readers took Andreas in differing ways, this study strongly supports a "Robertsonian" rather than a "Grabherian" (or "naturalist") understanding of Boccaccio's view of Andreas, especially in light of Boccaccio's probable sense of the propinquity of Andreas's to Dino del Garbo's similar definition of carnal love—see chapter 2, n. 83, above. For a discussion of another aspect of Boccaccio's debt to Andreas, see W. Trimpi, "The Quality of Fiction: The Rhetorical Transmission of Literary Theory," *Traditio,* 30 (1974), esp. 81–104.

5. The two central modern contributions to an understanding of Boccaccio's use of his own autobiography in his works are Branca's *Bibliofilia* article and Billanovich's various studies (most notably, in this connection, *Restauri boccacceschi*—for both items see preceding note). I shall not attempt to recon-

struct either their arguments or the rather imposing, if loosely built, structure of "biographical" criticism which has been reared up in modern times on the foundations laid by Crescini. Something about all this has been said in the Introduction to this study. Let us note a single piece of Branca's imposing array of evidence (*Bibliofilia,* 49 [1947], 7n.): from the texts of the *Filocolo, Comedia ninfe,* and *Decameron* we can variously deduce that "Fiammetta" was born before 1310, after 1313, and after 1321. We are likely, therefore, to have two or three actual "Fiammettas" or none.

6. See chapter 1, n. 10, above.

7. See chapter 3, n. 1, above.

8. V. Kirkham, "Reckoning with Boccaccio's *questioni d'amore,*" *MLN,* 89 (1974), 51, while referring to the "Maria/Fiammetta" of the frame, makes no attempt to discuss the relationship (or lack of one) between these two "Fiammettas." Her further sense that the "love story" concerning Boccaccio and this lady is not yet complete would make it seem that she has somehow accepted as legitimized the narrator's carnal desire for this Fiammetta—a desire that would seem to be sharply at odds with her own sense of the anti-venereal stance of the Fiammetta of the *questioni.*

9. In the *Rime,* on the other hand, although she is rarely named, she is called only Fiammetta: XLV.13; LXIX.41; XCVII.2: CII.10; CXXVI.7. If I have heretofore avoided the complications offered by Boccaccio's lyrics, this chapter offers an opportunity to consider them. See discussion below.

10. *Caccia* XVIII.37–38: "Ond'io priego ciascun divotamente,/che *subbietto* è, com'io, *a quel signore . . .*"; *Filostrato, Proemio,* 1: "quasi dalla mia puerizia infino a questo tempo *ne' servigi d'Amore* sono stato," and I.4.1–2: "Adunque, o bella donna, alla qual fui/e sarò sempre fedele e *suggetto"; Filocolo,* I, 1, 19: "*Amore* . . . che me . . . fece tornare disideroso d'esser*gli* per così bella donna *suggetto,*" and V, 97, 9: "Tu [the author addresses his 'libretto'] se' di tal donna *suggetto* che le tue forze non deono esser piccole"; *Teseida, ded.,* 2nd sentence: "La quale ['la bellezza' of Fiammetta], più possente che il mio proponimento, di sé e *d'amore,* giovane d'anni e di senno, mi fece *suggetto"; Comedia ninfe* II.45–47: "donna gentile, angelica figura,/a cui *suggetta* l'anima amorosa/di me dimora in pena . . ." and XLIX.91–92, where the narrator envies Ameto's state: "veggendo sé tornato, di *suggetto,*/ alto signor di donna . . ."; *Amorosa Visione,* sonn. III.15–16: "colei la cui biltate/questo [his

'libro'] mi mosse a ffar come *subgiecto,*" and L.89–90: "né più disio né disiar più voglio/fuor ch'essere di tal biltà *servente*"; *Ninfale fiesolano* 4.7–8: "priego preghiate la mia donna altera/che non sia contro a me *servo* sì fera," and 472.1–2 [where Amore is imagined accepting his 'libro']: "Ben venga l'ubidente *servo mio*/quanto niun altro che sia *a me suggetto* . . ." (italics added, passim). And see *Rime,* esp. XVIII.10; XXI.14; XXV.13.

11. It is interesting to note that while Amore is named and/or invoked in all seven of the frames alluded to in the preceding note, Venus, with a single exception (the "santa dea" of *Comedia ninfe* L.2), is mentioned only as part of the narrator's invocation of his muses, and then only twice (*Teseida* I. 3.3, *Comedia ninfe* II.8). The insistence on the god of Love, with his terrible and cruel power, as opposed to the at least possibly beneficent Venus, seems not to have been a casual one. In the *Rime* we will find the same configuration: continual recourse to Amore, while Venere is mentioned only twice (and then neither addressed nor treated as being present). And it is Amore to whom Fiammetta (in the *Elegia*) and the narrator of the *Decameron* each refer once in their addresses to their readers. Only the narrator of the *Corbaccio* will eschew his name.

12. See chapter 1, n. 46, above.

13. ". . . voi in essa [la presente opera] troverete quanto la mobile fortuna abbia negli antichi amori date varie permutazioni e tempestose, alle quali poi con tranquillo mare s'è lieta rivolta a' sostenitori" (I, 2, 1).

14. *Filostrato, Proemio,* 20: "Ahi, lasso, quanto m'è la Fortuna, crudele e inimica de' miei piaceri, sempre stata rigida maestra e correggetrice de' miei errori!"; *Teseida,* "A Fiammetta": "la nemica fortuna"; *Comedia ninfe* I.1: ". . . gli accidenti varii, gli straboccamenti contrarii, gli essaltamenti non stabili di fortuna . . ." (here the reference is neither personal nor complaining, one hastens to add); Fiammetta's *congedo* in the *Elegia* (IX) mentions Fortuna six times in tearful tones.

15. See discussion of Branca's judgment that Boccaccio himself took a positive view of Fortuna only late in his life, Ch. ii, n. 106, above. It seems more logical to argue that the negative view of Fortuna which we find in the early works is that of the love-struck characters or narrators, not Boccaccio's own.

16. The passage from the *Teseida* cited above is preceded by a sentence that seems fairly surely to be modelled on Dante's version (*Inf.* v.121–23) of Boethius's *De consolatione* ii, 4, and contains, as its final word, the word *consolazione.*

17. Or from her momentary and mutable blessings. See the momentary benediction of the poet-lover, *Rime* xxvi.11, "lodando Iddio, Amore e la fortuna."

18. The narrator in the *Corbaccio* speaks with his consoling friends of the "volubili operazioni della fortuna, della sciocchezza di coloro li quali quella con tutto il disiderio abbracciavano, e della pazzia d'essi medesimi li quali come in cosa stabile la loro speranza in essa fermavano" (49). He leaves them *consolato.* In the *Decameron* the author, hoping to bring *consolazion* to the ladies, also hopes "che per me in parte s'ammendi il peccato della Fortuna . . ." (*Proemio,* 13). He promises to recount in the *novelle* that will follow "piacevoli e aspri casi d'amore e altri fortunosi avvenimenti."

19. Some version of the phrase is found in each of the works in *ottava rima: Filostrato, Proemio,* 27: "l'antiche storie,": *Teseida,* "A Fiammetta": "una antichissima storia," i.2.2: "una storia antica"; *Ninfale fiesolano* 2.8: "storia molto antica."

20. This motif returns in *Comedia ninfe* i.12 and is rather dramatically overturned in the first paragraph of the *Corbaccio,* where God becomes the narrator's "muse." It also lies behind the important *apologia* offered in the narrator's equation of *Muse* and *donne* in the Introduction to the Fourth Day of the *Decameron* (35).

21. This "formula"—that the book is written to please a lady—recurs expressly in *Teseida,* "A Fiammetta": "disiderando di *piacervi*"; *Comedia ninfe* ii.66: "acciò ch'io possa parlando *piacere*"; *Amorosa Visione* l.71–72 (*A* text): "e fine faccio col *piacere/di voi. . . .*" See also *Decameron* iv, *Introd.,* 31: "Le quali cose io apertissimamente confesso, cioè che voi mi piacete e che io m'ingegno di *piacere a voi*" (answering the charge "che voi mi piacete troppo e che onesta cosa non è che io tanto diletto prenda di *piacervi* e di consolarvi"—italics added, passim).

22. The narrator of the *Filocolo* begins half Christian, half pagan (i, 2, 6): "E se le presenti cose, o voi, giovani e donzelle, generano ne' vostri animi alcun

frutto e diletto, non siate ingrati di porgere divote laudi a Giove e al nuovo autore." In the preceding sentence he had spoken of Amore as God. Nonetheless, his ambivalence contains the most in the way of Christian morality we will find in Boccaccio's narrators until we meet the author of the *Decameron.* In the *Filocolo* the narrator's *explicit* will—unlike that of the *Decameron*—anchor itself in other than Christian principles: the narrator is there a typical devoté of Amore. It is amusing that, while Florio and Biancifiore move from paganism to Christianity, the one who narrates their tale moves from what looks like a mixture of the two toward the univocal praise of the god of Love. For a much different view of Boccaccio's prologues see E. Levi, "Il prologo dell' Orlando Furioso," *Rendiconti della R. Accademia di archeologia lettere e belle arti di Napoli,* N.S. 18 (1938), 53, where the *proemi* of the *Filostrato* and the *Ninfale* are cited as examples of Boccaccio's break with the tradition of the "Christian invocation" (as found, for example, in Dante), and of his assumption of a carnal and pagan stance.

23. Thus Branca's remarks concerning the singularity of the dedication to Niccolò, "Profilo biografico," p. 58, require some adjustment.

24. But see Giuseppe Mazzotta, "The *Decameron:* The Marginality of Literature," *University of Toronto Quarterly,* 42 (1972), 69, who apparently believes that Boccaccio is ironic in claiming *utile consiglio* for his *Decameron:* "St. Augustine's esthetic doctrine of the 'uti et frui' . . . is depreciated." What the textual grounds are for this assertion is unclear. For Boccaccio's "quello che sia da fuggire e che sia similmente da seguitare" see *Remedia,* 796: "quos fugias quosque sequare, dabo." The formula had already been present in *Filostrato* VIII.32.3–5: "ciò ch'è da fuggire. . . . queste son da seguire. . . ."

25. See *Filsostrato* IX.3–4; *Filocolo,* V, 97, 1–2; *Teseida* XII.85–86; *Ninfale fiesolano* 465. And see *Ars amatoria* III.748 ("ut tangat portus fessa carina suos"); *Remedia* 811–12 ("fessae date serta carinae; contigimus portus. . .").

26. *Filostrato* IX.5.21; *Filocolo,* V, 97, 1–2; *Teseida,* concluding sonnet, 12–13; there is a slight variant in the *Ninfale:* the narrator (in this like the Fiammetta of the *Elegia*) prays to Love that he not allow the book to reach "ignoranti and villane persone"—470.4; Love replies that only his subjects will be allowed to read it—472–73.

27. None of the three works in *terza rima* (*Caccia, Comedia ninfe, Amorosa Visione*) has a formal *congedo.*

28. *Filostrato, Proemio,* 37: "priego colui [Amore] che *nelle vostre mani* ha posto la mia vita e la mia morte, che elli nel vostro cuore quello disio accenda che solo può essere cagione della mia salute"; see also *Proemio,* 32; the motif occurs within the narrative when Troiolo speaks to his letter to Criseida, II. 107.7–8: " 'Lettera mia,' dicendo 'tu sarai/beata, *in man di tal donna* verrai' "; it is repeated in the *congedo,* IX.5.5–8: "E come tu *nelle sue man* sarai/con festa ricevuta, umilmente/mi raccomanda all'alta sua virtute,/la qual sola mi può render salute"; *Filocolo,* V, 97, 2: ". . . la tua bellissima e valorosa donna . . . graziosamente ti porgerà, prendendoti *nelle sue dilicate mani,* dicendo con soave voce: 'Ben sia venuto'; e forse con la dolce bocca ti porgerà alcun bacio" (the phrase "ben sia venuto" is picked up in the *Corbaccio* when the wickedly painted wife complains that her husband no longer says to her, when she comes to bed, "Amor mio, ben sia venuta!"—216); *Teseida,* "A Fiammetta": "pensando che *in quelle dilicate mani* nelle quali io più non oso venire, una delle mie cose alcuna volta pervenga. . . . pregando colui [Amore] che mi vi diede . . . che se in lui quelle forze sono che già furono, raccendendo in voi la spenta fiamma, a me vi renda . . ."; *Elegia,* IX (the book is imagined as speaking to Panfilo): "O tu, più rigido che alcuna quercia, fuggi di qui, e noi *con le tue mani* non violare: la tua rotta fede è di tutto ciò che io porto cagione; ma se con umana mente leggere mi vuogli, forse riconoscendo il fallo commesso contro a colei, che, tornando tu ad essa, di perdonarti disidera, vedimi" (italics added, passim).

29. "Fatele onor secondo il su' valore,/avendo a tempo poi di me pietate" (sonn. II. 15–16): and see, more specifically, L.67–70: "rispetto avendo ancora alla salute/che da voi la speranza mi promette/per più allegiar le piaghe antevedute (a mitigar l'amorose ferute—*A*)/aggio legate (composte—*A*) queste parolette."

30. See 3.7–8; 4.7–8; 466.7: the narrator hopes his beloved will be more *pietosa;* that other lovers will pray to her so that she will not be so cruel; that Love will take his book with him when he visits his lady (and perhaps other lovers as well).

31. See "Sul testo del 'Decameron,' " *Studi di filologia italiana,* 1 (1927), 53–54.

32. See "Principe Galeotto," *Mélanges à E. Picot* (Paris, 1913), pp. 505–10.

33. Hauvette, p. 507.

34. See "Galeotto fu il libro e chi lo scrisse (Dante, *Inferno* v, 137)," *Sitzungsberichte d. Kgl. preussischen Akad. der Wissenschaften, Philos. histor. Klasse,* 63 (1916), 1118–38; and see rev. by E. Walser, *GSLI,* 70 (1917), 196–98.

35. "Nein, das 'Galeotto fu il libro' ist nicht der Fluch einer Bussfertigen. Francesca ist nicht bussfertig. Sie ist noch in der Hölle das liebende Weib. Das Buch wurde ihr Fatum, aber sie hasst und verwünscht es nicht" (p. 1133—this argument will be given in another form by Padoan—see n. 38, below). He further argues (p. 1137) that Boccaccio has for Galeotto "kein Wort des Tadels," either in the *Amorosa Visione* or in his commentary to *Inferno* v (see Branca's similar judgment, n. 37, below). Walser notes two reviews of Morf's study which are hostile to it (*La Critica,* 15, 198–99; *BSDI,* 23, 114). It now seems mainly to be fogotten, even if its basic notions are still in circulation.

36. ". . . il fier Galeotto, il cui valore/più ch'altri suoi compagni s'affigura"— XI.29–30.

37. *Opere,* III, 627. Strangely enough, Branca also finds a favorable representation of Galeotto in the *Esposizioni.*

38. "Mondo aristocratico e mondo comunale . . . ," pp. 124–25.

39. *Opere,* VI, 868.

40. *Esposizioni, Inf.* V, *esp. litt.,* 180.

41. For a most curious reading of the subtitle's meaning see S. Galletti, *Patologia al Decameron* (Palermo, 1969), 213–16. (One mentions this study despite the one-sentence review it received from C. De Michelis, *Studi sul Boccaccio,* 6 [1969], 270n.: "Non merita di essere discusso il libro di S. Galletti.") Galletti, whose work, in the tradition of A. Lipari, attempts wild allegoresis on the basis of the "etymologies" of the names of the ten tellers in the *Decameron,* also concludes that to be a "Galeotto" is to be morally positive. How? Boccaccio calls him "*Prince* Galeotto," that is, he is not a pander but a good soldierly companion (p. 215). Yet Boccaccio's commentary on *Inferno* V also calls Galeotto *prencipe,* a fact that Galletti might have noticed, and which, in my view, takes something from his argument (i.e., Galeotto was in fact, for Boccaccio, a prince). Galletti's Galeotto/*Decameron* "ha la pre-

tesa . . . di guidare l'uomo, smarrito e perduto nella peste morale del vizio, per la via della riconquista, alle Virtù" (p. 216). I may note that his reading of Galeotto is made all the less likely by his own previous use of the word (p. 12), where those who misunderstand the *Decameron* see it either as a "libro osceno e galeotto o libro ridanciano ed ozioso." And see A. Lipari, "Donne e muse," *Italica,* 15 (1938), 132–41; "The Structure and Real Significance of the *Decameron,*" in *Essays in Honor of Albert Feuillerat,* ed. H. Peyre (New Haven, Conn., 1943), pp. 43–83. For other important discussions of the framing elements of the *Decameron,* all of which, to one degree or another, attempt to "decode" the ladies and/or the settings of the frame, see Edith Kern, "The Gardens in the *Decameron Cornice,*" *PMLA,* 66 (1951), 506–21; Joan Ferrante, "The Frame Characters of the *Decameron:* A Progression of Virtues," *Romance Philology,* 19 (1965), 212–26; Marshall Brown, "In the Valley of the Ladies," *Italian Quarterly,* 18, No. 72 (1975), pp. 33–52.

42. See Maria Segre Consigli's headnote to the *Decameron* in Cesare Segre's 3rd. ed. (Milano: Mursia, 1972): "Ma il Boccaccio non vuole alludere a Galeotto come al paraninfo per antonomasia . . . , bensí solo come a simbolo del suo desiderio di compiacere, con la sua raccolta di novelle, alle lettrici, a cui essa è particolarmente dedicata."

43. See "The *Decameron:* The Marginality of Literature," *University of Toronto Quarterly,* 42 (1972), 68–69: ". . . Boccaccio seems intent on assigning to this text the role of erotic mediator, and thus unmasking the threats and seductions of his own artifact."

44. See the vigorously sexual appreciations—not only of Dioneo—but of the ladies: e.g., Filomena (III.3), Fiammetta (III.6), Emilia (III.7), all of whom pray to God that they may share the sexual joy of the protagonists of these tales.

45. In this connection see Jean-Jacques Rousseau's witty and scabrous reference to "books that one reads with one hand" (*Confessions,* Book I). I offer thanks to my colleague at Princeton, John Logan, for this observation.

46. *Epistola,* XXI (September 1372). See Branca, "Profilo biografico," pp. 180–81 and nn., for a brief discussion and pertinent bibliography.

47. See his similar protestation about himself in the *Proemio* (3): He is one who has been a lover since his earliest youth. The difference between the nar-

rator at this juncture and him of the *Proemio* and *Conclusione* is, nonetheless, striking. For there we find the *former* lover, here a continuing one. The contradiction was probably forced by the response to the first thirty tales, many of which were taken by Boccaccio's *morditori* as utterly and only lascivious. Boccaccio's strategy is to accept the charge of lasciviousness—which he cannot do as a *former* lover—and argue from it. The *morditori* are thus attacked on their own ground. While this argument is not advanced as a solution to a difficult problem, it is probably to be preferred, as a first step toward a solution, to those treatments of the Introduction to the Fourth Day which argue triumphantly from it that Boccaccio is a "naturalist," while paying little or no attention to the clearly stated Christian morality of the framing *Proemio* and *Conclusione.*

48. Some thirty years ago Vittore Branca, "Schemi letterari e schemi autobiografici nell'opera del Boccaccio," *La Bibliofilia,* 49 (1947), 19, had noted "l'inclinazione dell'artista ad accogliere schemi tradizionali secondo le libere preferenze della sua fantasia." He goes on to show that Boccaccio's letter *Mavortis miles extrenue,* itself a rhetorical exercise modelled on two of Dante's letters (see Billanovich, *Restauri boccacceschi,* pp. 47–78), offers a *schema* for literary enamorment (p. 21):

I) in eius [mulieris] apparitione stupor.
II) amor terribilis et imperiosus.
III) diutina lassitudo.
IV) tempusculum in auge rote volubilis.
V) in malorum profunditatem deiectio.
VI) amici solatio.

Branca indicates that all of these six conditions are found in the lovers of the *Filocolo, Amorosa Visione,* and *Fiammetta* (while most of them pertain in the *Comedia ninfe*), while various of these components are to be found in the *lettere dedicatorie* of the *Filostrato* and *Teseida* and in the opening and closing *strofe* of the *Ninfale,* which "replace" these in that work. While Branca's method and interpretation are somewhat different from my own, he had noticed the same basic phenomenon: the "literariness" of love in Boccaccio's fictions. See the earlier but less acute observation of G. Traversari, in his edition of *Le lettere autografe di Giovanni Boccaccio del Codice Laurenziano XXIX, 8* (Castelfiorentino, 1905), p. 21.

49. If we put to one side the question of the date of the *Ninfale fiesolano,* it seems likely that the *Elegia, Decameron,* and *Corbaccio* were the last to be written.

50. Here and elsewhere one sees the slight but clear shade of difference between the narrators of the *Decameron* and of the *Corbaccio.* Their messages are roughly equivalent, but the recently galvanized moralism of the latter cuts away the first half of the usual formula, "delight and instruct."

51. But see V. Branca, *Boccaccio medievale* (Firenze, 1956), pp. 23–24: "Il capolavoro del Boccaccio, invece, proprio perché appare nei suoi aspetti più costituzionali e più validi come la tipica 'commedia dell'umo' rappresentata attraverso i paradigmi canonici alla visione cristiana e scolastica della vita e insieme come una vasta e multiforme epopea della società medioevale italiana colta e ritratta nel suo autunno splendido e lussureggiante, non si oppone alla *Divina Commedia* ma in qualche modo le si affianca e quasi la completa."

52. E.g., Giorgio Padoan, "Mondo aristocratico e mondo comunale . . .," pp. 182–86; Aldo D. Scaglione, *Nature and Love in the Late Middle Ages* (Berkeley-Los Angeles, 1963), esp. pp. 113–25. With reference to this last see the negative reviews of R. H. Green and C. S. Singleton, *MLN,* 79 (1964), 58–70 and 71–76, along with Scaglione's responses to some of their charges, pp. 556–59 of the same volume. And see the remark of M. Ciavolella, "La tradizione dell' 'aegritudo amoris' nel 'Decameron,' " *GSLI,* 87 (1970), 516: "Se la nostra tesi è valida, la concezione d'amore del *Decameron* segue linee strettamente tradizionali e non è indice, come vorrebbe Aldo Scaglione, di un nuovo naturalismo." On the other hand, Mario Baratto, *Realtà e stile nel Decameron* (Vicenza, 1970), p. 58n., associates himself with Scaglione's position.

53. See "Dalla 'Commedia' e dall' 'Amorosa Visione' ai 'Trionfi,' " *GSLI,* 123 (1946), 14: "La revisione accalorata dell' *Amorosa Visione* subito dopo l'aprile del 1351, e quindi la composizione del *Trattatello in laude di Dante* e il riordino del corpo poetico dantesco a cui egli attende allora laboriosamente per un altro stimolo immediato dei colloqui e della corrispondenza col Petrarca, si accompagnarono e si accavallarono, incredibilmente per noi, intellettuali mediocri e perciò frigidi e lenti, colla esecuzione a pennellate larghe e fiammeggianti del *Decameron.*"

54. The passage is discussed in the preceding chapter, n. 62.

55. *Opere,* II, 891: "la punta di maggior civetteria nel fantasioso edificio dell' autobiografia del Boccaccio."

56. *Rime* II, 14: *fui preso* da virtù [of his lady and thus of Love] ch'io non vedeva"; XXV.2: *"fui* da Amore *preso;* XXXII.4: "nelle cui reti *son preso";*

LV. 11: "Amor *mi prese*"; XCVIII. 6: "*fui* ne' lacci d'amor *preso*" (italics added, passim).

57. For a recent full review of the *fortuna* of the *Rime* among the critics, see Rosario Ferreri, "Studi sulle rime," *Studi sul Boccaccio,* 7 (1973), 229–37.

58. Branca, *Tradizione delle opere del Boccaccio* (Rome, 1958), p. 306: "I due fatti salienti che per testimonianza del Petrarca e del Boccaccio caratterizzano la diffusione delle *Rime*—cioè la riduzione del famoso e favoloso rogo del Boccaccio a un gesto di impazienza tutta giovanile, limitato a qualcuna delle primissime liriche, e la rinuncia dello scrittore a raccogliere i suoi componimenti in un vero 'canzoniere'—trovano conferma piena e solida nella tradizione manoscritta delle *Rime* stessé."

59. *Tradizione . . .*, p. 292: ". . . la coscienza dell'impossibilità de eguagliare l'esperienza lirica petrarchesca."

60. *Tradizione . . .*, p. 320. He speculates: "Se potessimo raggiungere la sicurezza che la raccolta beccadelliana offerta da F [1] rispecchia un 'canzoniere,' sia pur provvisoriamente ordinato dall'autore, molti dei problemi ancora insoluti, che oppongono le *Rime* del Boccaccio, verrebbero chiariti."

61. A. F. Massèra, *Le Rime* (Bologna, 1914). Branca's first edition (Bari, 1939) was reviewed by Billanovich, *GSLI,* 116 (1940), 134–55, and by Roncaglia, *Annali della R. Scuola Normale Superiore di Pisa,* S. II, 8 (1939), 359–82. The edition and these reviews reflect the severe problems that afflict the authenticating and ordering of the various components. Branca has always been as tentative as one must be in handling such problems. But, to be fair, one must note that such is also the case, if to a lesser degree, in Massèra's work as well. See his "Giovanni Boccaccio nella sua lirica," *Miscellanea storica della Valdelsa,* 22 (1914), 53: "Le *Rime* del Boccaccio non sono, Voi ben sapete, una raccolta di poesie liriche organica, ed in sé chiusa, e dal poeta stesso riordinata secondo un determinato criterio."

62. See "Giovanni Boccaccio nella sua lirica," passim. For a treatment in a similar vein of the Baia sonnets, see G. Gigli, "I sonetti baiani del Boccaccio," *GSLI*, 43 (1904), 299–311.

63. See Dante Bianchi, "Petrarca o Boccaccio," *Studi petrarcheschi,* 5 (1952), 13–84. Bianchi has doubts about the authenticity of the following: I, XXI,

XXVII, XXXII, XXXIX, XL, XLVIII, LV, LXVI, LXVIII, LXXXVII; he claims that LXXI is by Petrarch, and that LXXX may also be.

64. Probably the most valuable recent discussion of the various problems (influence of Cino, Guido Cavalcanti, Dante; knowledge of Petrarch's lyrics, etc.) is to be found in Branca's introduction to the Liviana edition (Padova, 1958), pp. v-xxxix. And we do well to remember his warning, *Tradizione delle opere del Boccaccio,* p. 288: "Ogni tentativo di ricostruzione della tradizione manoscritta, cui restarono affidate le *rime,* deve partire obbligatoriamente dalla constatazione che il Boccaccio non volle mai costituire un *corpus* di questi suoi componimenti, né si interessò con impegno vivace—come pure fece per altre sue opere—alla loro diffusione. Tutta la tradizione frammentaria, dispersa, extravagante delle 'rime' porta così chiaramente le stigmate di queste condizioni di fatto che nessun dubbio è possibile né è stato mai avanzato su questi punti."

65. The sonnet ("Intorn' ad una fonte, in un pratello") put first by Massèra is surely of later composition, according to Branca. See his comment in his edition of the *Rime* (Padova: Liviana, 1958) and *Tradizione delle opere del Boccaccio,* p. 307.

66. While she has been referred to as "una fiammetta" (V, 12), this is the first time (in Massèra's ordering, at any rate) that her name appears. The sonnet is crucial. Fiammetta proclaims her innocence—it is *his* fault that he fell in love, not hers.

67. Boccaccio's power as lyric poet is much maligned. This group of obsessive sonnets is both disturbing and moving.

68. LIII exists only as a first line, "Dentro del cerchio, a cui intorno si gira."

69. These sonnets would function better *preceding* LIV.

70. These two sonnets seem to belong in a group with LIX. All three celebrate the joys of carnal satisfaction.

71. LXIX and LXX constitute the tripartite *ternario* "Contento quasi," and were possibly not destined to be included in a *canzoniere.* LXXI, according to Bianchi (see n. 63, above), is by Petrarch. At any rate it too does not "fit" here.

72. LXXVIII and LXXIX are responses to other poets (Riccio barbiere, Cecco di Meletto de' Rossi da Forlí); LXXX, according to Bianchi, is possibly by Petrarch (though it might well have served, if by Boccaccio, as the first of the "penitent group" that follows); LXXXI is addressed to Antonio Pulci; LXXXII might also have served as introduction to or component in a "penitent group."

73. LXXXIII, with its clear quotation of the first sonnet of Petrarch's *Canzoniere* (ll. 12–13: "ed hami fatto del vulgo noioso/favola divenire": see *Canz.* I.9–10: "al popol tutto/favola fui gran tempo"), announces a new theme, the poet's desire to repent his earthly love (the next poem is the first in which God's name appears). The last poem in this "group" takes the hardest line: "Ma più ch'altri mi par matto colui/ch'a femina, qual vogli,il suo onore,/sua libertà e la vita commette" (LXXXIX.9–11).

74. XCII–XCVI, probably following Petrarch's example (e.g., "Italia mia") are "political" poems. Following Petrarch's example Boccaccio might well have chosen to include them in a "*canzoniere.*" For our purposes they lie outside the scope of the "love plot" which concerns us.

75. Fiammetta's name occurs again in XCVII (it has occurred in LXIX, "Contento quasi"). On the model of the central *canzone* of the *Vita Nuova* Boccaccio has her ascending to heaven on a "nugoletta" (l. 3). This is all that we hear about the "death" of Fiammetta—but the rest of the poems that concern her all make her a celestial lady.

76. CXX–CXXI are *apologiae pro vita sua* against the attacks of an unnamed priest, and CXXII–CXXV are (touching) defenses of his public lectures on Dante.

77. The fifth chapter of Massèra's introduction to his edition of the *Rime* (Bologna, 1914), pp. CCXLIX-CCCXI, contains a similar attempt to break Boccaccio's putative "*canzoniere*" into subject groups. It does not differ from my own in any major respect, except for its initial pretext, which is that the poems are literally autobiographical.

78. Those who have dealt with the overt Christianity of the last of the *Rime* tend to see it as opposed to Boccaccio's own earlier sentiments in his lyrics. Massèra (*Misc. stor. della Valdelsa,* p. 60) seems at least faintly disgusted with the "decina di sonetti ad imitazion del Petrarca." For a more pleased

appreciation, see A. Bertoldi, "Del sentimento religioso di Giovanni Boccaccio e dei canti di lui alla Vergine," *GSLI*, 68 (1916), 82–107; G. de Felice, "Boccaccio poeta religioso," *La Tradizione,* 2 (1929), 233–42. And see V. Branca, "Boccaccio poeta di Maria," *Mater Dei,* 5 (1958), 466–70.

79. There he is singled out (V, 97, 5) as being particularly appropriate to the *Filocolo,* or at least to the narrator's amatory purpose in sending the book to his lady. Virgil, Lucan, Statius, and Dante are seen as having different literary purpose and effect, and the narrator advises his book to leave them to others while it speaks to his lady. The passage is not without its ironic intent. With or without irony, its literal meaning has escaped V. Kirkham, "Reckoning with Boccaccio's *questioni d'amore,*" *MLN,* 89 (1974), 50. Perhaps the best single study of Boccaccio's use of Ovid is by Vincenzo Ussani, Jr., "Alcune imitazioni ovidiane del Boccaccio," *Maia,* 1 (1948), 289–306, which deals primarily with the text of the *Filocolo,* but suggests a general sense of the importance and the nature of Boccaccio's debt to Ovid. For an indication of Ovid's presence in the *Rime,* see Rosario Ferreri, "Ovidio e le *Rime* di G. Boccaccio," *Forum Italicum,* 7–8 (1974), 47–55.

80. For an excellent brief study of this document, see S. Battaglia, "La tradizione di Ovidio nel Medioevo," *Filologia Romanza,* 6 (1959), 211–18. For the history and nature of Ovid's many medieval "biographies," see Fausto Ghisalberti, "Mediaeval Biographies of Ovid," *JWCI,* 9 (1946), 10–59. And for some bibliography, see Ettore Paratore's article, "Ovidio," in the *Enciclopedia Dantesca,* IV (Roma, 1973), 268a–68b.

81. *Esposizioni, Inf.* IV, *esp. litt.,* 116–26.

82. Apollo calls him "lascivi praeceptor Amoris" (*Ars am.* II,497); he characterizes what he teaches as follows: "Nil nisi lascivi per me discuntur amores" (III,27). Boccaccio's final responses to Ovid's frankness are troubled, but he hardly seems eager to dispense with even the *Ars* in the last years of his life. See *Genealogie,* XIV, XV (150a), where he grants the charge of lasciviousness against Ovid, but takes back with one hand what he gives with the other: "For example, Ovid, the Pelignian, a poet of great eminence but licentious imagination [*clari, sed lascivientis ingenii poetam*] wrote a book on the Art of Love in which, to be sure, he suggested many a wrong practice; yet it was in no respect really dangerous, since no youth is so mad with passion, and no young woman so simple, that under the impulse of carnal appetite they are not much keener in inventing expedients to achieve their desires than he who

thought to make himself an eminent advisor in such matters" (tr. C. G. Osgood, 2nd ed. [Indianopolis, 1956], p. 72). This defensive posture occurs again at XIV, xix (153c), where Ovid is admitted to have at times written in such a way as to have been worthy of expulsion from the state for having weakened its moral strength.

83. The major effect of Ghisalberti's article, "Mediaeval Biographies of Ovid," is to demonstrate the insisistent desire on the part of medieval commentators to make the *Remedia* focal and thus to "save" Ovid—even the *Ars* and the *Amores.* See also D. W. Robertson, Jr., *A Preface to Chaucer,* esp. pp. 356–57. C. S. Lewis, "What Chaucer really did to 'Il Filostrato,' " p. 36, refers to "Ovid's purely ironical worship of Venus and Amor in the *De Arte Amatoria.*" And see S. Battaglia, "La tradizione di Ovidio nel Medioevo," p. 192: "Egli fu accettato come il più coraggioso denunziatore del più umano dei peccati: *Ovidius amorigraphus,* secondo . . . Alano di Lilla." Some of the best evidence which we have as to what medieval readers were likely to think of Ovid's various *opere* is given in the documents published by R. B. C. Huygens, *Accessus ad Auctores,* 2nd ed. (Leiden, 1970). From these twelfth-century documents we find that the *Heroides* have the following purpose: "Intentio huius operis est reprehendere masculos et feminas stulto et illicito amore detentos . . ." (p. 29), or again "intentio sua est legitimum commendere conubium vel amorem, et secundum hoc triplici modo tractat de ipso amore, scilicet de legitimo, de illicito et stulto, de legitimo per Penolopem, de illicito per Canacen, de stulto per Phillidem" (p. 30), a judgment repeated at greater length in the third *Accessus* to the *Heroides* printed by Huygens (p. 31). The *Accessus* to the *de Amatoria Arte* (p. 33) sees that text as a manual for the use of amorous young men, offering no explicit moral judgment on its nature, but stating that the work comes under the heading of ethics: "Ethicae subponitur, quai de moribus puellarum loquitur, id est quos mores habent, quibus modis retineri valeant." The practical aim of the text and good morals are evidently at odds. However, the *Remedia,* in the construction of the *Accessus,* would clearly undo the moral turpitude wrought by the *Ars,* for that text "Instruit ad medici similitudinem: bonus enim medicus infirmis ut sanentur medicinum tribuit et etiam sanis, ut ab infirmitate non capiantur" (p. 34). All we can say is that the picture of Ovid's intention that emerges from the various *Accessus* is a mixed one and allows for either a positive or a negative reading of his frankly amorous works (see the *Accessus* to the *Amores,* p. 37), while insisting on the "proper" moral purpose of the *Heroides.*

84. Boccaccio accuses Ovid himself of having been utterly effeminate and lascivious. His evidence is the *Ars* and the *Amores* (*Esposizioni, Inf.* IV, *esp. litt.,* 371). In the *Amorosa Visione* he places Ovid among the poets of the fifth canto. In the *A* text he has in mind the author of the *Ars* ("lo qual poetando/iscrisse tanti versi per amore,/com' acquistar si potesse mostrando"—V,25–27), while in *B* he seems to be thinking rather of Ovid's unknown *error* (an affair with Livia??): "il qual già poetando/scrisse cotanti versi e alfine amore/troppo alto 'l fé morir misero in bando."

85. See *Esposizioni, Inf.* IV, *esp. litt.,* 119: "il quale alcun chiamano *Liber amorum,* altri il chiamano *Sine titulo,*" and ibid., 371: "il quale è intitolato *Sine titulo.*" J. E. Shaw, "Il titolo del *Decameron,*" *GSLI,* 52 (1908), 289–320, while noting G. Dionisi's brief attention to the possible derivation from Ovid, brushes by the Ovidian resonance of the phrase in order to assert that all Boccaccio meant was that the first three days circulated "senza iscrizione titolare," that is, without the name of the work and its author and without a dedication.

Conclusion

1. A. Gaspary, *Storia della letteratura italiana,* tr. V. Rossi (Torino, 1900), II, while seeing more clearly than most readers the Christian elements in Boccaccio's early work, also sees that work as being not particularly serious and describes the Christian morality of the *Amorosa Visione* as follows: "Ma dietro a questa castigattezza esteriore si nasconde uno spirito mondano, tutto rivolto alla terra" (p. 21); he also claims that it is only in the *De casibus* that the moral of the *Amorosa Visione* is taken seriously ("presa sul serio"—p. 31).

2. We may subtend here the "refreshment theory"—which holds that Boccaccio joins the tradition of writers who chose only to delight, with no other purpose in mind. See Glending Olson, "The Medieval Theory of Literature for Refreshment and its Use in the Fabliau Tradition," *Studies in Philology,* 71 (1974), 291–313, a study which takes Horace's "*Aut* prodesse *aut* delectare poetae" (italics added) as its starting point. While Olson is not specifically concerned with Boccaccio, his argument may be brought to bear as a theoretical framework for C. S. Singleton's article, "On Meaning in the *Decameron,*" *Italica,* 21 (1944), which makes the *Decameron* "escape literature," devoid of any purpose but to please.

3. Appended here are some judgments which have mainly been forgotten. The question of Boccaccio's religion is not one often addressed in our time. To simplify, there are two camps, one of which sees Boccaccio as lifelong Christian, but is usually content with that mere assertion, while the other insists on a "conversion," or at least a Boccaccio who espouses Christian principles only at the end of his life. (This second view usually also takes the early works as pagan in spirit and tends to consider the religious "finale" either uninteresting or unimportant). Among representatives of the first view are: Vincenzo Borghini, who defended Boccaccio against the clergy in 1571; see "Risposta alle censure fatte sopra il Boccaccio dal maestro del sacro pallazzo ed alcuni prelati di Roma," ed. P. Fanfani, *Letture di Famiglia* (Marzo 1859): "Noi pensiamo che egli fusse buono e fedele cattolico, mossi, non solo dalle azioni sue ma degli scritti di coloro che, come più vicini a quei tempi, lo potettero sapere, li quali lo fanno di modesti e buoni costumi" (p. 11). F. Corazzini, who, in the introduction to his edition of Boccaccio's letters (Firenze, 1877), sees Boccaccio as a Christian: "Niccolò Mauro lo accusò d'irreligione, come tutti i Monaci passati, presenti e futuri; ma non pensarono così ecclesiastici rispettabilissimi del suo tempo, il vescovo di Firenze, e papa Urbano VI. Egli fu cristiano, ma senza ipocrisia, senza superstizione ch'egli si adoperò a mettere in ridicolo; contrario all'intromittenza della Chiesa nelle cose civili, a del clero nelle famiglie" (pp. lxvii-lxviii). O. Hecker, *Boccaccio-Funde* (Braunschweig, 1902), p. 300, who is at least as firm: "Boccaccio ist sein lebenlang religiös gewesen. Fromme Gebete schickt er zum Höchsten auch in seinen Jugendwerken. Später vertieft sich sein religiöses Gefühl immer mehr." To A. Della Torre, *La giovinezza di Giovanni Boccaccio* (Città di Castello, 1905), p. 99, Boccaccio was a lifelong, if hidden, Catholic. In his *tesi di laurea* Silvio Segalla, *I sentimenti religiosi nel Boccaccio* (Riva, 1909), takes a similar view, and finds specific Christian elements in three of the *opere di gioventù:* the *Filocolo, Comedia ninfe,* and *Amorosa Visione,* but begins his treatment of the early works (pp. 18–32) with the usual perception of Boccaccio's "pagan" stance: "L'amore, com' è noto, fu la ragione di tutte le opere giovanili del Boccaccio" (p. 18). His view is that Boccaccio was a timid or a lukewarm Christian in the early works (as well as in the *Decameron*), but in this only reflected the defects in religiosity of his time; see review in *GSLI,* 56 (1910), 251–52, which holds that Boccaccio was a "pagan" until 1362, and only then converted. Gaetano de Felice, "Boccaccio poeta religioso," *La Tradizione,* 2 (1929), 232–42, who argues that his religious lyrics "non sono dunque rime venute sulla penna dopo la predica del Ciani e la famosa *conversione;* sono sospiri dell'anima contemporanei alle ottave ed alle novelle profane" (p. 239). And more recently,

M. Pastore Stocchi, "Prospettiva del Boccaccio minore," *Cultura e Sculoa,* 3, No. 9 (1964), 29–38, who opposes the theory of a "conversion," finding instead a basic continuity in all of Boccaccio's work without really taking up the question of his Christianity.

Somewhere between the two positions we find Gustav Koerting, *Boccaccio's Leben und Werke* (Leipzig, 1880), p. 368: "Aber freilich in seiner Jugend und bis in seine reiferen Mannesjahre hinein ist Boccaccio, wenn auch nicht unkirchlich, so doch schwerlich streng kirchlich gesinnt gewesen, sondern mag, ohne eigentliches Wissen und Wollen, praktisch einem religiösen Indifferentismus gehuldigt haben. Mit den zunehmenden Jahren aber wandte er sich von diesem Standpunkte ab und mehr und mehr positiver Gläubigkeit zu." In the other camp we find G. B. Baldelli, *Vita di Giovanni Boccaccio* (Firenze, 1806), p. 159: "L'ammonizione del Ciani, l'epistola del Petrarca, generarono nel Boccaccio un cambiamento convenevole alla sua dignità, al suo carattere. Detestando i trascorsi passati, si rivolse a studj utili e gravi; e ridusse a maggiore austerità il suo modo di vivere." G. Riva, "Sulle Vite de' Santi Padri, e sui principali sacri ed ascetici scrittori del Trecento," *Memorie di religione, di morale e di letteratura,* 2 (1822), 427–30, asserts that the conversion brought about by Petroni and Ciani at last brought Boccaccio around to being his true self. G. Perticari, "Intorno un antico poema tribuito a Giovanni Boccaccio," in his *Opere,* II (Bari, 1841), 162–63, adds the influence of Petrarch to explain Boccaccio's "nuova condizione di penitente." V. Crescini, *Contibuto agli studi sul Boccaccio* (Torino, 1887), p. 255, presents a classic statement of the "conversion theory": "Così il Boccaccio, pari a non pochi de' trovatori provenzali, dopo avere provato intero il sentimento della vita, si mostra vinto dallo spirito ravvivantesi del medioevo, onde pur come poeta dell'amore finisce quale un asceta, con gli occhi volti al cielo, nella speranza di salire ove sognava che fosse la donna sua fatta angelo." A. Bertoldi, "Del sentimento religioso di Giovanni Boccaccio e dei canti di lui alla Vergine," *GSLI,* 68 (1916), 82–107, while arguing (p. 90) that Boccaccio's faith becomes active only after Pietro Petroni's intervention, which was his "Mount Ventoux," also sees the young Boccaccio as religious (pp. 83–84): "Pur nelle opere giovanili . . . persino le forme esterne del culto sono pienamente rispettate, e nulla vi è in nessuna che possa far dubitare, anche in quel tempo, dell'ortodossia—inefficace e inoperosa fin che si voglia—del nostro autore." Bertoldi's position tends to move in the direction of Koerting's.

4. See Branca, "Profilo biografico," p. 125n. for bibliography. Branca does *not* accept this view.

5. Branca, pp. 124–26.

6. A *Corbaccio* written ca. 1354 is certainly something of an embarrassment to the theory.

7. See "Mondo aristocratico e mondo comunale . . .," *Studi sul Boccaccio,* 2, (1964), 187–203.

8. See chapter 1, n. 80, above.

9. See Branca, "Profilo biografico," p. 176.

10. Branca (p. 180) justly points to the humorousness of the letter (*Epistola* XXI), which is often treated as a prime document by the "conversionists." It was written in September of 1372—possibly not much more than a year after Boccaccio finished retouching the *Decameron.*

11. For consideration of what is probably the most important literary relationship in the middle age—or any other—see G. Billanovich, "Il più grande discepolo," in his *Petrarca letterato* (Roma, 1947), pp. 57–294, which removes the need for consultation of most of the earlier work in this area. See also V. Branca, "Per la genesi dei 'Trionfi,' " *La Rinascita,* 4 (1941), 681–708.

12. For quite a different sense of Petrarch's effect on Boccaccio, see F. Rizzi, "Petrarchismo boccaccesco e platonismo sensuale," *La Rassegna,* 30 (1922), 187: "E non sono rari gli esempi di platonismo o petrarchismo boccaccesco, cioè di concetti platonici sensualmente rappresentati (e si badi che non c'è evidentemente intento di parodia o di satira, ma piuttosto una specie di diletto nel giovarsi delle teorie platoniche, care a tutti, per un travestimento inaspettato ed audace)."

13. *Genealogie,* XI, v (114a), "De Amore XII° Iovis filio."

Index